Multiparty
Arbitration

DOSSIERS
ICC Institute of World Business Law

This text is the work of independent authors and does not necessarily represent the view of ICC. No legal imputations should be attached to the text and no legal responsibility is accepted for any errors, omissions or misleading statements caused by negligence or otherwise.

Copyright © 2010
International Chamber of Commerce

All rights reserved. No part of this work may be reproduced or copied in any form or by any means – graphic, electronic, or mechanical, including photocopying, scanning, recording, taping, or information retrieval systems – without written permission of ICC SERVICES, Publications Department.

ICC Services
Publications Department
38 Cours Albert 1er
75008 Paris
France

ICC Publication No. 701E
ISBN: 978-92-842-0083-2

CONTENTS

FOREWORD 5
by Serge Lazareff

INTRODUCTION 7
Multiparty Arbitration by Bernard Hanotiau, co-editor

1. **Fernando Mantilla-Serrano** 11
   Multiple parties and multiple contracts: divergent or comparable issues?

2. **Stephen R. Bond** 35
   Dépeçage or consolidation of the disputes resulting from connected agreements: the role of the arbitrator

3. **Kristof Cox** 49
   Dépeçage or consolidation of the disputes resulting from connected agreements: the role of the judge

4. **Karim Youssef** 71
   The limits of consent: the right or obligation to arbitrate of non-signatories in groups of companies

5. **John M. Townsend** 111
   Extending an arbitration clauses to a non-signatory claimant or a non-signatory defendant. does it make a difference?

6. **Georgios Petrochilos** 119
   The extention of the arbitration clauses to a non-signatory state or state entities: Does it raise different issues?

7. **Yves Derains** 131
   Is there a group of companies doctrine?

8. **Sébastien Besson**..147
    Piercing the corporate veil: back on the right track

9. **Simon Greenberg, José Ricardo Feris and Christian Albanesi**......161
    Consolidation, joinder and cross-claims: multi-party and multi-contract arbitration-recent ICC experience

10. **S.I Strong**..183
    Class arbitration outside the United States: reading the tea leaves

11. **Gerard Asken**..215
    Class actions in arbitration and enforcement issues: an arbitrator's point of view

12. **Pierre Mayer** 223
    The effects of awards rendered in multiparty-multicontract situations

CONCLUDING REMARKS 235
by Eric A. Schwartz, Co-Editor

KEY-WORDS INDEX...241

CONTRIBUTORS...263

ICC AT A GLANCE..273

FOREWORD

by Serge Lazareff

Member of the Paris Bar;
Chairman, ICC Institute of World Business Law

One of the most pleasant yearly tasks of the Chairman of the Institute is to write the foreword to our recurrent Dossier. This is especially true for this publication, as this will be my last foreword before I leave the Institute at the end of the year.

I am very grateful to all our friends who have contributed to each edition of the Dossier over the past years and have thus contributed to the renown of the Institute.

The mixture of theoretical knowledge and the pragmatism of practitioners, the quality of the writers, the fine-tuning of their contributions and the dedication of the successive co-editors have allowed the ICC Institute to continue publishing the Dossiers, now valued works of reference.

This edition, prepared under the keen supervision of both co-editors, Bernard Hanotiau and Eric A. Schwartz, is no exception, and it is a privilege for me to introduce it. With the development of arbitration, the number of multiparty cases is constantly increasing. As the statistics for 2009 show, 28.5% of ICC cases involved multiparty issues. This has raised questions of an academic and practical nature. Each issue is splendidly discussed in this book, which touches upon all aspects of this topic.

As usual, the contributors to this issue have produced some of the best work in this area.

This Dossier, as well as the Institute's activities, both as a think-tank for ICC and as a training centre, would not have been possible without the hard work of Laetitia de Montalivet, Director of the Institute. Son professionnalisme, sa fine intelligence, sa constante loyauté (une si rare qualité!), sa connaissance du monde des affaires et de ses principaux acteurs ont considérablement contribué au cours des dernières années aux activités de l'Institut. Qu'elle en soit ici remerciée ainsi que sa charmante et brillante équipe – Katharine Bernet, Sybille de Rosny-Schwebel… et les autres.

Good luck to all of you.

INTRODUCTION

By Bernard Hanotiau*
Co-Editor

The first seminar of the ICC Institute, which took place thirty years ago, was devoted to the subject of multiparty arbitration. Since then, many developments have taken place in this area. The Council of the Institute therefore decided to select the same subject matter for its 30th anniversary seminar. The topic is also of the utmost importance in current arbitration practice. According to ICC statistics, approximately 30% of all arbitrations governed by its rules involve multiple parties and/or multiple contracts.

Where a dispute arises that involves more than two parties, a series of contracts and multiple issues, the plaintiffs or potential plaintiffs may not be in a position to bring the various desired defendants to one single arbitration proceeding. Arbitration is, indeed, consensual by nature, with the consequence that privity of contract applies to the arbitration clause, limiting its effect to the contracting parties alone. Joining non-signatories or third parties often proves difficult, sometimes impossible.

The issues raised by multiparty, multicontract arbitration are multiple. They include:

- Who are the parties to the contract and/or the arbitration clause contained therein?
- May an arbitration clause be extended to non-signatories? Does the fact that the issue arises in relation to groups of companies make a difference?

- To what extent can one bring to a single arbitration proceeding the various parties that have participated in a single economic transaction through several contracts?
- May an arbitral tribunal that is hearing a dispute that arises principally from a specific contract decide issues arising from connected agreements entered into by the same parties, possibly alongside other contractors?
- If separate arbitration proceedings need to be started, can these different proceedings be consolidated and under what conditions?
- If they cannot be consolidated, how and to what extent can one over come the inconveniences that arise from having several parallel proceedings?
- Who can act as claimant and against which defendants? Can a defendant join other defendants, be they privy to the arbitration agreement or third parties? Can a party to the complex contractual structure intervene voluntarily in the proceedings?
- When there are several defendants who have divergent interests and therefore do not want to appoint the same arbitrator, how does one go about constituting the arbitral panel?
- Can a defendant in the arbitration proceedings bring a claim against another defendant?
- How does one handle these complex or parallel proceedings in the interests of the best administration of justice?
- What are the consequences of the answers to the above questions for the enforceability of the award?
- To what extent should an arbitral tribunal take into consideration an arbitral award rendered in a connected arbitration arising from the same project?
- Is class-wide arbitration possible and desirable?

It was of course impossible to deal with all these topics in one day. The organizers therefore decided to concentrate on some hot topics and fundamental issues.

One of the main problems arising from multiparty arbitration is the intellectual confusion that reigns in this field. This confusion has been generated by unfortunate court decisions and arbitral awards, not to mention poorly written legal articles, which, unfortunately, are legion in this area. For example, a clear methodological distinction should be made – and unfortunately is not often made – between issues arising from the fact that the project at the centre of a dispute has been negotiated and performed by one or more companies that belong to a group, some of which are not signatories to the arbitration clause, and issues arising from the fact that the dispute concerns problems originating from, or in connection with, two or more agreements entered into by the same and/or different parties that do not all contain the same – or at least compatible – arbitration clause(s). It was therefore decided to devote the first part of the seminar to the distinction between groups of contracts and groups of companies – are they two different subjects? Once the distinction has been clarified, the following question remains: on what basis should the judge or the arbitrator decide to treat separately or consolidate the disputes resulting from connected agreements, which in some cases constitute a single economic transaction?

Groups of companies have developed considerably in recent decades and with them the issue of the possible extension of an arbitration clause to non-signatories, although the issue does not only arise in relation to groups of companies but also to individuals within the group or to states and state entities. A lot has been said, decided and written on the topic. The organizing committee therefore decided to concentrate on fundamental issues and current problems, such as the limits of consent, whether it makes a difference if the issue of extension arises in relation to a non-signatory claimant or a non-signatory defendant and the extent to which the extension of the arbitration clause to a non-signatory state or state entity raises different issues.

As indicated above, confusion in the case law and doctrinal writings has complicated issues that at the outset were relatively simple. For example, reference is very often made to a so-called 'group of companies' doctrine. The undersigned considers that this doctrine is totally unnecessary and confusing. In the same vein, a lot of confusion surrounds the theory of piercing the corporate veil which – rightly or wrongly – has from time to time allowed the extension of an arbitration clause to a non-signatory. Asking two distinguished speakers to put the two doctrines 'back on track' was therefore judged appropriate.

Moreover, one cannot deal with groups of companies without addressing other complex procedural issues that frequently arise in this area, such as consolidation, joinder and cross-claims, as well as ICC practice in relation to these issues.

It was finally decided to devote the last part of the seminar to enforcement issues – which are particularly sensitive in multiparty, multicontract cases – and to a topic that has acquired great importance in theory and practice in the United States: class action arbitrations.

The seminar was a great success due to the efforts of many people who deserve our warm thanks: the ICC Council and, in particular, its President, Serge Lazareff; Eric Schwartz, who co-organized the seminar; Laetitia de Montalivet and Katharine Bernet and their whole team at the Institute, who took charge of the organization; and of course the speakers whose contributions are published in this volume. Their presentations were excellent. They have made a great contribution to the law of multiparty arbitration.

* Co-editor of Dossier VII; Member of the Brussels and Paris Bars; Partner, Hanotiau & van den Berg, Brussels; Council Member, ICC Institute of World Business Law.

CHAPTER 1

MULTIPLE PARTIES AND MULTIPLE CONTRACTS: DIVERGENT OR COMPARABLE ISSUES?

FERNANDO MANTILLA-SERRANO[*]

1. INTRODUCTION

The reality of complex international commercial transactions in today's expanding global market has given rise to complex arbitration. These complex transactions often result in multiparty arbitration, as well as arbitration involving multiple contracts. The often imperfect arbitration agreements that have been fashioned in an attempt to extend arbitral jurisdiction over these commercial transactions have resulted in complicated situations in which not all the relevant parties, or all the relevant contracts, were explicitly included in the arbitration agreement. These situations have given rise to a number of questions that arbitral tribunals, national courts and scholars have attempted to address. In response to these questions, the 'group of companies' and 'group of contracts' doctrines have developed. These doctrines have encountered varying levels of acceptance and application across national jurisdictions.

The proximity of both these doctrines to the issues often encountered in connection with complex international transactions may lead to confusion of the two and raises a number of questions. Are we in the same universe of complexity when we speak of multiparty arbitration and arbitrations involving multiple contracts? Are the 'group of companies' and 'group of contracts' doctrines necessary components of complex arbitration? Are these doctrines to be distinguished from or likened to one another given their, at least superficial, similarities?

Setting aside the relative acceptance or rejection of either of these doctrines in various national jurisdictions[1], this analysis aims to identify the basic differences and similarities behind the doctrines to better approach the questions raised. I will therefore consider these issues in the light of two opposing propositions. First, multiple parties and multiple contracts are two different subjects. Second, multiple parties and multiple contracts raise, in essence, the same issues. In conclusion, I will attempt to reconcile these seemingly incompatible propositions to achieve a more nuanced understanding of whether the 'group of companies' and 'group of contracts' doctrines are more likely to differ or overlap.

2. FIRST PROPOSITION: THE 'GROUP OF COMPANIES' DOCTRINE AND THE 'GROUP OF CONTRACTS' DOCTRINE ARE TWO DIFFERENT THINGS

In order to consider where the 'group of companies' and 'group of contracts' doctrines diverge, this section addresses the following basic issues: (a) each doctrine raises different fundamental questions regarding its application; (b) the economic aspects of the situation do not carry the same importance under both doctrines; and (c) procedurally, the doctrines arise in different scenarios.

a. Each doctrine raises different fundamental questions

In order to simplify matters and thus get to the essence of the two doctrines, it is necessary to isolate the two variables (i.e. contracts and parties) for each one. We will start with the 'group of companies' doctrine and assume that only one contract exists. With respect to the 'group of contracts' doctrine, we will assume a situation with multiple contracts entered into between the same parties.

The 'group of companies' doctrine concerns one contract and multiple parties, and necessarily concerns companies that all have a separate legal personality from the companies that are signatories of the contract[2]. The name 'group of companies' suggests that this doctrine only applies to companies. For this reason, among others, criticism has been directed at the usage of the term 'group of companies' in connection with this doctrine, for failing to adequately represent its scope. It has also been suggested that this term has led to an oversimplification of the doctrine by arbitral tribunals and courts, leading to shortcuts, when in fact deciding whether the doctrine applies in a given situation requires rigorous legal reasoning.[3]

Thus, it merits clarification that the 'group of companies' doctrine is not exclusive to companies and that it essentially involves the extension of arbitration clauses to parties that have not signed the agreement. Under the 'group of companies' doctrine, the arbitration agreement may be extended to one or several non-signatories as claimants or respondents. Where companies are concerned, non-signatories might include a parent company, a subsidiary, a sister corporation or other affiliate within the group. Non-signatories could also include individuals linked to the group of companies, such as a director, general manager, CEO, owner or majority shareholder. Finally, non-signatories may include a state or state entity.[4]

Despite the questionable adequacy of the term 'group of companies' in describing this extension of the arbitration clause to non-signatories, this is the term that will be used in this article, taking into account the above-mentioned caveats to its understood meaning. In addition to the advantage of brevity, this term presents an interesting linguistic partner for the 'group of contracts' doctrine: it is perhaps in part the phonetic similarity of the names of these doctrines that encourages their comparison.

When the application of the 'group of companies' doctrine is raised, the following question must be answered: Does the arbitration agreement apply to certain non-signatories, or has a non-signatory consented to be bound by the arbitration agreement? The question of the intent behind an arbitration agreement must be answered by examining the parties' positions and actions. In other words, it is a subjective analysis in which the conduct of the non-signatory plays a paramount role in determining whether or not it has agreed to be bound by the arbitration agreement.

In contrast to the 'group of companies' doctrine, the 'group of contracts' doctrine (taken in isolation, i.e. without complicating it with issues of multiple or different parties) concerns multiple related contracts that are not linked to the same arbitration agreement and which are entered into by the same parties. Note, however, that when multiple related contracts contain identical arbitration clauses, it can be inferred (in the absence of evidence to the contrary) that the parties intended to submit disputes arising under more than one contract to a single arbitration.

A 'group of contracts' situation could arise in either a two-party or multiparty scenario, unlike a 'group of companies' scenario, which necessarily involves multiple parties. A two-party situation would necessarily involve more than one contract signed by those two parties. Multiparty situations concerning multiple contracts could include varying contractual scenarios, including horizontal contractual relationships in which one party signs different contracts with multiple parties, vertical contractual relationships in which each party signs two related contracts with two different parties and consortium relationships in which a number of companies all sign different contracts.[5]

Application of the 'group of contracts' doctrine raises the following question: Does the arbitration agreement cover disputes arising from contracts other than the one in which it is contained or those that specifically incorporate it? In other words, the test is an objective one. What subject matter did the parties consent to submit to arbitration according to the arbitration agreement? In other words, what is the objective scope of the arbitration agreement?

Thus, we see that the 'group of contracts' and 'group of companies' doctrines, when reduced to their essence, concern fundamentally different issues. The 'group of companies' doctrine concerns 'who' has given consent to be bound by the arbitration agreement, whereas the 'group of contracts' doctrine concerns 'what' subject matter the parties consented to submit to arbitration. These questions must also be answered by examining different criteria. Understanding who has given consent to arbitration requires an examination of the subjective intent of the parties concerned. Determining what issues the parties have consented to submit to arbitration necessitates an examination of the objective meaning of the arbitration agreement and other relevant agreements as they were contracted. Thus, the application of the 'group of contracts' doctrine may require an inquiry into the intent of the parties, but this inquiry will focus on the objective scope of the arbitration agreement binding the parties, rather than on the parties' consent to be bound by the agreement.

b. Importance of economic considerations differs under each doctrine

As the *'group of companies'* doctrine has matured, it has shed the economic considerations that initially formed an important foundation of its application. In contrast to this development, economic considerations remain at the heart of the 'group of contracts' doctrine.

i. Economic considerations have lost importance in the 'group of companies' doctrine

The notion that a group of companies formed a 'single economic reality' was an important underlying concept in determining the existence of intent for non-signatory companies within a group to be bound by an arbitration agreement. Indeed, in the seminal case of *Dow Chemical Company v. Isover Saint Gobain*[6], the arbitral tribunal determined that it should take into account the existence of a single economic reality that formed the basis of a group of companies when determining jurisdiction.

The arbitral tribunal relied heavily on the parties' roles in various aspects of the contract to conclude that they were *'veritable parties'* to the contracts or that they were 'principally concerned' by the disputes concerning the contracts:

> *"[B]y virtue of their role in the conclusion, performance or termination of the contracts containing said clauses, and in accordance with the mutual intention of all parties to the proceedings, [the parties] appear to have been veritable parties to these contracts or to have been principally concerned by them and the disputes to which they may give rise."* [7]

However, the existence of a 'single economic reality' was an important element in the reasoning of the tribunal. Thus, the arbitral tribunal in *Dow Chemical* stated that 'irrespective of the distinct juridical identity of each of its members, a group of companies constitutes one and the same economic reality [*une réalité économique unique*] of which the arbitral tribunal should take account when it rules on its own jurisdiction'. [8]

The decision of the arbitral tribunal in Dow Chemical, emphasizing the existence of a single economic relationship, was upheld by the Paris *Cour d'appel*. [9]

In the first decisions concerning the 'group of companies' doctrine, this 'single economic reality' constituted a rather important element for the following reasons:

- At the time, under certain legal systems, the conditions of formal validity of the arbitration agreement were often more stringent: the agreement not only needed to be in writing but also had to be signed and sometimes notarized.
- Consent, in itself, was not sufficient to recognize the existence and validity of an arbitration agreement.
- The validity of an arbitration agreement incorporated by reference was not universally accepted.

Today, the importance of the existence of a single economic reality is attenuated in the 'group of companies' doctrine. This economic factor has diminished in importance as other indices of intention have come to the fore. Participation in the negotiation, conclusion, execution and resolution of an agreement, which was a significant consideration highlighted in Dow Chemical, has become more important, necessitating a more subjective analysis than that which is aimed at identifying a *'single economic reality'* underlying the existence of a group of companies.

Participation in the contract serves to indicate that a non-signatory had knowledge of the existence and scope of the arbitration agreement and intended to be bound by it, which is the 'test' that was evidenced by the decision of the Paris *Cour d'appel* in the *Jaguar case*[10]. In this case, an English company, Project XJ 220 ('Project XJ'), offered to manufacture and sell to individual buyers a limited edition of a new Jaguar model, type XJ 220. A French individual ('Mr. X') entered into a contract with Project XJ for the purchase of one of the vehicles. The contract was drafted in English, with a translation in French provided by Jaguar France, which participated in the execution of the contract but was not a party to the agreement.

The contract contained an arbitration clause providing for arbitration in England by a sole arbitrator appointed by the Chairman of the Law Society in London. After the first payment, Mr. X, who no longer wished to purchase the vehicle, refused to pay the remaining amount due and filed a claim against Project XJ and V 2000, successor-in-interest to Jaguar France, before the Paris *Tribunal de grande instance*, seeking the annulment of the contract. Project XJ argued that the court lacked jurisdiction because of the arbitration clause. V 2000 raised the same defence, arguing that though it was a non-signatory, it was bound by the arbitration clause because of the participation of its predecessor-in-interest in the execution of the contract.

The *Paris Tribunal de grande instance* having retained jurisdiction over the case, Project XJ and V 2000 lodged an appeal against the decision. The Paris Cour d'appel reversed the lower court's decision, holding that the arbitral tribunal had exclusive jurisdiction over both Project XJ and V 2000, since the latter, 'although not a signatory, had knowledge of the contract in dispute, which it decided to have translated, and in particular of the existence of the arbitration clause it is seeking to benefit from'[11]. The *Cour d'appel* further held that:

> *"in international arbitration law, the effects of the arbitration clause extend to parties directly involved in the performance of the contract*

provided that their respective situations and activities raise the presumption that they were aware of the existence and the scope of the arbitration clause, so that the arbitrator can consider all economic and legal aspects of the dispute." [12]

A similar line of reasoning was adopted by the French *Cour de cassation* in the more recent *Alcatel* case. In this case, Alcatel Business Systems (ABS) and Alcatel Micro Electronics (AME), French and Belgian companies belonging to the Alcatel group, had entered into a collaborative business relationship. AME contracted with Amkor, a company incorporated in the United States, for the purchase of computer chips. Amkor in turn entered into a contract with a Korean manufacturer, Anam, for supply of the computer chips to AME. The contracts between AME and Amkor, and between Amkor and Anam, contained arbitration clauses, both referring disputes to the American Arbitration Association (AAA), but in different locations. [13]

Anam delivered the goods to AME, after two French subsidiaries of Amkor had certified that they complied with the contractual specifications. AME delivered the approved computer chips to ABS. Arguing that the chips were defective, ABS brought a claim for damages against Amkor, its two French subsidiaries and Anam before a French *Tribunal de commerce*. All of the named defendants to the action objected to the court's jurisdiction, invoking the arbitration clause contained in the contract between AME and Amkor, referring disputes to AAA arbitration in Philadelphia. The *Tribunal de commerce* declined jurisdiction, and the *Cour d'appel* subsequently upheld this decision.

On appeal from the lower courts, the Cour de cassation considered whether the French subsidiaries of Amkor could invoke the arbitration clause contained in the contract between AME and Amkor, despite the fact that they were not party to it. The court held that they could, stating:

"the effect of the international arbitration clause extends to the parties directly involved in the execution of the contract and the disputes that may arise from it; [therefore the French subsidiaries of Amkor] were entitled to invoke, against ABS [...] the arbitration clause contained in the contract that tied their parent company to AME." [14]

The *Cour de cassation*, in emphasizing that Amkor's subsidiaries had been involved in the execution of the contract, thus implicitly recognized that the subsidiaries had knowledge of the arbitration clause and intended to be bound by it. However, the *Alcatel* decision can also be interpreted as the beginning of a new stage in French case law on the *'group of companies'* doctrine, with the absence of any explicit reference to the non-signatory's knowledge of the contract demonstrating the court's abandonment of the requirement that the non-signatory have knowledge of the arbitration clause.[15] In fact, the conduct of the non-signatory is such as to imply knowledge and, of course, consent.

In a very recent decision by the Paris *Cour d'appel* in the *Pujol* case, the court did not explicitly require knowledge of the arbitration agreement in order to extend it to a non-signatory[16]. In this case, an Italian company, Suba & Unico, had entered into a contract with a related French company, Suba France, for the multiplication and delivery of seeds. The contract contained an arbitration clause and authorized Suba France to conclude different multiplication contracts with other producers of seeds in order to be able to meet the quantity requirements of Suba & Unico under the main contract. Suba France therefore entered into a multiplication contract with Pujol, a French company. This contract, which also contained an arbitration clause, provided that Pujol would deliver the seeds to, and be paid by, Suba & Unico. A dispute arose from the second contract, leading Pujol to file a request for arbitration against both Suba France and Suba & Unico.

The arbitral tribunal found that it had jurisdiction over both respondents, since the two companies belonged to a group of companies and Suba & Unico participated in the execution of the contract between Suba France and Pujol. The Suba companies brought a claim before the Paris *Cour d'appel*, seeking the annulment of the award, with Suba & Unico notably arguing that it was not bound by the arbitration clause. The *Cour d'appel* rejected the claim, holding that:

> *"the arbitration clause contained in an international contract has a specific validity and efficiency, which calls for the extension of its applicability to the parties directly involved in the execution of the contract and the disputes that may arise from it."* [17]

On this sole basis, the *Cour d'appel* considered that Suba & Unico was bound by the arbitration clause, even though it was not a party to the contract between Suba France and Pujol. The court did not refer to the potential knowledge of Suba & Unico of the existence of the arbitration clause. More importantly, it did not respond to Suba & Unico's argument that no group of companies existed between itself and Suba France, thus demonstrating that participation in the execution of the contract was in itself sufficient to bind the non-signatory, regardless of any other consideration.

Accordingly, if the *Alcatel* and *Pujol* trend is confirmed, the importance of 'economic considerations' (i.e. the existence of economic ties between the companies involved), which at one time served to infer knowledge of the existence and scope of the arbitration agreement, will disappear completely in favour of a purely 'conduct-oriented' analysis of the intention of the non-signatories to be bound by the arbitration agreement.

ii. Economic considerations remain at the heart of a 'group of contracts' analysis

Considerations about the economic aspects of a multi-contract situation remain at the heart of the 'group of contracts' doctrine. This is because there must be an economic tie that creates a link between the contracts. Without this economic link to bind the contracts together, there would be little reason to consider that they should share a common arbitration agreement. One description of the underpinnings of the 'group of contracts' doctrine is particularly insightful in this regard:

> "[C]ontractual relationships usually involve long-term economic operations comprising a large number of distinct, but interrelated, contracts. In many cases, the different kinds of agreements seem to give rise to an indivisible transaction, an economical and operational unit 'hidden' behind a multi-contract façade, that actually amounts to one fundamental relationship." [18]

Of course, finding the existence of an economic link between the parties is only one part of the puzzle; there must also be intent and consent. French courts have thus far refused to extend the arbitration clause contained in one contract to the other contracts of the group for the *sole* reason that all contracts were part of a single economic operation. However, it is established in French case law that the indivisibility of a group of contracts subject to a dispute may justify the extension of an arbitration clause contained in one contract to all contracts concerned. When inquiring into the divisibility of contracts, French courts frequently take into consideration the economic links between the contracts in dispute.

Thus, in some cases, the economic unity of the operation will serve as evidence of the indivisibility of the contracts (an objective analysis), which can in turn lead to the extension of the arbitration clause to other contracts of the group. In other cases, this economic unity will be interpreted as showing the intention of the parties (a subjective analysis) to extend the applicability of the arbitration clause to other contracts in addition to the one containing the arbitration clause. Sometimes, both analyses will be applied to the same contractual situation, thus reinforcing the important role played by economic considerations. [19]

The decision of the Paris *Cour d'appel* of 23 November 1999 in the *Glencore* case is a good example of how economic aspects of multiple contracts are taken into account by French courts.[20] In this case, Glencore Grain Rotterdam BV ('Glencore'), a Dutch company, entered into a contract with Afric, a Congolese company, for the sale of a shipload of rice. The contract contained a clause providing for arbitration in Paris, under French law. Before the delivery could take place, both companies agreed that Glencore would take back the rice and reimburse Afric, as the latter was no longer in a position to receive the goods because of the ongoing war in Congo. The companies entered into a second contract to this effect, which did not contain any dispute resolution clause.

Difficulties arose with the execution of the second contract, and Afric initiated arbitration proceedings. The arbitral tribunal considered that the two agreements amounted to one contractual relationship and that it therefore had jurisdiction over the dispute. The arbitral tribunal ordered Glencore to proceed with the reimbursement and also awarded damages to Afric. Glencore filed for annulment of the award with the Paris *Cour d'appel*. The court rejected the application for annulment, holding as follows:

> *"[A]ssuming that they are independent from each other, two agreements concluded successively in a few weeks time and concerning the sale and the taking back between the same parties of the same merchandise have obviously constituted complementary or at least connected conventions; therefore, even though the exchange of telecopies that took place does not refer to the arbitration clause contained in the initial agreement, neither to any other form of resolution of potential disputes, it stems from the close economic links existing between the two phases of the operation, the second of which was only the continuation and consequence of the first one, that the implicit intention of the parties was necessarily to extend the effects of the arbitration clause to the whole set of disputes with inseparable components that may arise between them with respect to their situation."* [21]

Thus, in *Glencore* the fact that there was a 'close economic link' between the two agreements was a key factor in finding that the parties in fact intended the arbitration clause in the first agreement to apply to both agreements.

In a more recent case, the French *Cour de cassation* followed a similar method of interpretation to extend the arbitration clause to another contract within a group of contracts.[22] In this case, the French company Uni-Kod entered into a contract with certain Russian companies, including one called Ouralkali, to create a joint venture, called Uni. The joint venture contract contained a clause providing for arbitration under the auspices of the Court of Arbitration of the Chamber of Commerce of the Russian Federation. Uni-Kod and Ouralkali then entered into a second contract, according to which Ouralkali was to provide Uni-Kod with the funds necessary to buy raw materials that would be used by Uni.

A dispute arose with respect to the second contract, which was settled by an arbitral award that Ouralkali sought to enforce in France. Uni-Kod opposed the exequatur decision, arguing that the arbitration clause contained in the joint venture contract could not be extended to the second contract. The Paris *Cour d'appel* confirmed the exequatur judgment, and the Cour de cassation subsequently upheld the decision, finding that the arbitration clause was legally separable from the main contract. With regard to the intended scope of the clause, the *Cour de cassation* held that:

> *"both contracts were inseparable with a view to ensuring the economic viability of the operation and that all disputes and differences that might arise from the joint venture contract or in relation to it had to be submitted to arbitration, including the supply contract, so that the arbitration clause was tacitly but necessarily included in the [second contract]."* [23]

These two French cases provide examples of how economic considerations have been taken into account to determine that two contracts between the same two parties formed a group of contracts (although it should be noted that in the case of Uni-Kod the first contract was also signed by multiple parties, including the two parties that were the only signatories of the second contract). Economic aspects are also important in situations in which two parties have signed a succession of contracts that do not necessarily involve the same transaction. In that case, it is the significant ongoing business relationship that ties together a succession of contracts, as well as the existence of a prior practice in that business relationship showing that the parties intended to include a particular arbitration clause in their usual agreements. [24]

In situations involving multiple parties as well as multiple contracts, the economic link between the contracts necessarily becomes a key consideration in determining the existence of a group of contracts, as the existence of more than two parties eliminates the almost natural link that exists between the contracts when the same parties are the signatories of all of them.

c. Procedural aspects

Group of companies and group of contracts issues can also be distinguished on procedural grounds, as they arise in different procedural contexts and raise different procedural questions.

As explained above, the 'group of companies' doctrine concerns the inclusion of a non-signatory to the arbitration agreement as a party to the proceedings. The group of companies question is always a matter of jurisdiction, and thus often arises even before the constitution of the arbitral tribunal or at the beginning of the proceedings, such as in the request for arbitration or in the answer/counterclaim. This issue is to be distinguished from 'joinder', which in some national jurisdictions concerns the intervention of a *non-party* in the arbitral proceedings at the behest of the claimant or respondent.[25] The group of companies approach concerns the identification of parties to the arbitration, as either claimants or respondents, despite the fact that they have not signed the applicable arbitration agreement.

Under the 'group of companies' doctrine, there is often a single arbitration agreement that may apply to a single contract. In addition, there is generally only one set of arbitral proceedings. Finally, though courts may later review the decision, this jurisdictional question is for the arbitrator to decide, potentially in a partial award following a preliminary phase of the proceedings.

In contrast, the 'group of contracts' doctrine by definition concerns multiple contracts, thus raising the possibility of diverse clauses concerning jurisdiction. That is to say, there may be some contracts with arbitration agreements, others giving jurisdiction to national courts and yet others that contain no clauses concerning jurisdiction. This raises the possibility that multiple proceedings will be commenced in different forums. In any event, initial proceedings may be brought either before an arbitral tribunal or a national court. The 'group of contracts' doctrine is concerned with the question of whether disputes arising under these various contracts may be raised in a single arbitral proceeding. Here the issue, although it could be presented as an issue of jurisdiction, pertains rather to the consolidation of different proceedings, or case management. This situation raises complicated questions as to who has the power to make this determination. Indeed, insofar as groups of companies are concerned, no one seems to doubt that the arbitrator (subject to the control of the state courts in setting-aside or enforcement proceedings) has the power to rule on who is bound by the arbitration agreement. With respect to the consolidation of proceedings (a situation that arises more frequently in the case of groups of contracts than in the case of groups of companies), that power may be vested – sometimes even exclusively – in an arbitral institution or in state courts.

3. SECOND PROPOSITION: THE 'GROUP OF COMPANIES' DOCTRINE AND THE 'GROUP OF CONTRACTS' DOCTRINE ESSENTIALLY RAISE THE SAME ISSUES

Though useful from a conceptual point of view, the sterilized presentation of the 'group of companies' and 'group of contracts' doctrines made under the first proposition, in which certain variables are intentionally isolated, does not reflect the reality and complexity of commercial relations and arbitrations today. It is therefore useful at this point to consider the second proposition, namely that the 'group of companies' and 'group of contracts' doctrines are in fact comparable.

In actuality, the 'group of companies' and 'group of contracts' doctrines do share certain fundamental, common characteristics. These common characteristics include: (a) the convergence of multiple parties and multiple contracts in many cases; (b) the need for the consent of the parties; (c) the diminishing relevance of national laws; and (d) the solution to the issues raised by both doctrines.

a. Overlap of multiple parties and multiple contracts

Situations that involve multiple contracts can involve contracts that do not have identical parties. These situations, which involve both multiple contracts and multiple parties, may implicate various facets of group of companies and group of contracts analysis. In today's practice, it is rather common to find group of companies and group of contracts issues in a single case. The prominent case of *Kis France* v. *Société Générale*[26] provides a good example of a case in which these two doctrines have intersected.

In this case, the French company Kis France entered into a commercial relationship with Société Générale for the marketing of photography printing and development laboratory equipment manufactured by the former. The various agreements signed by the parties included the following: (a) a framework agreement between Kis France and Société Générale acting on their own behalf and on behalf of their subsidiaries; (b) an agreement for implementation of the framework agreement between Sogelese Corporation, a leasing subsidiary of Société Générale, and Kis Corporation (previously named Kis California), a subsidiary of Kis France; (c) a contract between Société Générale, acting for itself and for its subsidiary, and Kis Photo Industrie, acting on its own behalf and on behalf of its subsidiary Kis USA; and (d) an addendum to the framework agreement signed between Société Générale, acting in its own name and for its subsidiary Sogelese Corporation, and by Kis France, also acting in its own name and for its subsidiary Kis Corporation.

The framework agreement contained an ICC arbitration clause to which express reference was made in the local agreements and the addenda. A dispute arose between the parties and arbitration was initiated by Société Générale, Sogelese Corporation and Sogelese Pacifique (also a subsidiary of Société Générale) against Kis France and Kis Photo Industrie, jointly and severally, for monies allegedly owed to Sogelese Corporation by Kis Corporation under the framework agreement and two of the subsequent agreements. The arbitral tribunal considered that it had jurisdiction over all the claimants and respondents, as well as jurisdiction to decide all issues arising under the various agreements.

An action to set aside the arbitral tribunal's decision was filed with the Paris *Cour d'appel,* but the court confirmed the jurisdiction of the arbitral decision. The court held that, since the local agreements referred to the arbitration clause contained in the framework agreement and 'the parent companies played a dominant role *vis-à-vis* their subsidiaries, which were bound to abide by the former's commercial and financial decisions', it could be assumed that the main agreement and subcontracts were inexorably linked, forming part of a unified contractual scheme, that allowed for the consolidation of the disputes into a single proceeding. The court's observation about the dominant role of the parent companies over their subsidiaries shows that it implemented aspects of the 'group of companies' doctrine when determining that the 'group of contracts' doctrine applied to tie together all the disputes.

Thus, *Kis France* provides a good example of the potential overlap between the 'group of companies' and 'group of contracts' doctrines. It has been argued that when the issue of a group of contracts is raised, 'the fact that the parties to the contracts may belong to a group is a priori irrelevant', though the commentary also acknowledged that 'it may in some cases help clarify or resolve the issues that arise from the existence of a group of contracts'[27]. It has also been pointed out that the grounds for the arbitral decision in *Kis France* 'lay primarily in the contracts between the parties', and that 'it was not so much the existence of a group, but instead the intention of the parties – revealed in this case by the interrelated contracts – which justified the extension of the arbitration agreement'. [28]

Though the 'group of contracts' doctrine was undoubtedly central to the *Kis France* case, the group of companies aspect also played an important role. Importantly, the French *Cour d'appel* found that, given the subordination of the subsidiaries, it was not only possible to involve the parent companies in an arbitration of a dispute arising between the subsidiaries, but that the involvement of the parent companies was a necessary element of any arbitration brought: 'the arbitrators may decide the disputes concerning the execution of both the Basic and Local Agreement, but only upon the request of the two parent companies.'

b. Consent

Consent is the cornerstone on which the foundations of arbitration rest. Any court or arbitral tribunal seeking to apply either the 'group of companies' doctrine or the 'group of contracts' doctrine must establish that the parties consented to submit the disputes at issue to arbitration. Without consent, no amount of connections between multiple parties and multiple contracts would be sufficient to give an arbitral tribunal jurisdiction. It has thus been observed, in particular with regard to the 'group of contracts' doctrine, that:

> *"it is not simply because a number of contracts bind several parties with a view to performance together of certain obligations thereunder that arbitration is available for all of them on the basis of one or more arbitration clauses binding only some of them. It is only where there exists a true common intention to abide by such an arbitration agreement that contractual 'consolidation' by agreement is possible."* [29]

In other words, analyzing the issues raised by the 'group of companies' and 'group of contracts' doctrines serves the ultimate purpose of determining the intention of the parties. The essential underlying question in either doctrine must be: does an arbitration agreement exist that encompasses or links together all the parties and/or all the contracts? The primacy of the issue of consent was highlighted by the Paris *Cour d'appel* in *Kis France*, where it observed:

> *'The arbitrators' main consideration was that the parties intended by their agreements to carry out one economic operation by establishing a contractual unity, in which the subsidiaries would be very dependent on the parent companies, which retained the decision making power.'* [30]

The emerging trend in French case law, as revealed in the *Alcatel* and *Pujol* cases discussed above, is that consent is the key element that permits all construction around the 'group of companies' or 'group of contracts' doctrines.

c. Diminishing relevance of national laws

The foregoing analysis shows that arbitrators and state courts alike resort to factual analysis rather than legal considerations when resolving group of companies and group of contracts issues. Consequently, the resolution of these issues does not necessarily depend on the applicable law.

Arbitral practice has evolved to allow the application of the 'group of companies' and 'group of contracts' doctrines in a rather homogenous way (at least by arbitral tribunals), not only because the analysis for both is based on the common intention of the parties and commercial practice, but more so because of: (1) the homogenization of national laws that recognize the importance of determining consent (beyond the form of the arbitration agreement); and (2) a general acceptance that an arbitration agreement may be incorporated by reference.

Furthermore, both doctrines rely on the universal principles of good faith, estoppel and apparent authority.

d. A common solution to situations requiring application of both doctrines

The root of problems necessitating the application of both doctrines often lies in the imperfections of the arbitration agreement, which may fail to adequately express the scope of issues falling under its purview or may not have been signed by all of the parties intending to be bound by it. The common solution for avoiding the problems that may arise under the 'group of companies' and 'group of contracts' doctrines is therefore to go back to the basics and devise adequate arbitration agreements when drafting contractual instruments implementing complex economic transactions.

The problems giving rise to application of the 'group of companies' and 'group of contracts' doctrines could be prevented by drafting an adequate global arbitration agreement that can then easily be referred to in other contracts. This global agreement could take the form of a stand-alone agreement or be part of an umbrella or framework agreement. Of course, this solution is effective only to the extent that subsequent contracts clearly refer to the arbitration agreement and to the extent that all relevant parties sign contracts reflecting their consent to adhere to the arbitration agreement. Although such arbitration clauses remain relatively rare in practice, examples and model clauses have started circulating within the international arbitration community. [31]

One interesting example is offered by Euro Disney's arbitration clause.[32] This standard arbitration clause, apparently inserted in the construction contracts concluded by Euro Disney, covers both bipartite and multipartite arbitrations, providing for settlement of all disputes by three arbitrators under the ICC arbitration rules. Concerning multiparty arbitration, the clause aims at preventing the most frequent issues from arising by addressing the various possibilities that could arise in connection with consent to arbitration and procedural issues, such as the appointment of arbitrators.

Regarding consent to arbitration, the main contractor expresses in advance its consent to the client joining third parties to the arbitration and its consent to be joined to arbitrations between the client and third parties, under a set of circumstances specified in the clause. Similarly, the client agrees to be joined to an arbitration arising between the main contractor and a designated subcontractor. The arbitration clause further specifies the contracts that may be considered part of a group of contracts and the entities that may become party to an arbitration arising out of these contracts.

The original mechanism set up in the clause for the appointment of arbitrators is noteworthy for what is clearly a thorough contemplation of the possibility of multiparty arbitration. It provides that when filing a request for arbitration and the answer to this request, the initial parties will refrain from nominating an arbitrator, thereby departing from the ICC rules.[33] If the arbitration remains bipartite, the parties will proceed to agree on a sole arbitrator or nominate their respective arbitrators. If the arbitration becomes multipartite within the time limits set for joining other parties, the mechanism provides that all parties will try to agree unanimously on the names of the co-arbitrators and the president of the arbitral tribunal. Failing such agreement, any party will be free to request the President of the Paris *Tribunal de grande instance* to appoint the arbitrators from a list of candidates prepared by the ICC.

Even in the absence of such a carefully crafted arbitration clause, it has been argued that 'one should not exaggerate the difficulties raised by resolving disputes pertaining to interdependent contracts' and that the problems caused by multiparty and multi-contract arbitrations are 'not always complex ones, and even if they are, more often than not an acceptable solution is found'. [34] This point is highlighted by the decision of the Swiss *Tribunal*

Fédéral of 8 December 1999 in *Arthur Andersen Business Unit (AABU) Member Firms v. Andersen Consulting Business Unit (ACBU) Member Firms*, in which it found that, despite imperfections in the implementation of a revised arbitration agreement, the intention of the parties to adhere to the revised arbitration agreement was clear. [35]

In the *Andersen case*, the Swiss *Tribunal Fédéral* held that an arbitration agreement among no fewer than 142 parties was valid and enforceable. The very complex and elaborate structure of the Arthur Andersen group was at the heart of the dispute in this case.

In 1999, the global entity Andersen Worldwide Organization comprised Andersen Worldwide Société Coopérative (AWSC), its partners, its member companies ('member firms') and other affiliated entities. AWSC was a cooperative incorporated under Swiss law, with the purpose of organizing a global services network among the member firms. Within AWSC, two separate commercial units coexisted: the Andersen Consulting Business Unit (ACBU) and the Arthur Andersen Business Unit (AABU). Every member firm belonged to one of these two commercial units.

The member firms were interdependent national entities that had each entered into a contract with AWSC called the 'Member Firm Interfirm Agreement' (MFIA), so that the Andersen group could operate as a whole to provide their services globally to international clients. The MFIAs were essentially based on a standard contract approved by AWSC's partners. Each MFIA was concluded between the member firm (and/or its partners, shareholders, etc.) and AWSC, acting on its own behalf and on behalf of the other member firms. Under the standard MFIA, each member firm accepted that all the rights and obligations contained in the MFIA could be enforced by or against the other member firms and that the MFIAs could only be amended in writing through agreements signed by both parties.

Section 22 of the standard MFIA provided for the resolution of all disputes arising out of or relating to the MFIA through arbitration by a sole arbitrator. Generally, these arbitrations would take place in Geneva under the rules of the *Concordat intercantonal sur l'arbitrage* (CIA), with a Swiss court as the appointing authority, although the parties could agree to a seat outside Switzerland, where the arbitration would take place under the ICC arbitration rules. Section 22 of the standard MFIA was amended over time. Under the revised version of Section 22, any arbitration would take place under the ICC rules, with the ICC as the appointing authority, irrespective of the seat of the arbitration. However, only a handful of the individual MFIAs signed with member firms were actually amended to reflect the changes to the standard MFIA.

In 1997, 44 member firms belonging to ACBU initiated an ICC arbitration in Geneva against AWSC and 97 member firms of AABU. Sixty-eight of the respondents challenged the jurisdiction of the sole arbitrator appointed by the ICC on the ground that most MFIAs contained older versions of Section 22 providing for arbitration under the CIA rules and/or appointment of the sole arbitrator by a Swiss court.

In a partial award, the sole arbitrator found that he had jurisdiction over all parties to the dispute, considering that only the 1994 (revised) version of the arbitration clause was in force. The respondents who had disputed the arbitrator's jurisdiction challenged the award before the *Swiss Tribunal Fédéral*, which upheld the arbitrator's decision. The court held that these member firms were bound by the latest version of the standard MFIA arbitration clause even though the MFIAs they had signed did not contain the same version. Because AWSC entered into the various MFIAs on its own behalf and on behalf of the other member firms, the fact that the new version of the standard MFIA was included in only one MFIA was enough to make it binding on all other member firms. Furthermore, this interpretation was in line with the intention of AWSC's partners in 1994 when they formally approved the changes to the standard MFIA, including a revised arbitration clause.

> The *Tribunal Fédéral* concluded: *'All things considered, it is difficult to understand why the claimants criticize the sensible solution of giving a sole arbitrator responsibility for resolving this multiparty conflict.'* [36]

The *Andersen case* thus illustrates a number of points. First, it is possible to draft effective arbitration clauses suitable for even the most complex multiparty situations. Of course, *Andersen* also shows that in drafting and implementing such clauses, the possibility for future revisions should always be taken into account. In this respect, when the arbitration clause is to apply to a multiplicity of contracts, it might be wise to proceed by way of reference to a stand-alone arbitration agreement, rather than actually inserting the clause itself in every contract. On the other hand, the *Andersen case* also shows that even if the implementation of such a clause is not executed perfectly, arbitral tribunals and national courts can still uphold the manifest intention behind such a global arbitration clause.

4. CONCLUSION

Following this analysis, it is apparent that there are grounds for arguing that the 'group of companies' and 'group of contracts' doctrines are either divergent or comparable. Though they cannot be said to be identical, it is clear that the similarities between the two are more than superficial. The answer that this analysis points to, when considering the results of each proposition, is that the 'group of companies' doctrine and the 'group of contracts' doctrine are two different subjects, but they essentially raise the same fundamental issues.

Both the 'group of companies' doctrine and the 'group of contracts' doctrine will likely continue to arise in the context of complex international transactions, although the proliferation of complex arbitrations may encourage parties to draft their arbitration clauses with these issues in mind.

However, if arbitral tribunals and courts alike opt for an analysis that concentrates only on the conduct and intention of the parties, one may legitimately wonder whether the interest in and importance of the 'group of companies' and 'group of contracts' doctrines are still justified. Maybe these doctrines have already passed their time and, as some commentators on the *Pujol* and *Alcatel* cases have suggested with respect to the 'group of companies' doctrine[37], perhaps these doctrines have become 'obsolete'.

END NOTES

* Partner, Shearman & Sterling LLP. The author gratefully acknowledges the able assistance of Rachel Boynton-Laut, Associate, and Jérémie Kohn, intern, at Shearman & Sterling LLP, in the preparation of this article.

1 Since the 'group of companies' doctrine originated under French law, and French law has also explored the 'group of contracts' doctrine, this article focuses mainly on French arbitration and case law examples. As noted, the relative acceptance of either the 'group of companies' doctrine or the 'group of contracts' doctrine is outside the scope of this article. For an overview of the reception of the 'group of companies' doctrine in various jurisdictions, see Gary Born, *International Commercial Arbitration* (Kluwer, 2009) p. 1174 et seq.; Stephan Wilske, Laurence Shore and Jan-Michael Ahrens, 'The "Group of Companies Doctrine" – Where Is It Heading?', *The American Review of International Arbitration* 17 (2006) p. 73 at p. 78 et seq.; Noah Rubins, 'Group of Companies Doctrine and the New York Convention', *Enforcement of Arbitration Agreements and International Arbitral Awards: The New York Convention in Practice* (Cameron May, 2008) p. 455 et seq. For a thorough review of case law relating to the 'group of companies' and 'group of contracts' doctrines, see Bernard Hanotiau, *Complex Arbitrations: Multiparty, Multicontract, Multi-issue and Class Actions* (Kluwer, 2005).

2 Emmanuel Gaillard and John Savage (eds.), *Fouchard, Gaillard, Goldman on International Commercial Arbitration* (Kluwer, 1999) at para. 500.

3 See Bernard Hanotiau, 'Non-signatories in International Arbitration: Lessons from Thirty Years of Case Law', *International Arbitration 2006: Back to Basics?* (Kluwer, 2007) p. 343; Hanotiau, supra note 1, at pp. 49-50.

4 For a detailed description of the group of companies scenarios with which courts and arbitral tribunals have been confronted, see Hanotiau, supra note 1, at pp. 54-55.

5 For examples of group of contracts scenarios, see Hanotiau, *supra* note 1, at pp. 101-104.

6 In *Dow Chemical,* various companies within the Dow Chemical group brought an arbitration claim against Isover Saint Gobain, though not all of the Dow Chemical companies were signatories to the contracts containing the relevant arbitration clause. See Interim Award of 23 September 1982 in ICC case No. 4131, *Isover-Saint-Gobain* v. *Dow Chemical France*. See the original French version in Revue de l'Arbitrage (1984) p. 137. For the English version, see Sigvard Jarvin and Yves Derains, *Collection of ICC Arbitral Awards 1974-1985* (ICC Publishing/Kluwer, 1994) p. 146.

7 See Jarvin and Derains, *supra* note 6, at p. 151. See also Born, *supra* note 1, at pp. 1168-1169 (citing this passage).

8 Ibid.

9 *Societe Isover-Saint-Gobain* v. *Societe Dow Chem*. France, Paris Cour d'appel, 21 October 1983. See the original French version in Revue de l'Arbitrage (1984) p. 98, and the commentary by André Chapelle. See also Born, supra note 1, at p. 1169.

10 *Société V 2000 v. Société Project XJ 220 ITD et autre*, Paris Cour d'appel, 7 December 1994. See the original French version in Revue de l'Arbitrage (1996) p. 245, and the commentary by Charles Jarrosson.

11 Ibid., at p. 250 : '[...] bien qu'elle n'en soit pas signataire, elle a eu connaissance de la convention litigieuse qu'elle a pris l'initiative de faire traduire et notamment de l'existence de la clause compromissoire dont elle revendique elle-même le bénéfice.'

12 Ibid. See also Gaillard and Savage, *supra* note 2, at para. 499 (citing this passage and

providing the translation used here).

13 *Société Alcatel Business Systems* (ABS) et al. v. *Société Amkor technology et al.*, Cour de cassation, 27 March 2007, pourvoi n° 04-20842. See the original French version in *Revue de l'Arbitrage* (2007) p. 785, and the commentary by Jalal El-Ahdab. See also the commentary by Cécile Legros in *Journal du Droit International 'Clunet'* (2007) p. 968.

14 *Société Alcatel Business Systems (ABS)*, *supra* note 13, at p. 787 : '[...] l'effet de la clause d'arbitrage international s'étend aux parties directement impliquées dans l'exécution du contrat et les litiges qui peuvent en résulter; [...] ces sociétés étaient en droit de se prévaloir, à l'égard de la société ABS [...] de la clause d'arbitrage stipulée au contrat liant leur société mère à la société AME.'

15 See Jérôme Barbet, 'Extension des effets de la clause compromissoire à des parties non signataires du contrat: les juridictions françaises persistent... et signent', *Petites affiches* 159/160 (2009) p. 10 at p. 18. See also Christophe Seraglini, *Société Alcatel Business Systems (ABS)*, commentary in *La semaine juridique – Edition générale* I 168 (LexisNexis JurisClasseur, 2007) p. 19 at p. 20.

16 *Sociétés Suba France et Suba & Unico v. Société Pujol*, Paris Cour d'appel, 7 May 2009. See the original French version in *Petites affiches* 159/160 (2009) p. 10.

17 Ibid., at p. 12 : 'la clause compromissoire insérée dans un contrat international a une validité et une efficacité propres qui commandent d'en étendre l'application aux parties directement impliquées dans l'exécution du contrat et dans les litiges qui peuvent en résulter.'

18 Philippe Leboulanger, 'Multi-Contract Arbitration', *Journal of International Arbitration* 13/4 (1996) p. 43 at p. 46.

19 See Eric Loquin, 'Différences et convergences dans le régime de la transmission et de l'extension de la clause compromissoire devant les juridictions françaises', *Gazette du Palais* 157 (2002) p. 7, in particular paras. 25 to 45.

20 *Société Glencore Grain Rotterdam* BV v. *Société Afric*, Paris Cour d'appel, 23 November 1999. See the original French version in *Revue de l'Arbitrage* (2000) p. 501, and the commentary by Xiao-Ying Li-Kotovtchikhine.

21 Ibid., at p. 503-504 (emphasis added): '[...] à les supposer même juridiquement indépendants l'un de l'autre, les accords successivement conclus à quelques semaines d'intervalle [...], qui concernaient la vente et la «reprise» entre les mêmes parties d'une même marchandise ont constitué à l'évidence des conventions complémentaires ou à tout le moins connexes; que dès lors et même si l'échange de téléfax intervenus [...] ne fait pas référence à la clause compromissoire figurant dans l'accord initial ni d'ailleurs à aucune autre forme de règlement des litiges éventuels, il se déduit des liens économiques étroits existant entre les deux phases de l'opération dont la seconde [...] n'était que la suite et la conséquence de la première, que la volonté implicite des parties a été nécessairement d'étendre les effets de la clause compromissoire à l'ensemble du contentieux aux composantes indissociables, pouvant survenir entre elles à propos de leur exécution.'

22 *Société Uni-Kod* v. *Société Ouralkali*, Cour de cassation, 30 March 2004, pourvoi n° 01-14311. See the original French version in *Revue de l'Arbitrage* (2005) p. 959, and the commentary by Christophe Seraglini. For the English version, see *Yearbook of Commercial Arbitration*, Vol. 30 (Kluwer, 2005) p. 1200.

23 Ibid., at p. 960 (emphasis added) : '[...] les deux contrats étant indissociables en vue d'assurer la viabilité économique de l'opération et [...] la soumission à l'arbitrage concernait tous les litiges et divergences pouvant naître du contrat de coopération ou en liaison avec celui-ci, comme l'était le contrat de fourniture, de sorte que la clause compromissoire était tacitement mais nécessairement incluse dans le [second contrat].'

24 See Gaillard and Savage, *supra* note 2, at para. 523.

25 See Hanotiau, *supra* note 3, at p. 346.

26 *Kis France* v. *Société Générale*, Paris Cour d'appel, 31 October 1989. See the original French version in Revue de l'Arbitrage (1992) p. 90, and the commentaries by Laurent Aynès and Daniel Cohen. For the English version, see Yearbook of Commercial Arbitration, Vol. 16 (Kluwer, 1991) p. 145.

27 Hanotiau, *supra* note 3, at p. 342 (citing Kis France).

28 Gaillard and Savage, supra note 2, at para. 506.

29 Jean-Louis Delvolvé, Jean Rouche and Gerald Pointon, French Arbitration Law and Practice (Kluwer, 2003) p. 72.

30 Kis France v. Société Générale, supra note 26, at pp. 148-149.

31 See Hanotiau, supra note 1, at para. 226, and the selection of multiparty arbitration clauses provided in Appendix 2, p. 313.

32 Ibid., at Appendix 2, p. 321.

33 At the time, under the ICC Rules then in place (the 1988 version), no provision for designation of arbitrators in a multiparty setting existed (such a provision was inserted as Article 10 in the 1998 revision of the ICC Rules).

34 Hanotiau, *supra* note 1, at para. 225.

35 *Arthur Andersen Business Unit (AABU) Member Firms* v. *Andersen Consulting Business Unit (ACBU) Member Firms*, Swiss Tribunal Fédéral, 8 December 1999. See the original French version in ASA Bulletin 18/3 (2000) p. 546. For the English version, see *The American Review of International Arbitration* 10 (1999) p. 559.

36 Ibid., at p. 557 : 'Au demeurant, on ne comprend guère pourquoi les recourants critiquent la solution judicieuse consistant à charger un arbitre unique de démêler un conflit multipartite.'

37 See Barbet, *supra* note 15, at p. 21.

CHAPTER 2

DÉPEÇAGE OR CONSOLIDATION OF THE DISPUTES RESULTING
FROM CONNECTED AGREEMENTS:
THE ROLE OF THE ARBITRATOR

STEPHEN R. BOND*

1. INTRODUCTION

Consider the following situation. A company plans to build a facility for the liquefaction of natural gas on a sandy island in the Persian Gulf. The liquefaction takes place by placing the gas into tanks and freezing it into a liquid state at extremely low temperatures. The tanks in which the process takes place are huge: a hundred yards in diameter and a hundred feet tall. To build these tanks, the company hires a contractor, who in turn hires a subcontractor for the specific purpose of supplying certain building materials and incorporating them into the tanks as they are being built.

Unfortunately, after the facility goes into operation, defects are noticed in the structure of the tanks. Cracks appear, and tanks have to be repaired at a cost of millions of pounds. The company blames the contractor for the problem, claiming that the tank design was defective. The contractor blames the sub-contractor, claiming the materials were inadequate for the sandy soil of the island. The contract between the facility owner and contractor has an arbitration clause, and so the owner brings a claim against the contractor. The contract between the contractor and the sub-contractor also has an arbitration clause, albeit one that differs significantly from the one in the main contract, and so the contractor brings a separate claim against the sub-contractor.

The question then is whether there must be separate arbitrations for the two contracts or whether there should be only one proceeding. Separate proceedings could result in inconsistent rulings on points of common concern – such as what actually caused the cracks in the walls of the tanks and who was responsible – but a single proceeding would seem to conflict with the intent of the parties, as expressed in their decision to have two contracts between three separate parties, each with its own arbitration clause.[1]

This paper considers such situations from the perspective of an arbitrator charged with this question – *dépeçage* or consolidation. In some instances, an arbitrator considering whether to consolidate or keep separate related disputes must inquire into his or her authority under national legislation or the rules of international arbitral institutions. In other instances, the answer to this question is driven more by an interpretative analysis, namely whether the parties intended for multiple, connected agreements to be considered as part of a single proceeding. In all instances, however, the arbitrator must weigh two competing principles. First, the fundamental notion that the arbitration derives its authority from the consent of the parties.[2] Second, the idea that arbitration should be a system of dispute resolution that is relevant to the needs of international commerce, actually resolves disputes and does so with a minimum of unnecessary delay and expense.

This paper suggests that, while the policy-oriented goals of effective and efficient dispute resolution are highly appropriate from a systemic perspective, in a case-specific context they must yield to the clearly expressed will of the parties. To conclude otherwise is to make the best the enemy of the good and to threaten the foundation of consent upon which the international commercial arbitration system is based.[3]

2. LEGISLATIVE AND INSTITUTIONAL RULES AS A SOURCE OF AUTHORITY FOR CONSOLIDATION OR *DÉPEÇAGE*

Often, the decision of an arbitrator whether or not to consolidate is fundamentally impacted by national legislation and the institutional rules under which the arbitration is taking place.[4] In a few instances, the arbitrator's job is made easier by the fact that the power to consolidate is consigned to the courts, rather than the arbitrator.[5] In these cases, the arbitrator's role is naturally limited.

Where national legislation empowers the arbitrators to consolidate, it commonly authorizes consolidation only in the presence of the parties' positive consent. For example, Section 35 of the English Arbitration Act of 1996 provides that:

"(1) The parties are free to agree –
(a) that the arbitral proceedings shall be consolidated with other arbitral proceedings, or
(b) that concurrent hearings shall be held, on such terms as may be agreed.
(2) Unless the parties agree to confer such power on the tribunal, the tribunal has no power to order consolidation of proceedings or concurrent hearings."

Other Commonwealth and former Commonwealth countries, such as Singapore and Ireland, have passed similar legislation.[6]

While these laws make clear that consolidation is permissible under some circumstances, they do not add much insight to any of the more complicated permutations of the consolidation analysis, such as when both parties do not agree to consolidate or when the consolidation would implicate a separate proceeding that is already ongoing.

In this regard, the Australian International Arbitration Act represents a marked departure from the model generally embraced by the Commonwealth community. Section 24 of the Act allows for a party to arbitral proceedings before an arbitral tribunal to apply to the tribunal for a consolidation order on any of three grounds: (1) 'a common question of law or fact arises in all those proceedings'; (2) 'the rights to relief claimed in all those proceedings are in respect of, or arise out of, the same transaction or series of transactions'; or (3) 'for some other reason specified in the application, it is desirable that an order be made [for consolidation]'.[7] Importantly, this procedure provides for consolidation whether or not all the proceedings at issue are before the same arbitral tribunal. Where related proceedings are being heard by different tribunals, the law directs the panels to communicate, jointly deliberate and, if possible, issue a joint order determining whether to consolidate the proceedings, sequence them according to an agreed-upon timeline or, alternatively, stay any of the proceedings pending the determination of any other proceeding.[8]

By clarifying the procedure for consolidation and allowing consolidation based upon a single party's application, the Australian law takes a stronger pro-consolidation approach than the laws of most other countries.[9] The problem with this law, however, is that in setting out a detailed procedure for consolidation, it also limits the parties' autonomy to craft an arbitration agreement that takes a different position with respect to consolidation. Parties may have legitimate interests in opposing an arbitral framework that allows for easy consolidation – such as, for example, an interest in arbitration as a vehicle for targeted dispute-resolution involving parties that can be reliably identified in advance – and these interests could be substantially frustrated under this law.

The same tension is present in the rules of international arbitral institutions that relate to consolidation. Several prominent international arbitral institutions allow for consolidation by the relevant institution (not the arbitral tribunal) of multiple proceedings in the absence of both parties' consent. For example, Article 4(6) of the Rules of Arbitration for the International Chamber of Commerce (ICC) authorize the ICC Court[10] to consolidate multiple proceedings when several conditions are met: (1) consolidation is requested by a party; (2) the two (or more) related arbitrations are proceeding under ICC Rules; (3) the arbitrations concern the 'same parties'; and (4) the arbitrations arise from the same 'legal relationship'.[11]

Other international arbitral institutions have adopted similar provisions, some of which allow for consolidation in situations where neither party has so requested.[12] In a certain sense, these provisions are more sympathetic to consolidation than the British legislative model, insofar as they allow consolidation in the absence of the parties' agreement. Furthermore, at least in theory, they do not depart from the intent of the parties, since by agreeing upon a particular arbitral institution in their arbitration agreement, the parties are submitting to a certain set of procedural devices – including any rules that provide for consolidation even in the absence of both parties' agreement. The reality, though, is that when arbitral institutional rules depart from parties' reasonable expectations regarding their procedural rights – particularly in situations where the procedural rules result in a real or perceived inequality between the parties – party autonomy can be fatally undermined.

This concern was made manifest in the watershed *Dutco* case.[13] The case arose from a consortium agreement that involved three parties – BKMI, Siemens and *Dutco* – entering into a contract to build a cement factory.[14] The consortium agreement included an arbitration clause that provided for ICC Rules and the appointment of three arbitrators. *Dutco* initiated the arbitration against Siemens and BKMI and chose its arbitrator. Given that their interests were not fully in alignment, Siemens and BKMI were unable to agree upon a joint party-appointed arbitrator. In order to avoid having the ICC appoint a single arbitrator on behalf of both respondents, they eventually nominated an arbitrator, but only under protest. After the arbitration was concluded, Siemens and BKMI initiated an action in the French courts to set aside the award on jurisdiction on the grounds that it violated the fundamental principle of equality between the parties, notwithstanding that the ICC Rules had mandated the arbitrator-selection procedures employed. [15]

The case eventually reached the French *Cour de cassation*, which invalidated the award, concluding that 'the principle of the equality of the parties in the designation of the arbitrators is a matter which concerns public policy, which can only be waived after the dispute has arisen.'[16] While many arbitral institutions reacted swiftly to *Dutco* by changing their rules to preclude situations where parties have unequal power over the constitution of the panel,[17] *Dutco's* continuing importance should not be underestimated. By suggesting that even advance waivers are in some circumstances void for reasons of public policy, *Dutco* lends support to the broader proposition that arbitrators must be wary of consolidation – even when provided for by the relevant arbitration rules – when it appears to interfere with the principle of party autonomy and the equal treatment of the parties in the constitution of the arbitral tribunal.

In sum, while national legislation or arbitration rules sometimes authorize the courts or arbitral institutions to consolidate cases over the objections of a party, arbitral tribunals themselves appear not to have been accorded this power through the relevant laws or arbitration rules.

3. DERIVING AUTHORITY FOR CONSOLIDATION OR *DÉPEÇAGE* FROM THE ARBITRATION AGREEMENT ITSELF

Where national legislation or the rules of the relevant international arbitral institution do not provide guidance regarding consolidation or *dépeçage*, an arbitrator must commonly engage in an interpretative analysis of the arbitration agreement (or agreements in the case of a multiple-contract dispute). Except in the rare case where a consent to consolidate appears to be present in the arbitration clauses, in the face of a party's objection the arbitrator is obliged to determine whether the parties' consent to consolidate is fairly implied from the terms of their agreement.

As an arbitrator undertakes this analysis, it is appropriate to consider whether there exists a presumption, either in favour of consolidation or opposed to it. While arbitrators are familiar with the traditional notion of interpreting arbitration agreements in *favorem validitatis*,[18] that is to say, interpreting arbitration agreements broadly, there is little discussion of the question whether it is appropriate to apply a specific presumption for or against consolidation.

Two US courts of appeal have grappled with this question as it relates to the courts' power to consolidate. In *American Centennial Insurance Co. v. National Casualty Co.*,[19] the Sixth Circuit considered a case in which an insurance company embroiled in a complex reinsurance dispute sought to have all aspects of the dispute resolved in a single proceeding. When the respondents resisted, the claimant filed an action in federal court seeking to have the proceedings consolidated. The court rejected the effort, explaining that 'a district court is without power to consolidate arbitration proceedings, over the objection of a party to the arbitration agreement, when the agreement is silent regarding consolidation.'[20] By seemingly requiring a clear statement that consolidation is permissible – and by refusing to allow for the possibility that an arbitration agreement, by itself, while silent on the exact question of consolidation, may yet strongly suggest an agreed upon intent to consolidate[21] – the Sixth Circuit adopted a strong presumption against consolidation.

The Sixth Circuit's approach was explicitly rejected in 2000 by the Seventh Circuit, which refused to adopt a presumption either in favour of or against consolidation. In *Connecticut General Life Insurance Co. v. Sun Life Assurance Co. of Canada*,[22] the Seventh Circuit confronted a similar situation involving a multi-party dispute with multiple contracts among insurers and reinsurers. In determining whether or not to allow for consolidation, the court explicitly rejected a rule requiring a clear statement in the arbitration agreements authorizing consolidation. The court explained that 'we cannot see any reason why, in interpreting the arbitration clause for purposes of deciding whether to order consolidation, the court should (as the language [...] from the *American Centennial case* might, if read literally, be thought to suggest) place its thumb on the scale, insisting that it be "clear", rather than merely more likely than not, that the parties intended consolidation.'[23]

Applying this debate to the context of an arbitrator's decision whether or not to consolidate, there is considerable merit to the Seventh Circuit's approach. As noted, a principal objective of the arbitrator in structuring the proceedings is to give effect to the intent of the parties. This is a familiar jurisprudential posture, not just for arbitration matters but, as the court in *Connecticut General* noted, for issues of contract interpretation generally.[24] For an arbitrator to require a clear statement allowing consolidation is to indulge in a policy preference against consolidation. This might be appropriate from the perspective of a legislative body or an international arbitral institution, but it is not the role of the arbitrator.

Indeed, if there is to be any presumption, it might be said to lean in favour of consolidation. As Lord Denning noted in the *Abu Dhabi* case referred to in note 1: 'It is most undesirable that there should be inconsistent findings by two separate arbitrators on virtually the self-same question, such as causation. It is very desirable that everything should be done to avoid such a circumstance.' (p. 427).

Concluding, then, that an arbitrator should investigate the intent of the parties regarding consolidation as an issue to be proven, one way or another, without any presumption against consolidation and bearing in mind that most business people would most probably have intended to avoid the problems pointed out by Lord Denning, the next question is whether there are any *indicia* that allow an arbitrator to find implied consent or objection to consolidation. In a multi-contract setting, this question is typically answered by reference to the relationships among the contracts themselves, including the degree of similarity of the wording of the arbitration clauses. Where multiple parties are involved, the relationship among the parties also impacts the analysis. [25]

With respect to these *indicia*, it is instructive to compare two cases, ICC case No. 4367[26] and ICC case No. 8420.[27] In the first case, the arbitration was initiated by a US claimant who sold certain industrial equipment. The respondent was an Indian company that used the claimant's equipment to process and sell products in India. In 1964, the two parties entered into a sales agreement that included an arbitration clause. In 1982, a dispute arose between the parties on account of unpaid interest on certain promissory notes relating to their ongoing business relationship. The respondent argued that the promissory notes (which did not have arbitration clauses) were separate agreements from the original 1964 contract and thus that there was no arbitral jurisdiction to hear the dispute. The panel disagreed, reasoning that 'even if, which we dispute, the promissory notes were separate contracts, we would find that the arbitration clause was sufficiently wide to embrace disputes between the parties arising from them.'[28] Thus, for purposes of its holding, the panel relied on the relationship between the contracts as the dispositive *indicia* to support consolidating the multiple contracts into a single proceeding. Because the promissory notes were ordinary incidents to the underlying 1964 contract, the panel concluded that they were fairly within the scope of the original contract's arbitration clause. [29]

The tribunal came out in the opposite direction in ICC case No. 8420. In this case, the claimant, a Syrian purchaser, and the respondent, an Italian supplier, concluded an agency agreement whereby the claimant undertook to promote the respondent's products and provide general assistance to its business. Four years later, the two parties entered into two secondary contracts, both of which related to a discrete, specific project. When a dispute arose in relation to these secondary contracts, the claimant initiated an arbitration, relying on an arbitration agreement in the principal agency contract. The tribunal concluded that '[t]he two "secondary" contracts [...] represent neither a fulfillment nor an amendment of the previous contractual relationship, i.e. the agency agreement, but something completely new, which gives the parties different duties and obligations which are not directly connected with the agency.'[30] Thus, while focusing on the same dispositive *indicia* as the panel in ICC case No. 4367 – the relationship between the contracts – here the tribunal came out in the opposite direction.

An intriguing conceptualization of *indicia* relating to the connectedness of contracts was employed by the tribunal in the Zurich Chamber of Commerce award in case No. 273/95 of 31 May 1996.[31] The panel was confronted with a complex and interconnected group of contracts involving the supply of raw materials to the claimant's processing plant in Hungary. Even though the various contracts and agreements were signed by different parties and used different wording, and even though some contracts had arbitration clauses and some did not, the panel concluded that it had jurisdiction over the whole group. Its discussion resembles the analyses of the panels above insofar as it focused on the relationship between the contracts – what the panel in this case referred to as the 'group of contracts theory' – but what makes the discussion of this decision unique is that it conceives of contracts as existing in multiple layers, with 'top' layer agreements setting up frameworks between the parties, and 'bottom' layer agreements executing specific transactions.[32]

In the tribunal's view, so long as the top layer agreements have arbitration clauses, lower layer contracts would be covered by them: '[w]here in the top layer agreements the parties have provided for a particular type of arbitration any dispute that arises under a contract of a lower layer such as the disputes leading to claimants' claims will be governed by the top layer arbitration clause unless there is a different arbitration clause or a different jurisdiction clause on a lower level or in the contract under which a particular, specific dispute arises.'[33] By categorizing the contracts at issue in the case into layers and fashioning a general rule along these lines, the panel took what is often a factor-based standard (i.e. whether the parties intended to provide for consolidation) and reframed it as more of a bright-line rule.

However helpful such a rule might be in situations involving contracts that can be intelligibly sorted into multiple layers, the analysis is of less assistance when an arbitrator is confronted with a multiple contract group involving multiple parties where each contract belongs to the same layer. Such a case was confronted by the tribunal in a matter before the Chamber of National and International Arbitration of Milan in 1996.[34] In the case, claimant A entered into an agreement with respondent C to develop a new pharmaceutical product. Claimant A had also entered into identical contracts with claimants B and company D. The costs of research were to be shared by parties A, B, C and D. Each of these contracts had an identical arbitration clause, even though B and C had no arbitration agreement between them. The question before the panel was whether these contracts constituted one multilateral agreement that would allow claimant B to initiate, jointly with claimant A, an arbitration against defendant C. The tribunal decided that a single agreement had not been created. Rather, in the panel's view, what had been created by the parties was merely a series of bilateral agreements, each with an arbitration clause limited by the terms of the contract in which it was located.[35] Although requiring claimant B to proceed against respondent C in state court risked inconsistent judgments and measured costs, the panel reasonably concluded that it was inappropriate to bind respondent C to an arbitration against a party with which it had neither expressly nor implicitly manifested an agreement to arbitrate.

A final consideration that bears mentioning is cost. In assessing the intent of the parties, an arbitrator may reasonably assume that the parties did not intend for any arbitrations arising between them to be unduly costly. This is a slightly different matter from considering the issue of cost from a system-wide perspective. For example, in an arbitration between A and B, it might decrease overall costs to allow B to implead a third respondent, C. However, this would certainly increase the costs for C, and probably for A as well. An arbitrator using unnecessary cost avoidance as an *indicia* of the will of the parties in this circumstance would not find much support for consolidation.

A case where the panel did appropriately consider cost was in a 2002 award of the Hamburg Chamber of Commerce.[36] In that case, a dispute arose between the claimant and respondent as to whether the principal claim and counterclaim should be consolidated into a single arbitration, or, alternatively, whether they should be allowed to proceed separately. In deciding against consolidation, the panel considered several *indicia,* including cost to the parties. The panel explained that: '[t]he separation of the proceedings does not disadvantage the parties, in particular from the point of view of costs. The fees of the arbitral tribunal are namely charged separately for claim and counterclaim if no set-off is allowed. This rule applies also when both [claim and counterclaim] are heard by one and the same arbitral panel.' [37]

4. CONCLUSION

An arbitrator's decision regarding consolidation or *dépeçage* is appropriately informed by each of the considerations described above: national legislation, arbitral rules, the relationship between the contracts, the relationship between the parties and cost. At the heart of the issue, though, where the decision is truly left to the arbitrator's discretion (as opposed to the arbitral institution itself or the national courts), there is really only one question: did the parties intend to allow for the related disputes to be considered as part of a single proceeding?

Gary Born encapsulated this author's view on the litmus tests to be applied by arbitrators who must decide on *dépeçage* or consolidation when he wrote that these issues:

> *"have [been] resolved [...] in favor of party autonomy and contractual privity. The foundation of international commercial arbitration is the parties' agreement to arbitrate and their procedural autonomy. Equally important, parties agree to arbitrate with particular other parties, according to specified procedures – not to arbitrate with anybody, in any set of proceedings."* [38]

To this may be added that Article IV(1) of the New York Convention should not be disregarded. A court must be shown the arbitration agreement in writing between or among the parties as a precondition for the enforcement of an arbitral award. Thus, it could be a grave error to allow considerations of procedural efficiency or cost considerations to trump the principles set out above, lest arbitrators find that they know the price of everything, but the value of nothing.

In the final analysis, consolidation is a useful tool in cases where it can be fairly reconciled with the parties' intent. However, arbitrators must never confuse their role with that role of national courts, nor should they forget that, even when consolidation is authorized by national legislation or institutional rules, the ultimate source of the arbitrator's authority is the consent of the parties.

END NOTES

* Senior of Counsel in the London office of Covington & Burling LLP. The views set out in this article are the author's. The author expresses his gratitude to Alexander Berengaut, associate in the Washington DC office of Covington & Burling, for his invaluable assistance in the preparation of this article [paper].

1 The facts of this hypothetical case are drawn from Abu Dhabi Gas Liquefaction Co. v. Eastern Bechtel Corp. [1982] 2 Lloyd's Rep. 425. In that case, decided under the English Arbitration Act, 1950, the Court of Appeal appointed the same sole arbitrator for both arbitrations.

2 See *Dell Computer Corp. v. Union des consommateurs*, 2007 SCC 34, at § 51 (Canadian S. Ct.) ('arbitration is a creature that owes its existence to the will of the parties alone'); see also *Alexander v. Gardner-Denver Co.*, 415 U.S. 36, 53 (1974) ('As the proctor of the bargain, the arbitrator's task is to effectuate the intent of the parties.').

3 In addition to the overall risk to the system, there are also specific risks to enforcement where an arbitrator or arbitral institution chooses procedural rules that are at odds with the expressed will of the parties. The New York Convention allows for non-recognition of an arbitral award if '[t]he composition of the arbitral authority or the arbitral procedure was not in accordance with the agreement of the parties, or, failing such agreement, was not in accordance with the law of the country where the arbitration took place.' Convention on the Recognition and Enforcement of Foreign Arbitral Awards, Art. V(1)(d), 10 June 1958, 330 UNTS 38.

4 Note though that several important model and national laws do not address the subject of consolidation. See, e.g., UNCITRAL Model Law on International Commercial Arbitration, UN Docs. A/40/17, A/61/17 (2006); US Federal Arbitration Act, 9 U.S.C. § 1 et seq.; French New Code of Civil Procedure, Arts. 1492 et seq.

5 One prominent example of national legislation that empowers the court, as opposed to the arbitrator, to consolidate is the Netherlands Arbitration Act, which provides that:

"If arbitral proceedings have been commenced before an arbitral tribunal in the Netherlands concerning a subject matter which is connected with the subject matter of arbitral proceedings commenced before another arbitral tribunal in the Netherlands, any of the parties may, unless the parties have agreed otherwise, request the President of the District Court in Amsterdam to order a consolidation of the proceedings."

Art. 1046 of the Code of Civil Procedure (Netherlands Arbitration Act of 1 December 1986).

Another variant on this type of law is the Hong Kong Arbitration Ordinance, which grants the court the power to consolidate even in the absence of a party's request:

"(1) Where in relation to two or more arbitration proceedings it appears to the Court

(a) that some common question of law or fact arises in both or all of them, or

(b) that the rights to relief claimed therein are in respect of or arise out of the same transaction or series of transactions, or

(c) that for some other reason it is desirable to make an order under this section, the Court may order those arbitration proceedings to be consolidated on such terms as it thinks just or may order them to be heard at the same time, or one immediately after another, or may order any of them to be stayed until after the determination of any other of them."

Section 6B of the Hong Kong Arbitration Ordinance (5 July 1963).

6   See Section 9 of the Irish International Commercial Arbitration Act of 1998; Section 26 of the Singapore Arbitration Act of 2001.

7   Australia International Arbitration Act of 1974, § 24(1)(a)-(c).

8   Ibid., at §§ 24(2), (5) and (6).

9   Though the law is in parity with the legislation of countries that allow courts to consolidate in the absence of both parties consent. See supra note 5.

10   The ICC Court is not a panel appointed for a particular case, but rather the ICC's standing body tasked with ensuring the application of the Rules of Arbitration and overseeing the overall ICC arbitration process.

11   Article 4(6) of the ICC Rules of Arbitration (1998).

12   See, e.g., Belgian Centre for the Study and Practice of National and International Arbitration (CEPANI), CEPANI Arbitration Rules (2005) Article 12: 'When several contracts containing a CEPANI arbitration clause give rise to disputes that are closely related or indivisible, the Appointments Committee or the Chairman is empowered to order the joinder of the arbitration proceedings. This decision shall be taken either at the request of the Arbitral Tribunal, or, prior to any other issue, at the request of the parties or of the most diligent party, or upon CEPANI's own motion.' Stockholm Chamber of Commerce, Arbitration Rules (1 January 2010) Article 11: 'If arbitration is commenced concerning a legal relationship in respect of which an arbitration between the same parties is already pending under these Rules, the [SCC's] Board may, at the request of a party, decide to consolidate the new claims with the pending proceedings.'

13   Siemens AG and BKMI Industrieanlagen GmbH v. Dutco Construction Co., 119 J.D.I. (Clunet) 707 (French Cour de cassation civ. lre) (1992).

14   See Bernard Hanotiau, Complex Arbitrations (2005) pp. 200-207 (detailed treatment of Dutco's background, holding and implications).

15   In the interests of full disclosure, the author was Secretary General of the ICC International Court of Arbitration at the time.

16   Dutco, supra note 13, at p. 708.

17   See, e.g., Article 10 of the ICC Rules of Arbitration (1998) (requiring that, in Dutco situations, where co-claimants or co-respondents are unable to agree on an arbitrator, the ICC Court may appoint the panel). Commentators have also suggested an alternative solution to the Dutco problem in a three-party arbitration: allow each party to select an arbitrator, at which point the three party-appointed arbitrators will select two neutral arbitrators. This was the approach applied by the Second Circuit in Compania Española de Petroleos, S.A. v. Nereus Shipping, S.A., 527 F.2d 966 (2d Cir. 1975), though the decision was subsequently overruled in United Kingdom v. Boeing, 998 F.2d 68 (2d Cir. 1993). See Irene M. Ten Cate, 'Multi-Party and Multi-Contract Arbitrations: Procedural Mechanisms and Interpretation of Arbitration Agreements Under U.S. Law', Am. Rev. Int'l Arb. 15 (2004) pp. 133, 143-144.

18   ICC partial award in case No. 8420 of 1996, Y.B. Com. Arb. 25 (2000) p. 328 (identifying the 'trend in international arbitration to interpretate [sic] arbitration agreements in the widest possible way in favorem validitatis […] arbitration [being] a usual practice in international business matters' [second alteration in original]).

19   951 F.2d 107 (6th Cir. 1991).

20 Ibid., at p. 108.

21 As discussed infra, there are several indicia that might suggest an agreed-upon intent to consolidate a multi-contract or multi-party disagreement.

22 210 F.3d 771 (7th Cir. 2000).

23 Ibid., at p. 774.

24 Ibid.

25 See, e.g., ICC interim award in case No. 6000 of 1988, ICC Ct. Bull. 2 (1991) p. 31 (suggesting that where parties are closely related, it can be justified to extend the arbitral clause of a contract binding one of the parties to the other parties as well). This factor, which is also termed the 'group of companies' question, is the subject of a separate analysis in this publication by Yves Derains.

26 ICC interim award in case No. 4367 of 16 November 1984, YCA 11 (1986) pp. 134-139.

27 ICC partial award in case No. 8420 of 1996, YCA 25 (2000) pp. 11-432.

28 ICC interim award in case No. 4367, YCA 11 (1986) p. 137.

29 A similar conclusion was reached by the court in Fletamentos Maritimos SA v. Effjohn International BV [1996] 2 Lloyd's Rep. 304. The parties in Fletamentos signed an agreement to start a cruise business which included an arbitration clause. They later agreed to jointly purchase a cruise ship in a contract that did not have an arbitration clause. The court allowed an arbitration to move forward with respect to a dispute involving the ship purchase agreement, notwithstanding the fact that the agreement lacked an arbitration clause because, in the court's view, the arbitration clause in the initial agreement encompassed the related dispute arising under the ship purchase agreement.

30 ICC partial award in case No. 8420, YCA 25 (2000) p. 339.

31 Zurich Chamber of Commerce award in case No. 273/95 of 31 May 1996, YCA 23 (1998) pp. 128-148.

32 Ibid., at pp. 128-130.

33 Ibid., at p. 134.

34 Chamber of National and International Arbitration of Milan, award of 2 February 1996, YCA 22 (1997) pp. 191-196.

35 Ibid., at pp. 192-193.

36 Hamburg friendly arbitration award of 27 May 2002, YCA 30 (2005) pp. 17-21.

37 Ibid., at p. 18. Though cost is appropriately considered in this situation, one might quibble with the tribunal's conclusion that cost to the parties would be the same whether or not the two claims were consolidated. The fees of the arbitral tribunal might be the same, but that is no guarantee that other costs, such as legal fees, would be similar as well.

38 G. Born, *International Commercial Arbitration* (Kluwer Law International, 2009) p. 2072.

CHAPTER 3

DÉPEÇAGE OR CONSOLIDATION OF DISPUTES RESULTING FROM CONNECTED AGREEMENTS: THE ROLE OF THE JUDGE

Kristof cox*

1. INTRODUCTION

Modern industrial and commercial transactions have reached such a degree of complexity that the classic one-contract-two-parties model is threatened with extinction. Rather, multiple parties enter into multiple contracts for the completion of a single economic transaction. The rights and obligations of the parties in such transactions are intrinsically linked and interdependent. As a result, one event may give rise to a multi-party dispute. Like in a game of dominoes, the first piece topples the second, which topples the third, and so forth. Ideally, such multi-party disputes would be resolved in one proceeding, by means of one decision. Ideally indeed, since another side-effect of the growing complexity of trade and commerce is that parties progressively opt for arbitration, attracted by the efficiency of its procedures and the expertise of the arbitrators. That choice as such does not create a problem if parties coordinate their (arbitration and other) dispute resolution clauses. Unfortunately, they rarely do so. In one transaction, parties A and B may opt for LCIA arbitration with three arbitrators sitting in London; parties B and C for ICC arbitration with a single arbitrator sitting in Paris; parties C and D for *ad hoc* arbitration under the UNCITRAL Rules; and parties D and A for the courts of New York. The multi-party dispute is spread over several proceedings, each including some of the parties. Since all these proceedings deal with the same transaction, the judges and arbitrators are presented with connected and even identical questions of fact and law.

Two arguments plead in favour of the consolidation of such related proceedings. Firstly, overall procedural efficiency is generally higher if the same questions are only discussed and decided once. Secondly, if the first decision-maker's findings have no binding effect on the decision-makers in parallel or subsequent proceedings, the decision-makers may well render inconsistent decisions on related or identical issues of fact and law. However, '[t]he lawyer's truth is not Truth, but consistency or a consistent expediency.'[1] If that be so, what is left of the reliability of courts and arbitral tribunals when they reach inconsistent decisions in disputes resulting from connected agreements? Inconsistency violates the normal sense of judicial propriety in cases where a party loses a certain argument while another party in a similar or identical position wins the same argument.[2] The losing party may feel that it is the victim of unequal treatment.[3]

For these reasons, the consolidation of disputes resulting from connected agreements is often presented as a welcome or even necessary solution. So far, the focus in legal writing has been mostly on the consolidation of related arbitration proceedings. For multiple reasons, which we will examine further on, the role of the judge in such situations is rather limited. A question that is rarely looked into, however, is whether parallel court and arbitration proceedings resulting from connected agreements may be consolidated and, if so, what the role of the judge may be in such consolidation. These are the core questions of this article.

Part I examines why the court-ordered consolidation of arbitral proceedings is so rare and whether the same reasons also speak against the court-ordered consolidation of court and arbitral proceedings. As the analysis shows that the appeal of such consolidation may be even lower than that of consolidated arbitral proceedings, Part II examines whether there may be situations in which the consolidation of court and arbitral proceedings is necessary, rather than merely convenient.

2. INSURMOUNTABLE OBSTACLES?

There are numerous arguments against the consolidation of arbitration proceedings by the court. The fact that the legislation of most countries does not provide for such consolidation is both a consequence of those arguments and an obstacle to consolidation. At times it has been tried to consolidate arbitration proceedings on the basis of the statutory provisions for the consolidation of court proceedings.[4] However, since such an extension is clearly not in line with the *ratio legis*, it is generally rejected.[5]

The few cases in which the court-ordered consolidation of arbitration proceedings is explicitly provided for may be divided into two categories: those where consolidation requires the consent of all parties and those where it does not. In the first category we find such examples as the English Arbitration Act and the law of British Columbia. Likewise, the US Court of Appeals for the Second Circuit confirmed that consolidation requires consent in the famous case of *UK v. Boeing*.[6]

By contrast, the Netherlands Arbitration Act,[7] the Hong Kong Arbitration Ordinance,[8] the New Zealand Arbitration Act 1997[9] and the US Uniform Arbitration Act leave the question of consolidation to the discretion of the court. It suffices that a party to one of the arbitration proceedings requests consolidation. The main objection against these systems is that court-ordered consolidation violates party autonomy. Firstly, the intervention of the court would violate the parties' will to resort to arbitration and to stay as far away from the courts as possible.[10] Moreover, since parties may end up in arbitration with parties they do not have an arbitration agreement with, fundamental rights such as the right of access to a court may come into play.[11] Furthermore, if Article V(1)(a) of the New York Convention may be interpreted as covering not only situations in which the arbitration agreement is invalid but also situations in which there simply was no arbitration agreement between the parties, courts in other jurisdictions may refuse to recognize an arbitration award resulting from a consolidated arbitration. Finally, as a matter of practical necessity, the appointment of the tribunal and the arbitral procedure after consolidation will almost inevitably deviate from the rules established by at least one of the arbitration agreements. Thus, in consolidated multi-party arbitration, parties may lose their opportunity to appoint their own arbitrator. On that basis, too, courts in other jurisdictions may refuse to recognize the award (Art. V(1)(d) of the New York Convention).[12]

These arguments are mostly rebutted via an opt-out system and a presumption of implied consent. The Dutch Act and the US Uniform Arbitration Act, for instance, explicitly provide the parties with an opportunity to exclude consolidation by the court in their arbitration agreement. Parties that opt for arbitration in one of these countries and fail to exclude consolidation are presumed to have agreed to the rules on consolidation, including the power of the court to appoint the tribunal and determine the procedural rules.[13] The New York Convention, too, may provide escape routes, as the relevant provisions of Article V refer to the law of the country where the arbitration took place or where the award was made. Since the consolidation itself and the resulting appointment of the tribunal and procedural rules are in accordance with that law, there is no reason to refuse recognition of the award.[14] Furthermore, the consolidation of arbitration proceedings between A and B and arbitration proceedings between B and C may technically be said not to amount to an arbitration between A and C. Therefore, the right of A and C to resort to the courts for their mutual disputes would not be violated.[15] This reasoning, however, presupposes that A and C cannot directly claim relief vis-à-vis each other in the consolidated arbitration, but only *vis-à-vis* B. That limitation may undermine the practical use of consolidation.

These arguments in favour of court-ordered consolidation are not of equal force when it comes to the consolidation of parallel court and arbitral proceedings. Such consolidation will necessarily result in proceedings for which at least one of the parties has not opted. Either the consolidated proceedings are referred to the court, in which case the arbitration agreement is disregarded, or they are referred to an arbitral tribunal, in which case at least one of the parties is undeniably deprived of its right of access to a court. Implicit consent cannot even be an option in those countries where consolidation is provided for by statute, since these provisions only cover the consolidation of arbitration proceedings or the consolidation of court proceedings, but not the consolidation of court and arbitral proceedings.

On the upside, a judgment resulting from proceedings that were consolidated into one court proceeding cannot be refused enforcement on the basis of the New York Convention.[16] Moreover, there is generally no ground for refusing such enforcement in national legislation either if a judgment is rendered in breach of an arbitration agreement. This, however, may change in the (near) future. The European Commission's proposal to include such a ground in the new Brussels I Regulation was one of the (only) suggestions in the Green Paper that could count on unanimous support from its commentators.

Where official consolidation is unavailable, certain procedural alternatives may alleviate the negative consequences. The best known examples are the appointment of the same arbitrator(s) for all arbitration proceedings and joint hearings.[17] These alternatives, however, cannot be applied in the case of parallel court and arbitral proceedings. Clearly one cannot appoint the judges in the court proceedings as arbitrators,[18] let alone appoint the arbitrators as judges. Likewise, the (private) arbitration hearings cannot take place in a public court room and *vice versa*.

Furthermore, the practical difficulties that arise from the consolidation of arbitration proceedings are equally harsh, or even harsher, in the case the consolidation of court and arbitral proceedings. These difficulties include such issues as the point in the proceedings up to which one may request consolidation,[19] who pays the fees of the arbitrators that are dismissed,[20] how to deal with confidentiality,[21] and so forth. The discussion on these issues may in itself cause considerable delay.[22] For these reasons, the English legislator decided not to provide for court-ordered consolidation of arbitration proceedings in the 1996 Act.[23]

Finally, even in cases where there is a legal basis for court-ordered consolidation and the practical problems can be overcome, the fact of the matter is that consolidation is mostly impossible if the concurrent arbitrations have their seat in different jurisdictions. Thus, the Dutch Arbitration Act only provides for the consolidation of two arbitrations taking place in the Netherlands.[24] Moreover, some have argued that both proceedings must also be governed by the same law.[25] In international arbitration, these restrictions make the prospects for a successful consolidation very bleak. It is almost impossible to agree on a criterion for determining which court may assume jurisdiction to consolidate arbitration proceedings in different countries.[26] On this point, the situation may be slightly easier for the consolidation of court and arbitral proceedings. The obvious solution would be that the court where one side of the dispute is pending assumes jurisdiction over the entire dispute by way of consolidation. As long as the New York Convention grants every member state the authority to assess the applicability of an arbitration agreement under its own law, the court may have the possibility to set an arbitration agreement aside for the purpose of consolidation in appropriate cases.

This brings us to our next question. Under what conditions is the consolidation of court and arbitral proceedings – hypothetically into one court proceeding – appropriate? Considering the lack of statutory provisions, the risk of unenforceability, the practical problems and the problems of jurisdiction surrounding the issue, not to mention the necessary dismantling of the arbitration agreement between some of the parties, these conditions must be very strict. These questions are examined in greater depth in the next section.

3. EXCEPTION FOR 'INSEPARABLE' DISPUTES

a. Joinder and intervention

The existing criteria for the court-ordered consolidation of arbitral proceedings generally derive from the efficiency and consistency rationale. Thus, the Dutch Act allows for consolidation when the subject matter of both arbitrations is connected, while the Hong Kong, New Zealand and US arbitration acts allow for it when the dispute involves some common question of law or fact or arises from the same transaction.[27] These criteria, however, may be too liberal in an international context, particularly when the consolidation of court and arbitral proceedings deprives some of the parties of their arbitration agreement. Therefore, we need a much stricter criterion.

That criterion may be found in the concept of 'inseparable' disputes as applied in such jurisdictions as France and Belgium. Article 12 of the Belgian Code of Civil Procedure, for instance, provides that:

> *"Claims can be handled as connected claims when they are so closely related that it is desirable to consolidate them and judge them together, in order to avoid an outcome that would be incompatible, if said disputes would have been handled separately."*

There is discussion among the Belgian courts as to what degree of incompatibility in the outcome of disputes is required to allow the consolidation of court and arbitral proceedings or the joinder or intervention of third parties that are bound by an arbitration agreement. On the one hand, some courts seem to be guided by the need for consistency in a wider sense. Thus, in one case, the Court of Appeal of Antwerp assumed jurisdiction over both the claimant's contractor and his insurer, even though the insurance contract contained an arbitration clause. The court based its decision on the need for legal certainty, uniformity of proceedings and consistency of judicial decisions.[28] The Court of Appeal of Brussels took a similar position.[29] In a claim brought by the victim of a fire, the court assumed jurisdiction over both the insurance company and the insurance broker even though the insurance contract contained an arbitration clause. The court was of the opinion that the same court should decide in these connected cases, as this was the only way to avoid inconsistent decisions.

The majority of courts, by contrast, are of the opinion that the need for consistency is not sufficient to disregard the arbitration agreement. Thus, in a case before the Court of Appeal of Liège, the owner of a property filed claims against the architect, the contractor and the sub-contractor. All parties except the sub-contractor were bound by an arbitration agreement. The court was of the opinion that, the unity of the dispute was no criterion in the Code of Civil Procedure that could be used to consolidate disputes that fell under different jurisdictions if they included the jurisdiction of an arbitrator. The court could assume jurisdiction despite the arbitration clause only if the cases were 'inseparable'. Such inseparability could only flow from 'the absolute material impossibility to enforce inconsistent decisions together'.[30] In the case at hand, the claims could only lead to individual orders for payment of money. Such orders could always be enforced simultaneously.[31] The mere fact that the findings of an award and a judgment might be inconsistent was not sufficient to consolidate the cases, 'even if the inconsistency is shocking'.[32]

Similarly, the Commercial Court of Hasselt decided that the claims of an owner against two contractors did not form an inseparable dispute, even though a decision on the liability of one might entail an implicit decision on the liability of the other. In the court's opinion, a judgment that rejected the claim against the first contractor would not be inconsistent with an arbitration award that rejected the claim against the second contractor.[33] Alternatively, a judgment in which one claim was rejected and an award in which the other claim was accepted were simultaneously enforceable. The court did not consider a situation in which both claims were accepted. Nevertheless, those decisions would technically also be simultaneously enforceable, even though this would imply that the owner would receive double compensation.[34]

Under this strict test of inseparability, the Courts of Appeal of Antwerp and Brussels should have reached a different result in the cases cited above. As to the former, an arbitral award ordering the insurer to cover the damage because it was caused by a natural disaster could be enforced simultaneously with a court judgment deciding that the contractor was liable for the damage because he committed a fault in the construction. Similarly, an arbitral award deciding that the insurance contract was valid could be enforced simultaneously with a judgment in which the broker was held liable because the court was of the opinion that the contract was invalid.

The same inseparability test is applied when a defendant in court proceedings claims indemnification from a third party with whom he has an arbitration agreement.[35] This was confirmed by the *Cour de cassation*. The Court of Appeal of Antwerp had decided that the main claim against the insured and the latter's claim for indemnity against the insurer were so closely connected that they should be decided simultaneously to avoid a situation in which the court and the arbitrator would reach inconsistent results.[36] The Cour de cassation quashed this decision, stating that the rules of connection do not set the arbitration clause aside and do not prevent the parties from bringing a claim for indemnity before an arbitral tribunal. [37]

The French *Cour de cassation* has taken a similar position. Thus, in *Quarto Children's Books* v. *Editions du Seuil and Editions Phidal*,[38] the *Cour de cassation* stated:

> *"Méconnait le principe de Kompetenz-Kompetenz la Cour d'appel qui, saisi, d'une part du litige opposant une société française à une société anglaise et portant sur l'étendue des droits cédés en vertu d'un contrat de diffusion en France d'un ouvrage édité par la société québécoise pour avoir mis en vente en France un ouvrage identique, écarte la clause compromissoire stipulé dans le contrat de diffusion de l'ouvrage en se fondant sur l'indivisibilité de ces deux litiges et en précisant que l'existence d'une contrefaçon dépendait de la détermination des droits résultant du contrat, alors que la seule constatation d'une indivisibilité ne suffisait pas à faire obstacle au jeu de la clause d'arbitrage."* [39]

Even though the facts did not warrant consolidation in any of these cases, these decisions do not exclude that there may be situations in which the possibility of inconsistent outcomes may be strong enough to set the arbitration agreement aside in order to bring all disputes resulting from connected agreements before the same court. This will be the case when it is physically impossible to enforce both the orders of the arbitral award and the court judgment. The criterion excludes claims for payment, but leaves room for claims to do or not to do something or to give or not to give something.

b. *Tierce opposition*

i. Criterion of inseparability

The criterion of inseparability may further be illustrated by situations in which proceedings were not consolidated and a third party to the proceedings that are first to come to a decision claims a result that is inconsistent with that decision. In such situations, the question is whether the second claim may simply be continued and, if so, whether the conflict between incompatible orders will simply be 'solved' by means of a race to enforcement in which the right of the fastest prevails? Alternatively, does the party have to challenge the prior decision before it may claim the incompatible relief?

In that regard, the third party's recourse, which is known in France and Belgium as *tierce opposition*, is highly interesting. Article 582 of the French Code of Civil Procedure provides an accurate definition of this means of recourse:

> *"La tierce opposition tend à faire rétracter ou reformer un jugement au profit du tiers qui l'attaque.*
>
> *Elle remet en question relativement à son auteur les points jugés qu'elle critique, pour qu'il soit à nouveau statué en fait et en droit."*

In common law systems, there is no recourse against judgments or awards that is specifically reserved to third parties. Sometimes the term *tierce opposition* is translated as 'third-party action'. However, in common law jurisdictions, and the United States in particular, a third-party action may refer to the (forced) intervention of a third party in ongoing proceedings. Therefore we use the original French term *tierce opposition* to avoid confusion.

Unlike a challenge or appeal, a successful *tierce opposition* does not necessarily quash the original decision. In normal circumstances, it merely implies that the decision is no longer 'opposable' against the third party. However, between the parties and *vis-à-vis* all other third parties, the decision does not cease to exist. Thus, the first part of Article 591 of the French Code of Civil Procedure reads:

> *"La décision qui fait droit à la tierce opposition ne rétracte ou ne réforme le jugement attaqué que sur les chefs préjudiciables au tiers opposant. Le jugement primitif conserve ses effets entre les parties, même sur les chefs annulés. [...]"*

Likewise, Article 1130 of the Belgian Code reads:

> *"La juridiction qui accueille le recours en tierce opposition, annule, en tout ou en partie, la décision attaquée, à l'égard du tiers seulement. [...]"*

Therefore, a successful *tierce opposition* results in two inconsistent decisions: the original decision and the decision on *tierce opposition*.

The only exception to this limited effect occurs in cases where the resulting inconsistency is of such importance that the original decision and the new decision are irreconcilable. Thus, Article 591 of the French Code of Civil Procedure continues:

> "[...] Toutefois la chose jugée sur tierce opposition l'est à l'égard de toutes les parties appelées à l'instance en application de l'article 584."

This Article 584 states that, in the case of inseparability, *tierce opposition* is only admissible if all parties are called to the suit.[40] Likewise, Article 1130 the Belgian Code states that *tierce opposition* annuls the decision *vis-à-vis* all parties if the enforcement of the original decision would be irreconcilable with the enforcement of the new decision.[41] The Belgian and French *Cours de cassation* used to apply a similar concept of inseparability, namely the impossibility 'd'exécuter en même temps deux décisions'.[42] Such a situation may, for instance, occur when a tenant successfully contests a decision ordering the demolition of the building he occupies.[43]

In other words, the criterion is identical to the criterion for consolidation of court and arbitral proceedings.

In recent cases, however, the French courts tend to apply a more lenient approach to inseparability based on the 'legal' impossibility of enforcing the original decision and the decision on *tierce opposition* simultaneously. Thus, in a case before the French *Cour de cassation*[44], a court had annulled the life insurance contract of Ms X and ordered the insurance company to refund the sums paid by Ms X, which the insurance company immediately did. The beneficiary of the life insurance, however, successfully filed a *tierce opposition* against that judgment. The court ordered the insurance company to pay the sums due under the insurance to the beneficiary, since meanwhile Ms X had passed away. The insurance company objected to such an order, arguing that the judgments were inseparable given the fact that the first judgment found that the contract was null while the second judgment ordered the company to perform that same contract. The Court of Appeal of Nîmes, however, rejected the argument, stating that it was not impossible to execute the orders of both judgments simultaneously.

The *Cour de cassation* quashed this decision:

> "Qu'en statuant ainsi, alors qu'il existait une impossibilité juridique d'exécution, tenant à la contrariété entre les deux décisions, l'une annulant les contrats et l'autre en ordonnant l'exécution, la cour d'appel a violé les textes susvisés".

Likewise, after a leaseholder was informed that part of the lands under the lease could not be utilized as a vineyard under the appellation 'AOC Graves', he claimed damages from the lessor for breach of contract and against the notary for professional misconduct. The court convicted both the lessor and the notary in *solidum*. Subsequently, the insurance company of the notary filed a *tierce opposition* against this judgment. The Court of Appeal of Bordeaux accepted the challenge in as far as the judgment found that the notary was liable and ordered the notary to pay. However, the court rejected the claims in as far as they concerned the liability of the lessor, arguing that there was no inseparability between a claim based on the contractual liability of the lessor and a claim based on the liability *'quasi-délictuelle'* of the notary.

Again, the *Cour de cassation* quashed this decision, stating that the first judgment found that the lessor was liable since he had not delivered lands that were entirely fit as a vineyard under the appellation AOC Graves, while the judgment on *tierce opposition* rejected the liability of the notary, finding that the lease in question did not require that the lands were entirely fit for that purpose. In the opinion of the *Cour de cassation*, such an inconsistency necessarily implied that the first judgment would be annulled in its entirety.[45]

Boyer referred to this type of case to support his claim that a successful *tierce opposition* should have an absolute effect – i.e. an effect *vis-à-vis* all parties and third parties – whether or not the first judgment and the second judgment can be enforced simultaneously.[46] He illustrated his opinion by reference to a case in which the first judgment between Primus and Secundus found that Primus had a right of passage across the lands of Secundus. Subsequently, Tertius, the co-proprietor of those lands, successfully contested that decision by means of *tierce opposition*. Both judgments cannot be enforced simultaneously. Therefore, these decisions were inseparable, even under the strict (Belgian) definition of inseparability. However, in Boyer's opinion, the real inseparability in this case does not lie in the fact that Primus cannot be prevented and allowed to pass across the lands at the same time but in the fact that the right of passage would exist and not exist at the same time. If the arguments and/or evidence presented by the third party had convinced the court that the original decision was inaccurate or simply wrong, it would be unfair if this decision would continue to affect the parties and all other third parties. Therefore, Boyer suggests that *tierce opposition* should always restore the inaccuracy of the first decision *erga omnes*.[47]

Even though such a larger effect would avoid inconsistency to the greatest possible extent, it would also foster legal uncertainty and inefficiency. No decision would be final as long as there were third parties with a potential interest in contradicting any of the findings of that decision. Moreover, each time that one of the findings of a prior decision, whether factual or legal, would come under discussion in subsequent proceedings, all parties to the prior decision would have to be offered an opportunity to be heard, since they would be bound by the result of the re-litigation. Furthermore, not only would the finding itself have to be re-litigated, but the second decision-maker would also have to consider and decide on the implications of a contrary finding on the remainder of the original decision. As such, other findings and decisions, including the operative part of the decision, might also have to be reconsidered. Potentially, the practical consequences of the execution of the original decision would have to be undone.

In as far as the original decision and the decision involving the third party are simultaneously enforceable, these consequences of the generalized absolute effect of *tierce opposition* unnecessarily undermine the finality of the first decision.[48]

Moreover, if we apply the broad definition of inseparable disputes to the consolidation of court and arbitral proceedings, the courts would have the power to consolidate all disputes involving overlapping issues of fact or law, thus setting the arbitration agreement aside. Nevertheless, such consolidation is still preferable to a situation in which the arbitration proceedings would first be completed, where after a third party would challenge the findings of the award in order to obtain a different decision in court proceedings on a common issue. Such a challenge would involve all parties to both the arbitration and the court proceedings, and the result of a successful challenge would be binding on all of them. Therefore, the result would be almost identical to a consolidation before the end of the arbitration, with the exception that the entire arbitral proceedings would have been completely useless.

ii. Jurisdiction

A broad definition of inseparability does not only undermine finality and the will of the parties to resort to arbitration; it would also give rise to multiple questions of jurisdiction and procedure. Even in those countries where *tierce opposition* against court judgments exists, third-party recourse against arbitral awards is not generally known. The Belgian Code of Civil Procedure, for instance, does not provide for *tierce opposition* against arbitral awards at all.

The French Code, by contrast, does provide for *tierce opposition*, but only against awards in national arbitration (Art. 1481 Code of Civil Procedure). Moreover, while tierce opposition against a judgment is brought before the court that rendered the judgment or the court that is next in the hierarchy, there may be much discussion on the question before whom the *tierce opposition* against an arbitration award should be brought. Neither *tierce opposition* before the arbitral tribunal nor before the courts may count on general approval.

Consolidation of court and arbitral proceedings raises similar questions of jurisdiction. Should the consolidated proceedings be brought before a tribunal or a court and, if the latter, which court? Therefore, we will now examine the jurisdictional and procedural debates surrounding *tierce opposition* against arbitral awards.

On the one hand, it is mostly impossible to require a third party to institute *tierce opposition* before the tribunal that has rendered the arbitration award. The third party may not agree to arbitration with the parties and *vice versa*. The only situation in which they would not have a legitimate reason to object to the jurisdiction of the arbitral tribunal would be where the parties and the third party all agreed to the same arbitration agreement that covers the issues in dispute. However, even such an agreement may not guarantee that the *tierce opposition* can be brought before the same arbitral tribunal that rendered the contested decision. It may be impossible to reconvene that tribunal, or the third party may invoke its right to appoint its 'own' arbitrator. Moreover, there is serious reason to doubt whether the original tribunal may still decide on an impartial and independent basis, since it has already formed *and* expressed its opinion on the issues. This raises questions that go to the very heart of the third party's rights of defence.

On the other hand, some scholars have also objected to the possibility of *tierce opposition* against an arbitration award before the courts, since re-litigation of the issues falling under the parties' arbitration agreement in court would violate their expectations[49] To evaluate this argument, one must again make a distinction on the basis of the risk of irreconcilable decisions, since this has an impact on the parties that take part in the *tierce opposition* and the effects of a successful *tierce opposition*.

Only if acceptance of the third party's objections would result in an order that cannot be simultaneously enforced with the order of the contested award should all parties to that decision necessarily take part in the re-litigation on *tierce opposition* before the court. Moreover, only in such cases of inseparability could the finality of the arbitral award between the parties be reversed by the decision on *tierce opposition*. This would imply that the arbitration agreement between the parties is no longer effective, which may indeed violate their expectations.

However, cases of inseparability form a particularly strong threat to the unity of the legal order. Therefore, it is no coincidence that the Belgian *Cour de cassation* generally does not allow the courts to assume jurisdiction over those parties that are bound by an arbitration agreement in connected multi-party disputes, whereas it does allow the courts to assume jurisdiction over all parties – including those that are bound by an arbitration agreement – in the case of inseparability (cf. *supra*). The only difference between the situation in which a party invokes the arbitration agreement before the court and the situation of *tierce opposition* against an award that may lead to an irreconcilable decision is that the arbitral award has already been rendered. The actual existence of the award may strengthen the expectation of the parties that their dispute is finally settled by arbitration. This, however, cannot prevent the need for one consistent decision that respects the rights of defence of all parties involved in the inseparable multi-party dispute, whether parties or third parties to the arbitration agreement. Such an effect can only be reached by allowing consolidation or intervention by third parties, or by allowing third parties to challenge the findings of the award in such a manner that the resulting decision will be binding on all parties, including all parties to the original award.

In these cases, where the third party does not only seek to rebut the findings of the award but also seeks to prevent or undo the enforcement of the award, the suggestion of certain authors to allow *tierce opposition* before the court that has ordered the enforcement of the award may seem attractive.[50] However, such a rule would imply that the third party cannot institute a *tierce opposition* as long as there have been no enforcement proceedings. This would be particularly problematic if the order of the award is performed voluntarily and this performance causes harm to the third party. Moreover, neither the enforcement proceedings nor the *tierce opposition* against a judgment in such proceedings are the appropriate forum to discuss the merits of the arbitration award, let alone to render a new decision on the contested findings of that award. This is witnessed by the fact that the court may only refuse enforcement of the award on very limited grounds, none of which relate to the merits of the decision, except in the extraordinary circumstance that the award would be contrary to public policy. However, the third party's objections in *tierce opposition* would most likely not be directed against the reasons why the court allowed the enforcement of the award but against the findings of the award itself. The evaluation of such arguments goes far beyond the tasks of the court of enforcement. Furthermore, a refusal to enforce, whether between the parties or as a result of tierce opposition, does not set the award aside, so that enforcement might still be sought in another country. The third party would thus be required to re-institute *tierce opposition* each time enforcement is being sought.

In cases where there is no risk of inseparability, it is not necessary to bring all parties to the arbitral award before the court since the decision on the *tierce opposition* would not affect the finality of the award between its parties. Therefore, the parties' expectations are fully respected. The *tierce opposition* merely decides a dispute between a party and a third party that are not connected through an arbitration agreement. Admittedly, certain issues in that dispute also fall under an arbitration agreement between the party and another party. However, the parties to the arbitration agreement do not expect those issues to be decided by means of arbitration in their relations with third parties. Neither could their arbitration agreement oblige third parties to resort to arbitration.

By contrast, if the party and the third party are also bound by an arbitration agreement that covers the contested findings, a *tierce opposition* before the courts *would* violate their expectations. Therefore, it should be possible for them not to resort to the courts and have the tierce opposition decided in accordance with their arbitration agreement. As long as there is no risk of irreconcilability between the first and second award, no other parties to the first award would have to intervene in this '*tierce opposition* arbitration' or would be bound by the second award. Moreover, under these circumstances, there is no reason why a party and a third party would not be allowed to exclude the jurisdiction of the courts in favour of an arbitral tribunal, just as they can for any other dispute that is 'arbitrable'.

Those statutes that provide for *tierce opposition* against an arbitration award have generally attributed jurisdiction to the courts. Thus, Article 1481 of the French Code of Civil Procedure provides that *tierce opposition* may be instituted against the arbitral award before the court or tribunal that would have had jurisdiction in the absence of an arbitration agreement, subject to the rules on incidental *tierce opposition* (Article 588.1).[51] Similarly, since the 2006 reform of the articles on arbitration in the Italian Code of Civil Procedure, third parties can lodge an *opposizione di terzo* before the court of appeal of the district in which the arbitration has its seat.[52]

However, the French provisions cannot be used for international cases, since they do not provide for tierce opposition in such cases. Moreover, in international cases, a foreign court may be 'the court that would have had jurisdiction in the absence of an arbitration agreement'. Clearly, while the French legislator may *recognize* the jurisdiction of a foreign court, it cannot grant jurisdiction to a foreign court. For the same reason, the Italian provision cannot be used for awards that are rendered outside Italy. This, too, would grant jurisdiction to a non-Italian court of appeal.

It is very difficult to decide which court or arbitral tribunal should have jurisdiction to decide a *tierce opposition* against an international arbitration award.

In cases where there is no risk of inseparability, the obvious solution would be that the court or arbitral tribunal before which the dispute is already pending has jurisdiction to decide an incidental *tierce opposition*. A *tierce opposition* by means of a main claim could be brought before a court or arbitral tribunal that has jurisdiction to decide the matter in dispute between the third party and the party or parties against which the third party directs the *tierce opposition*. As to the courts, this would depend on their rules of private international law. As to an arbitral tribunal, it would depend on the existence and scope of the arbitration agreement.

In cases where there is a risk of inseparability, the *tierce opposition* must be brought before a court or tribunal that may assume jurisdiction over the third party and all parties to the arbitration award, in spite of the arbitration agreement between the parties to the award and/or any other arbitration agreement. If the *tierce opposition* is instituted as a main claim, the third party will have to determine which court or arbitral tribunal may actually assume jurisdiction over all these parties. If the *tierce opposition* is instituted incidentally, the court or arbitral tribunal before which the action is already pending must have authority to order the forced intervention of the 'missing' parties to the award. If that is not the case – which is very likely with regard to an arbitral tribunal – the court or tribunal would have to decline jurisdiction over all issues that may potentially lead to an irreconcilable order in favour of a court or tribunal that does have such authority. The initiative to initiate new proceedings before the competent court or tribunal is most likely to come from the third party, since it is the one that seeks to prevent or undo the enforcement of the award. Nevertheless, the initiative may also come from a counterparty or even one of the other parties to the award, depending on their relative interests.

The same rules on jurisdiction should apply *mutatis mutandis* to the pre-award/judgment consolidation of court and arbitral proceedings. If the disputes are not inseparable, the proceedings should not be consolidated, and each combination of parties should resort to the court or tribunal that has jurisdiction over their personal relations depending on the existing arbitration agreement(s) and/or the rules of private international law. If the disputes are inseparable, the consolidated proceedings may only be brought before the tribunal or court that may assume jurisdiction over *all* parties to the inseparable dispute, again depending on the existing arbitration agreement(s) and/or the rules of private international law.

4. CONCLUSION

Consolidation of court and arbitral proceedings by the court should be inadmissible, except in those rare situations where the disputes are 'inseparable'. The best approach is to interpret the criterion of 'inseparable disputes' in a strict manner, namely by limiting it to cases where the orders resulting from the disputes physically cannot be enforced simultaneously. In all other cases, the court should honour the arbitration agreement and refuse consolidation. If a rare situation of inseparable disputes occurs, it is preferable to consolidate the disputes as early as possible, even if this implies that all parties – even those that are bound by an arbitration agreement – will be brought before the court. The rules of private international law will determine which court may assume jurisdiction over such consolidated proceedings. The alternative course – in which some of the disputes are first decided in arbitration proceedings between some of the parties – only to be brought before the court in a subsequent *tierce opposition* – is the least attractive of all possible solutions.

END NOTES

* The author is a Senior Legal Consultant at Deloitte Belgium, specializing in commercial contracts (international sale of goods, distribution, construction, etc.). He sits as an arbitrator in national and international arbitrations. He is an Affiliated Senior Researcher at the Institute for International Trade Law of the Katholieke Universiteit Leuven (Belgium). His doctoral dissertation on arbitration awards and third parties was awarded the first CEPANI scientific prize.

1   Henri David Thoreau, *Civil Disobedience* (1849).

2   Brian King, 'Consistency of awards in cases of parallel proceedings concerning related subject matters', in Emmanuel Gaillard (ed.), Towards a uniform international arbitration law? (IAI, 2005) p. 295.

3   J.C. McCoid, 'Inconsistent judgments', Wash. & Lee L. Rev. 48 (1991) p. 489.

4   For example, on the basis of Rules 42(a) and 81(a)(3) of the US Federal Rules of Civil Procedure; see Dominique Hascher, 'Consolidation of arbitration by American courts: fostering or hampering international commercial arbitration?', *Journal of International Arbitration 1*(2) (1984) p. 127.

5   Alberta Court of Queen's Bench, 2 February 2004, *Western Oil Sonds Inc. v. Allianz Insurance Co. of Canada, 2004 ABQB* 79.

6   *Government of UK v. Boeing Co.*, 998 F. 2d 68 (2d Cir. 1993).

7   Article 1035.

8   Article 6B. For an application, see High Court of Hong Kong, 12 September 1986, *Shui On Construction Co. Ltd. v. Moon Yik Co. Ltd.* e.a., in Yearbook Commercial Arbitration, Vol. XIV (1989) pp. 215-223; Peter Schlosser, 'The competence of arbitrators and courts', Arbitration International 8(2) (1992) pp. 194-195.

9   Section 2. Under this Act, however, a party must first apply for such a measure to the arbitral tribunal(s). Only if (one of) the tribunal(s) refuses consolidation, or the tribunals make inconsistent orders, should the party resort to the High Court. The court may then render or alter an order for coordination or consolidation.

10 Michael Mustill, 'Multipartite arbitrations: an agenda for law-makers', *Arbitration International 7*(4) (1991) p. 393.

11 In the Netherlands, consolidation is not considered to be in breach of that fundamental right, at least in as far as all parties have clearly opted for arbitration; see Pieter Sanders, Het *Nederlandse arbitragerecht nationaal en internationaal*, 4th edn. (Kluwer, 2002) p. 125; Henk Snijders, Nederlands Arbitragerecht, 3rd edn. (Kluwer, 2007) p. 208.

12 Mustill, *supra* n. 10, at p. 393; Sigvard Jarvin, 'Canada's determined move towards international commercial arbitration', *Journal of International Arbitration 3*(3) (1986) p. 111; Adam Samuel, 'Arbitration in Western Europe – A generation of reform', *Arbitration International 7*(4) (1991) p. 319; Hascher, supra n. 4, at p. 127, referring to a case in which an Italian court refused recognition of an American award: *Corte di Appello de Firenze*, 13 April 1978, in *Yearbook of Commercial Arbitration,* Vol. IV (1979) p. 294.

13 Mustill, *supra* n. 10, at p. 393; Samuel, *supra* n. 12, at p. 319; see also Hascher, supra n. 4, at p. 130.

14 As to Article V(1)(d), this is not entirely correct, since the reference to the law of the place where the arbitration took place is only by default of an agreement between the parties. Some commentators note that there rarely is such an agreement as to the appointment of the arbitrators or specific procedural rules. At best, the agreement refers the rules of an arbitral institution; see Michael Cohen, 'A missed opportunity to revise the Arbitration Act 1996', *Arbitration International* 23(3) (2007) p. 462.

15 Hascher, *supra* n. 4, at p. 131.

16 Unless one argues that a member state has violated its obligations under Article II of the New York Convention by enforcing a judgment in violation of an arbitration agreement.

17 Schlosser, *supra* n. 8, at p. 194-195.

18 In certain countries, there is a restriction on the possibilities for judges to sit as arbitrators. In Belgium, for instance, it is not officially forbidden for judges to do so, but they cannot accept remuneration, which mostly suffices as a disincentive.

19 High Court of Hong Kong, 12 September 1986, Shui On Construction *Co. Ltd. v. Moon Yik Co. Ltd. e.a.*, in *Yearbook Commercial Arbitration*, Vol. XIV (1989) p. 221.

20 See, e.g., Hong Kong Arbitration Ordinance, Article 6B.

21 Appendix C to 'Consolidation: The Second Report of the United Kingdom Departmental Advisory Committee on Arbitration Law', *Arbitration International* 7(4) (1991) p. 390; Mustill, *supra* n. 10, at p. 399; Anthony Diamond, 'Multi-party arbitrations. A plea for a pragmatic piecemeal solution', *Arbitration International* 7(4) (1991) pp. 405-406.

22 Hascher, *supra* n. 4, at p. 135.

23 Appendix C, *supra* n. 21, at p. 391; Mustill, supra n. 10, at p. 399.

24 Article 1046 of the Netherlands Arbitration Act.

25 Appendix C, *supra* n. 21, at p. 390.

26 Mustill, *supra* n. 10, at p. 397.

27 Or, in New Zealand and Hong Kong, if 'for some other reason it is desirable to make the order'.

28 Court of Appeal of Antwerp, 3 June 1997, unpublished.

29 Court of Appeal of Brussels, 24 September 1980, *De Verzekering* 1981, p. 285. The court based its decision on the case law of the Cour de cassation, which states that a dispute is inseparable from the moment that there is an inseparability of facts, so that it is necessary to evaluate the validity of different allegations to determine the liabilities and to examine the facts in which the parties played a role: Belgium, *Cour de cassation*, 9 May 1963, J.T. 1963, p. 529. The Commercial Court of Brussels (30 September 1986) remarks correctly that this point of view is no longer valid since the introduction of Article 31 of the Code of Civil Procedure. See also Court of First Instance of Nivelles, 17 June 1975, *Res Jur Imm.* 1976, p. 29: in a case between the owner as claimant and the architect and several (sub-)contractors as defendants.

30 Article of the 31 Belgian Code of Civil Procedure.

31 Court of Appeal of Liège, 25 June 1982, J.L. 1982, p. 341.

32 Labour Court of Appeal of Mons (Belgium), 15 November 1979, R.R.D. 1980, p. 141.

33 This is the situation in which the owner would get 'caught' between two inconsistent decisions.

34 Commercial Court of Hasselt, 4 December 2002, P.&B. 2004, p. 160.

35 Court of Appeal of Ghent, 28 October 1980, T.H.A. 1981-82, p. 169; Commercial Court of Brussels, 9 August 1973, J.T. 1974, p. 623; Commercial Court of Liège, 27 June 1985, Eur. Vervoerr. 1985, p. 572; Justice of the Peace of Berchem, 10 August 1976, R.W. 1976-77, p. 1835; contra Court of First Instance of Oudenaarde, 5 January 1984, R.W. 1985-85, p. 1098. The latter court decided that the connection between the claim of the victims and the claim for indemnity against the insurer warranted that these claims be decided by the court, notwithstanding the arbitration clause in the insurance contract. In the court's opinion, the decisions would be irreconcilable if the court were to find that there was liability and damage and the arbitrators were to decide that there was not.

36 Court of Appeal of Antwerp, 8 February 1993, unpublished.

37 Cour de cassation, 9 November 1995, Arr. Cass. 1995, p. 986; J.T. 1997, p. 97.

38 Cour de cassation, 16 October 2001, *Revue de l'Arbitrage* 2002, No. 4, pp. 919-920. See also French Cour de cassation, 6 February 2001, *Peavy Company v. Organisme Général des Fourrages e.a.*, No. 98-20.776. In this case, the court quashed a decision of the court of appeal in which that court assumed jurisdiction over multiple defendants, some of which were bound by an arbitration clause.

39 Cohen correctly remarks how difficult it is to determine whether a multi-party dispute is inseparable, particularly at the preliminary stage when the court decides whether it has jurisdiction. Moreover, the notion of inseparability 's'entoure d'un halo d'imprécisions ou d'hésitations'.

40 By contrast, the Belgian Code requires in all cases that all parties to the original judgment are party to the tierce opposition; see Art. 1125 Code of Civil Procedure.

41 Under the Belgian Code, all parties to the decision must be parties to the *tierce opposition*, whether there is a risk of inseparability or not.

42 See, for instance, Cour de cassation, 27 June 1990; Cour de cassation, 21 June 1995; Cour de cassation, 21 November 1996.

43 Cf. Serge Guinchard, *Droit et pratique de la procedure civile*, 5th edn. (Dalloz, 2006) p. 1158.

44 Cour de cassation, 30 April 2003, *Compagnie les Assurances générales de France-Vie (AGF) v. Mme Rignon-Bret e.a.*, No. 00-22.712.

45 Cour de cassation, 20 March 2007, EARL Les Domaines de la Mette v. M. Gilles Sautarel, No. 05-11.296.

46 Louis Boyer, 'Les effets des jugements à l'égard des tiers', R. Dr. Civ. (1951) pp. 194-195.

47 Guinchard, supra n. 43, at p. 1171.

48 This is probably how Mourre's opinion that tierce opposition should not be allowed has to be understood. The author states: 'ouverte pendant trente ans et impliquant la dévolution du litige à une juridiction étatique, la tierce opposition serait probablement contraire à la sécurité juridique et à l'exigence de confidentialité qui caractérise l'arbitrage international.' Alexis Mourre, 'L'intervention des tiers à l'arbitrage', *Gazette du Palais* 24 (2001) p. 21.

49 Charles Jarrosson, 'L'autorité de chose jugée des sentences arbitrales', Procédures n° 8, August 2007, étude 17, p. 49; Emmanuel Gaillard and John Savage (eds.), *Fouchard, Gaillard, Goldman on International Commercial Arbitration* (Kluwer Law International, 1999) p. 918.

50 See Jacques van Compernolle, 'Le droit de recours du tiers contre une sentence arbitrale obtenue par fraude', *Revue Critique de Jurisprudence Belge* (1994) p. 657; Beatrix Vanlerberghe, 'De vordering tot vernietiging van een arbitrale uitspraak door een derde', *Proces en Bewijs 6* (1993) p. 160. Vanlerberghe suggests that a third party should have the possibility to institute *tierce opposition* against the judgment that declares the award enforceable. In his opinion, such a *tierce opposition* would also allow the third party to resist the evidential value of the award.

51 Van Compernolle, supra n. 50, at pp. 660-662, suggests the same solution for Belgium, thus agreeing with Garsonnet and Cézar-Bru, who suggest this solution by analogy to the *requête civile* with regard to arbitration awards.

52 Previously, the section on international arbitration in the Code of Civil Procedure excluded the applicability of *tierce opposition*.

CHAPTER 4

THE LIMITS OF CONSENT: THE RIGHT OR OBLIGATION TO ARBITRATE OF NON-SIGNATORIES IN GROUP OF COMPANIES

Karim Youssef *

"Legal' arrangements are generalized for an entire class; 'equitable' arrangements are particularized for a specific case in order to remedy a grievance there without changing the general legal arrangement."
W.M. Reisman, *Law in Brief Encounters (1999) p. 164.*

1. CONSENT?

a. Doubt

'There'll be the breaking of the ancient Western code [...]'. Leonard Cohen's cynical prophecy in 'The Future' is being fulfilled today in the field of arbitration with regard to the foundational principle of consent to arbitrate. Only a stranger to the field could think that consent is no longer the *main* criterion of jurisdiction. However, with pervasive practices of extension based on criteria of jurisdiction that seem to either minimize or even disregard consent, one is legitimately entitled to question whether arbitral practice has developed limits on the once *exclusive* rule of consent as the basis for compelling non-signatories or for compelling signatories beyond their consent.

In recent years, studies of problems of jurisdiction and of the topic of non-signatories in particular focused on the role of consent. Reflections on the 'dimensions of consent'[1] and the 'quest for consent'[2] evidence mounting doubt that consent remains the undisputed and sole criteria by reference to which non-signatories may be compelled to arbitrate. Other worthwhile inquiries into how to '[do] justice without destroying consent'[3] in assessing jurisdiction *vis-à-vis* non-signatories are based on the fundamentally correct premise that, not infrequently, the requirement of consent may conflict with considerations of justice (or jurisdictional efficiency) in the specific case and hence may have to be undermined or sacrificed if justice is to be done.

b. Beyond doubt

Doubt is justified. Arbitration's ancient code has been broken. Case law reveals that, not infrequently, the search for the parties' intentions is neither the sole purpose nor the main criteria of the exercise of assessing jurisdiction. When consent is searched for, the *specific context* of the jurisdictional inquiry (the existence of an economic group and the participation of non-signatories in the contract containing the arbitration clause) exercises a distorting effect, sometimes to the point of giving contextual elements a role beyond merely ascertaining consent. They contribute directly to the decision to extend or not to extend. A systematic application of arbitration law (the requirement of consent) is also limited by the concurrent application of other branches of law, such as contract law or the law of corporate entities. Finally, developed practices of *objective* extension take place independently from any inquiry into consent, even if one could possibly be presumed from the facts.

A number of commentators have provided evidence of this growing reality of arbitral life and have called it many names: marginalization of consent, '*forçage de consentement*',[4] 'manufacturing consent'[5] and the 'decline of consent'.[6] A declining requirement of consent has been identified in rulings on the extension to non-signatories in groups of companies, the context where it probably all started. Studies of the issue of extension in this specific context divide the grounds of extension into 'grounds linked to consent' and 'grounds unrelated to consent'.[7] However, the decline of consent seems to be a broader phenomenon of modern arbitration. It has been identified in the context of groups of contracts,[8] investment arbitration[9] and public international adjudication.[10]

c. Importance of the inquiry into limits of consent

Enquiry into the *limits* of consent, albeit inconsistent with prevailing dogma, is of crucial conceptual and practical importance. Since consent is the cornerstone of the notion and the regulation of arbitration, a fading requirement of consent, if proved a reality, would send out shockwaves. It would defy conventional dogma, a ubiquitous norm of national laws and the traditional concept of arbitration as *justice by consent.* It would also defy the thinking habits of people involved in the business of arbitration for whom arbitration is consensual by nature or can only be 'a creature of contract'.[11]

Fundamentally, the assessment or control of jurisdiction beyond the ambits of consent dramatically alters the nature of the jurisdictional exercise and induces significant complexity in the tasks of arbitrators and courts. Whether the jurisdictional finding (to extend or not to extend) is made by reference to consent or transcends consent affects the methodology of applicable law and the contours of the duties of the arbitrator, in particular the extent of his or her compliance with the basic duties to observe due process[12] and to render a reasoned and enforceable award.

A decline in the role of consent also challenges the ongoing relevance of international arbitration standards and distorts the operation of fundamental principles of arbitration law (such as *separability*). A court that lets stand or enforces an award that entitles or compels a non-signatory to arbitrate, absent its consent, *necessarily* goes beyond the minimum standards of the New York ("NY") Convention and ignores the basic requirements of national arbitration laws, whether or not they are based on the UNCITRAL Model Law.[13] This raises important questions regarding how, on the level of *technique,* tribunals and courts overcome basic hurdles of a normative universe protective of consent.

Additionally, third-party issues in groups of companies touch upon general questions that go beyond arbitration (or consent) theory, for instance whether arbitration agreements should be treated as ordinary contracts. If they are, the application of arbitration law, built on the requirement of autonomous consent, may be set aside in favour of the application of contract law premised on the absence of such autonomy. The consequence, simple yet dramatic, is that a search for separate arbitral consent is simply excluded.

Finally, the implications of such question as whether and to what extent parties may be compelled to arbitrate beyond consent extend beyond arbitration and exercise a significant distorting effect on the operation of other branches of law, such as the law of corporate groups. Limits on consent involve limits on the principle of the independence of legal entities. The risk that overly expansive approaches to jurisdiction may place excessive burdens on corporate law is thus real and has been noted.[14] Such approaches could reduce the effectiveness of corporate forms in terms of shielding from liability or jurisdiction and, in a group context, could even undermine the notion of corporate groups.[15]

d. Approach

A detailed study of the grounds and principles for extending arbitral jurisdiction to non-signatories in comparative case law is neither needed nor possible, due to constraints of space. Such analysis has been ably conducted elsewhere.[16] In addition, while few general trends can be discerned in case law (for example, the application of national contract principles to arbitration agreements or the importance of involvement in performance), the field, more than ever before, is in dire need of reflections of a *general* nature. Case law is in a state of flux, and uncertainty is a main element of the *décor*. Solutions are elaborated outside the baseline of the NY Convention and materialize in significant divergences among national laws in dealing with similar problems. Uncertainty and lack of uniformity are exacerbated by the fact that jurisdictional assessment is invariably fact-intensive, with the inevitable result that diametrically opposite solutions (to extend or not to extend) may be reached in fact settings that differ only on points of detail.

In a spirit of back-to-basics,[17] these reflections would naturally centre on arbitration's *essentiala:* consent. In this article, which builds on broader analysis of contemporary jurisdiction practices through the prism of consent,[18] I explore and attempt to identify with more certainty this evasive *'somewhere beyond consent'* that most people know exists, but which is foggy, unfamiliar and perilous.

As a preliminary caveat, I do not address the question of whether a *practical* difference exists between extending the obligation as opposed to the right to arbitrate. The question is addressed elsewhere in this dossier. In terms of the conceptual analysis of consent, this article sees no *a priori* difference between compelling a non-consenting party to arbitrate and compelling a consenting party to arbitrate beyond its initial consent (with claimant(s) that it did not consent to arbitrate with). In both cases, jurisdiction is exercised beyond – and hence without the support of – the consent of those submitting.

e. Gradation of the role of consent in jurisdictional assessment

Analysis of case law reveals the existence of not one, but a multitude of approaches to jurisdiction. At opposite ends of the spectrum, one finds cases where consent is the exclusive basis of jurisdiction and cases where consent is simply excluded. A spectrum of degrees of consent ensues. Consent is interpreted broadly, undermined, presumed, indifferent and sometimes even marginalized to a vanishing point. To remain methodological, it is possible to identify four patterns of ruling on jurisdiction in practice.

1. Consent is the sole purpose of jurisdictional inquiry. It is found by ordinary contractual interpretation or a search for possible intent to arbitrate in the specific context of the dispute.
2. Consent is one of a number of elements of decision-making. The jurisdictional exercise is less focused on consent *per se* and consists of a global, factual assessment that looks at both subjective intentions and objective contexts that are deemed determinative.
3. Consent is *indifferent.* The decision to extent or not to extend is made by application of objective principles or doctrines that are indifferent, i.e. that apply without regard to whether consent to arbitrate exists. An active search for it is simply *excluded,* and the actual degree of consent involved (or imputed) to the non-signatory in the specific case depends on a large variety of factors.
4. Not only consent but also rigorous legal analysis is excluded in favour of a realist and pragmatic approach, which takes into account and sometimes relies primarily on conceptions of efficiency and equity.

This article will explore three limits on the *rule* of consent. These limits are: context, objective assessment and national contract law. Case law also contains evidence of a fourth potential limit on the *process* of ruling on jurisdiction. Considerations of equity constitute a broad practical limit on a rigorous search for consent in complex settings.

2. CONSENT IN CONTEXT[19]

The first limit on consent derives from the very context of jurisdictional assessment in groups of companies. The inquiry relates to the extent to which the existence of such a group distorts, and possibly undermines, the process of searching for the consent of non-signatories involved in the transaction. This inquiry naturally takes as a starting point the doctrine that first advanced the proposition that the specific context of an economic group may have an effect on the assessment of jurisdiction.

a. The dosage of consent in the 'group of companies' doctrine

How much consent there is in the so-called group of companies doctrine is not a straightforward matter. Like a religious or spiritual text, the formulation of the doctrine in *Dow*[20] and subsequent case law is sufficiently ambiguous to permit more than one interpretation of the true nature of the basis of jurisdiction. The understanding often depends on the eyes of the beholder: consensual, less consensual or objective.

Another source of difficulty is the constant dynamism of 'rules' and methods of decision-making in groups of companies. As we shall see, case law has constantly altered the relative importance of the various elements of the doctrine of groups of companies in a way that has affected the degree of consent in the composition of the basis of jurisdiction.

As a first approximation, the popular misconception that the doctrine is a domain of pure objectivity, where consent is simply excluded, should be dismissed as a selective or hasty reading.

i. Consent (derived from context) as *the* basis of jurisdiction

The doctrine, at least in its original version formulated in *Dow*, is consensual *en principe.* The tribunal, in the famous yet overrated passage, clearly noted that jurisdiction *vis-à-vis* non-signatories is assessed 'in accordance with the mutual intention of all the parties to the proceedings'.[21] The existence of a 'single economic reality' and the involvement of non-signatory entities in the conclusion, performance or termination of the contract are both *indices*[22] of – and not substitutes for – a finding of consent. Fouchard, Gaillard and Goldman explain: 'It is not so much the existence of a group that results in the various companies of the group being bound by the agreement signed by only one of them, but rather the fact that such was the true intention of the parties.'[23] Subsequent awards confirmed the consensual nature of jurisdiction. It is necessary to 'look for the actual and common intention of the parties at the time of the facts, or, at the very least, that of the non-signatory third party.'[24] Pre-*Dow* awards also assessed jurisdiction based on consent, while referring to the economic context of a group, albeit using less sophisticated language.[25]

Consensualism dominates jurisdictional assessment in groups of companies, whether or not the jurisdictional exercise is made under the conceptual sophistication of a doctrine of 'group of companies'. Studies by leading experts in the field of complex arbitrations, a number of whom contributed to this dossier, generally highlight the centrality of consent to decisions on jurisdiction involving non-signatories. Bernard Hanotiau, analyzing thirty years of case law, finds that '[i]n most cases, courts and arbitral tribunals still base their determination of the issue on the existence of a common intent of the parties and, therefore, on consent.'[26] In particular, in the context of groups of companies, '[e]xpress consent or conduct as an expression of implied consent – or a subtitle for consent – is still the basis on which most courts and arbitral tribunals reason to decide on the "extension".'[27]

The non-essential nature of the existence of an economic group *en soi*

To say that the group of companies doctrine is consensual is effectively to say that the doctrine has no autonomous standing, i.e. that it does not really exist as a separate basis for compelling non-signatories to arbitrate. As we shall see, French courts and ICC tribunals seem to have understood this conceptual flaw in their subsequent application of the doctrine. The relevance of the existence of an economic group has been undermined in some cases,[28] before being dispensed with as a non-essential element of decision-making. Since consent is the key element, involvement in the contract containing the arbitration clause (or other elements of fact) may evidence consent, *whether or not the facts relate to a group of companies.*[29]

Indeed, the notion of a 'single economic reality' is a term of social engineering that could not serve as legally rigorous basis to establish jurisdiction. Groups of companies are structures that are defined under national corporate laws. This loose social construction,[30] taken into consideration by the *Dow* tribunal and other tribunals before and after it, does not operate a *renvoi* towards specific national corporate structures. In a legal context, it can only be taken to mean that economic realities are important *contextual* elements that need to be considered when ruling on jurisdiction, i.e. when assessing consent. The basic idea could not be expressed any better than in Otto Sandrock's judgment of the group of companies doctrine:

> "Where traditional rules of law developed through decades are available, an international arbitral tribunal should refrain therefore from experimenting with any social engineering of its own. For, normally, it is not the task of an international arbitral tribunal to invent new law, but just to apply the law as it already exists."[31]

ii. Consent as *an* element of decision-making (among others): consent *and* context

The predominantly *contextual* nature of searching for consent in groups of companies has been expressed in a variety of ways. The jurisdictional inquiry is highly fact-specific.[32] Similarly, 'the issue of consent to arbitration may take on a special dimension when one (or more) company(ies) to a complex international transaction is (are) member(s) of a group of companies, given the nature of the relationships which exist between companies of such a group [...]'.[33] The essence – and consensus – is that the existence of a corporate group, like a prism, exercises *some* distorting effect on the issue of consent. However, this statement, albeit basically sound, is legally vague and does not say much about the true nature of the jurisdictional exercise.

One could think of two possible meanings for the proposition that, in a group of companies, consent is analyzed *in that context*. First, that the consent of non-signatory entities of the group (or that of the third party to arbitrate beyond its initial intent) remains the sole basis for extension, but that it may be derived from a number of objective *indices*, primarily the existence of a 'single economic reality' and/or the implication of non-signatory members of the group in the transaction.[34] However, that is not to say much. Every search for implicit consent is contextual by nature.[35] As proposed earlier, in a large number of awards and court decisions, searching for consent consumes the jurisdictional exercise *vis-à-vis* non-signatories.

A second and more interesting interpretation for one who inquires into the limits of consent suggests that the contextual elements, such as the structure of the group, the degree of integration of different entities and the extent of cross-involvement in the economic operation, may play a role of a *different* nature. A tribunal or court may take these elements not merely as indication of consent but as self-standing elements that feed, in their own right, the decision to extend or not to extend, within a larger context of complication of the process of ruling on jurisdiction. This second pattern of assessment of jurisdiction, which downgrades consent from being *the* element to merely an element of decision-making, is identifiable in both the language and reasoning of arbitral awards. Noah Rubins explains:

> "*Ostensibly, this analysis [of the full panoply of facts in each given case] is an attempt to ascertain whether the parties to the contract and the non-signatory intended ex ante that the non-signatory be implicated in arbitral proceedings. [footnote omitted] However, some courts and tribunals applying the group of companies doctrine have sought to conform the arbitration agreement to the non-signatory's role in the facts surrounding a given contract's signature, performance and/or termination, even in the absence of direct evidence concerning the parties' ex ante expectations.*"[36] *[Emphasis added]*

In a number of ICC awards, the tribunal has enumerated, without order of priority, the elements that it took into consideration in ruling on jurisdiction. Consent is merely one of them, and not even the first one. The Tribunal in ICC case No. 9517 [37] noted that:

> "[T]he question whether persons not named in an agreement can take advantage of an arbitration clause incorporated therein is a matter which must be decided on a case-to-case basis, requiring a close analysis of the circumstances in which the agreement was made, the corporate and practical relationship existing on one side and known to those on the other side of the bargain, the actual or presumed intention of the parties as regards rights of non-signatories to participate in the arbitration agreement, and the extent to which and the circumstances under which non-signatories subsequently became involved in the performance of the agreement and in the dispute arising from it."[38]

This suggests that the contextual elements characteristic of a group setting *stand side-by-side with consent* rather than merely helping to prove its existence as sole basis of jurisdiction. The dividing line is slim and hazy, and one is permitted to wonder whether the distinction is always clear, or even perceptible as relevant, in the minds of tribunals and courts. Nevertheless, the conceptual leap is fundamental. It makes the difference between a jurisdictional exercise limited to consensual analysis and one that transcends consent, and is fundamentally more *sophisticated* in terms of admission of decision-making by reference not to one, but to a multitude of criteria and factual elements. On the level of *technique*, the factual and legal analysis moves from being a single-minded exercise whose sole purpose is to find consent to a more complicated endeavour that is both more global in purpose[39] and less legalistic in nature.[40]

The fundamental conceptual implication is that consent moves from being the exclusive to the *default* basis of jurisdiction. Non-signatories may be compelled to arbitrate, absent *ex ante* consent, if sufficient support for this outcome is found in the facts. Blessing suggests that the context that would justify extension absent consent must be *compelling*:

> "All individual elements of a case will have to be weighted very carefully, respecting the basic principle of the *privity* of contract and the clear notion that legal entities are distinct from each other and that, therefore, such fundamental principles cannot easily be removed by an arbitral tribunal unless very specific circumstances demand such a removal."[41]

iii. The *principe de l'apparence* in the group of companies doctrine

In light of the previous analysis, I am inclined to classify the *Dow* award in this second category (where consent is not the exclusive factor of decision making). On second look, the doctrine does not seem to be merely consensual analysis given a sexy name. While the parties' intention is 'the key issue',[42] as pointed out by Fouchard, Gaillard and Goldman, a measure of objectivity is an integral part of the principle of extension formulated in the award. Moreover, the source of objectivity is not the existence of an economic group en soi. A different reading of *Dow* is suggested.

One aspect of the award has passed largely unnoticed. Specifically, the théorie de *l'apparence* is not only implicit in the rationale of the award (the reference to the existence of a single economic group that acts as such vis-à-vis third parties) but also explicit in its language. The arbitration agreement signed by members of a corporate group should bind other companies of the group 'which by virtue of their role in the conclusion, performance, or termination of the contracts containing said clauses, and in accordance with the mutual intention of all parties to the proceedings, *appear to have been veritable parties to these contracts* [...]'.[43] One is tempted to think that the fact that the non-signatory entities *appeared* to have been parties is *the* true basis for including them in the arbitral circle, rather than the systematic analysis of their consent.[44] All the other elements that the *Dow* tribunal took into account, namely the specific context of a group, the parties' intentions and the involvement in the transaction, are indices that contributed to creating such an appearance.

'Common' or 'mutual intention': Does it exist?

Pursuit of the linguistic exercise would provide further support for this conclusion. *Dow* and a number of awards ruling under the name of the group of companies doctrine refer to 'the mutual intention of all parties to the proceedings [including that of the non-signatory]'. However, there is no such thing as mutual intent *as a basis of jurisdiction*. Consent is the ultimate expression of individualism in the realm of legal institutions and can only be assessed *per persona*. The expression either reveals a lack of attention to the use of language [45] or suggests that this mutual intention plays a role other than establishing a consensual basis of jurisdiction. The expression could only mean that individual consents 'concur' or converge towards creating a certain understanding (*en l'occurence*, that non-signatories should nevertheless be treated as parties) or perhaps *appearance* that they are acting as such. This common intent or understanding is *irrelevant* to whether the non-signatory defendant has consented, or whether the third-party defendant has consented beyond its initial consent, because only their consent – and no one else's – matters for this purpose. Nevertheless, the use of the expression suggests that the intention of signatories matters in binding the non-signatory, and vice versa. It would matter only if we admit that concepts such as legitimate expectations or protection of appearances are involved. The 'mutual intention' makes sense only if read together with its objective implication, expressed in *Dow*, namely that the non-signatories '*appear* to have been veritable parties to these contracts'.[46] *The mutual intention to appear as parties, to the extent that it actually contributes to creating this appearance,* may serve as the basis for legitimate reliance or beleif that the group is acting as a block and is making its resources available as such. This appearance justifies the third party's right, as well as its obligation, to arbitrate.

Despite its central role in *Dow*, reliance on apparent positions or the *principe de l'apparence* is undervalued as a basis of extension. The principle could provide a reliable and well-recognized basis to entitle a third party to bring a claim against non-signatory entities of a group or to entitle non-signatories to bring a claim against the third party that contracted with the group *en connaissance de cause* (the *Dow* scenario).

b. Global assessment of jurisdiction

In final analysis, in a group of companies context, one finds subjectivity in objectivity (consent derived from objective contextual elements) and objectivity in subjectivity (objective elements that are called consensual). The assessment of jurisdiction, whether conducted under the name of a group of companies doctrine or otherwise, is neither entirely consensual nor entirely objective. The *Dow* decision and those that followed in its footsteps relied on a number of elements, including the interpretation of the contracts, the search for the implicit intent of non-signatories, the existence of a group, the involvement of non-signatories in the transaction and the appearance that all these elements may have created in the minds of third parties. The exact role that consent played in the basis of jurisdiction, compared to these other elements, is difficult to ascertain and would require the reading of minds.

It is suggested that, once tribunals and courts have stopped assessing *jurisdiction solely* by reference to consent, they are less inclined to assign a determinative role to a particular contextual element. Instead, they proceed with a *global* factual assessment of subjective intentions and objective context, which helps them to make up their mind with respect to the decision whether or not to extend. This necessarily involves a significant measure of equitable decision-making.

Even when the jurisdictional exercise is explicitly self-described as purely consensual, one is entitled to wonder whether, in the intellectual process of decision-making, a difference beyond semantics really exists between looking for indices of consent in the context of the dispute and looking for both intent and context in a global fashion. In groups of companies, the search for good old consent undergoes a significant distortion imposed by its context, like light passing near a black hole. Describing the jurisdictional exercise as a simple and single-minded search for evidence of the existence of consent fails to reflect the current complexity of the task of arbitrators ruling on such matters.

c. Changing roles of contextual elements (and uncertainty)

i. Dynamism

Normatively, the evolution of the group of companies doctrine is one of constant metamorphosis. If a group of companies doctrine exists, there is not one, but many. The respective roles of different elements of the basis of jurisdiction have varied significantly in case law, giving rise to many judicial restatements of the doctrine. In the immediate aftermath of *Dow*, French courts emphasized the existence of a group as an element that must be taken into account.[47] Then, a few years after it had confirmed the *Dow* award, the Paris Court of Appeal dropped any reference to the initial birth context of the doctrine. Focus shifted to involvement in performance regardless of the existence of a *'réalité économique unique'*, which remained more as a *façade* rather than as a condition of extension. In turn, the role of involvement in the contract containing the arbitration clause has itself varied significantly in relation to consent. Depending on the case, it was considered: the main element from which consent was derived; the main element upon which extension was decided, regardless of its implication as to the existence of consent;[48] or, on the contrary, as a simple *indice* of consent.[49] At times, the relevance of the economic group resurfaced.

ii. Consent presumed from context

Arbitration by *default*

In a number of cases, the existence of a group limited the requirement of consent not by reducing its exclusive role as basis of jurisdiction but by giving rise to a presumption that it existed in the specific case. 'The analysis of arbitral awards also leads to the emergence of a rebuttable presumption that a parent company binds its subsidiaries.'[50] ICC case No. 6000 of 1988 is a clear example. The tribunal held that:

> "[I]t is largely admitted that by virtue of a usage of the international trade, where a contract, including an arbitration clause, is signed by a company which is a party to a group of companies, the other company or companies of the group which are involved in the execution, the performance and/or the termination of the contract are bound by the arbitration clause, provided the common will of the parties does not exclude such an extension."[51] [Emphasis added]

The presumption in favour of the extension of the obligation to arbitrate undertaken by a parent to its subsidiaries is authoritatively cited as a principle of the *lex mercatoria*.[52] It is noteworthy that the presumption arises from the combined effect of the existence of a corporate group and the involvement in the contract containing the arbitration clause, and not from the sole effect of the existence of a group. A simple presumption of consent does not alter in *essence* the consensual nature of jurisdiction. Nevertheless, its effect is dramatic. It reverses the basic structure of jurisdiction in favour of private justice. Extension of the arbitration agreement does not take place if consent is found; it takes place unless excluded by agreement of the parties. Arbitration prevails *by default*.

iii. Drifting away (from consent)

It is perhaps this uncertainty concerning the respective roles of consent versus context that led subsequent French case law to bring objective elements such as involvement in performance to the surface of the basis of jurisdiction as a *substitute* for consent (section 3). On the other hand, comparative law shows that appropriate solutions to the third-party problem in the context of groups of companies may be reached by application of national contract law principles. These principles do not necessarily exclude a measure of consent or provide a more solid basis for disregarding it (section 4).

3. OBJECTIVE ASSESSMENT OF JURISDICTION

a. Involvement in performance *per se* and the notion of knowledge under French law

i. Consent substituted

While the majority of ICC tribunals ruling under the name of the group of companies doctrine continued to reason in consensual terms, or on the basis of a multi-layered analysis of consent and context, French courts ventured into more objective grounds. In a number of cases, involvement in the negotiation, performance or termination of the contract containing the arbitration clause was considered not as an *indice* of consent but per se as a self-standing basis for jurisdiction, without examining whether it constituted evidence of consent or even whether or not consent existed otherwise. On a number of occasions,[53] the Paris Court of Appeal held that:

> "[T]he arbitration clause inserted in an international contract has self-standing validity and effectiveness which require that its application be extended to parties that are directly implicated in the performance of the contract and in the disputes that may arise therefrom as long as their respective situations and activities give rise to the presumption that they were aware of the existence and the scope of the arbitration clause, even though they were not signatories of the contract which stipulates it."

In these different cases, rendered in a group context, the court analyzed the non-signatory's situation and activity and identified elements of fact that supported the conclusion that the non-signatory probably knew of the existence of the arbitration clause. Of course, to the extent that it gives rise to the presumption that the non-signatory knew of the existence of the clause, substantial involvement in the performance of the contract may be evidence of consent to arbitrate. However, the various decisions seem to have been satisfied with a relatively low threshold for finding knowledge. For instance, in Korsnas, the court relied on the non-signatory's character as a 'subsidiary' and its position as the *'bureau parisien'* in charge of implementing the contract.[54]

Fundamentally, what the *Cour d'appel* formulated in these cases is a modified principle of extension that involves no active verification of consent. A search for consent is simply dismissed from the court's *démarche*. Whether it exists or not seems to be an issue of less relevance. In Poudret's analysis of this line of case law, he underlines the shift in focus from the analysis of the relations between signatories and non-signatories, which could unveil an intention to be bound, to an emphasis on the object of the contract and a perception of the arbitration clause as a 'technical modality' of enforcement of the obligation arising under it.[55] A notion of involvement in performance *per se* replaces a search for consent. The arbitration clause simply extends to non-signatories 'directly implicated in the performance of the contract'.[56] Poudret concludes: '[L]e caractère volontaire de l'arbitrage en sort nettement amoindri.'[57] From this finding Hanotiau derives the normative corollary that involvement and knowledge 'have a standing of their own, as a substitute for consent'.[58]

ii. Autonomy transcended

Such a sweeping departure from the consent paradigm is expected to send shockwaves through the broader regulation of arbitration. Indeed, it does. The exclusion of consent from the jurisdictional inquiry in scenarios of involvement in performance collides with the principle of autonomy of the arbitration clause. Fundamentally, separability dictates that parties need to emit a specific consent to arbitrate that is separate from their consent to the substantive contract. This fiction is vital for purposes of initial *validity,* but it is inconsistent with a determination of the scope of the arbitration clause by reference to the conditions surrounding the performance of the main contract. The jurisdictional exercise consists in retracing the scope *ratione personae* of the arbitration agreement in order to align it with the substantive rapport. This technique of determination ratione materiae of the scope *ratione personae* of the arbitration agreement is clear in the *Westland* award.

> *"The question whether the four states are bound by the arbitration clause concluded by the AOI in its own name [...] is exactly the same as the substantive law question whether the four states are bound in general by the obligations contracted by the AOI."*[59]

One practical consequence of this entanglement of jurisdiction and merits is that tribunals will often find it necessary to join the question of jurisdiction to the final decision on the merits. Although it might be advisable to request an interim award on jurisdiction in cases of uncertain assertion of jurisdiction *vis-à-vis* non-signatories, granting such a request would not necessarily be possible.

iii. Consent transcended

In a critical assessment, the substitution of consent intrigues and may be unwarranted in a factual context where a first attempt to find consent is likely to yield. In this line of cases, consent is not the *first* basis of jurisdiction, absent a finding of which the courts proceed to more objective grounds. French courts relieved themselves of the burden of finding consent, or even of signalling its existence, even if consent may be reasonably presumed from the facts. While a language of consent would be consistent with the *droit commun* and would enhance the chances of enforcement abroad, dropping such language is probably intended to avoid a perilous – and perhaps artificial – fact-intensive search for subjective intentions. In a word, the purpose, as a matter of judicial policy, may be to *simplify* jurisdictional assessment and control in scenarios where consent may in any case be reasonably presumed to exist from the jurisdictional context.

The application of national contract law to arbitration agreements is an alternative method for injecting simplicity into the 'rules' governing jurisdiction *vis-à-vis* non-signatories. It nevertheless constitutes a third – and significant – limit on the systematic search for arbitral consent.

4. NATIONAL CONTRACT LAW

It is increasingly accepted that general principles of contract law apply mutatis mutandis to arbitration agreements.[60] Their application may result not only in the creation of substantive rights or obligations but also in the transmission or extension of the right or obligation to arbitrate to third parties. Even opponents of the *lex mercatoria* (and hence of the group of companies doctrine) feel comfortable admitting that exceptions to the principle of *privity* may be derived from 'the national proper laws of contract'.[61] This involves admission of the proposition that, if the applicable law dictates that consent to arbitrate need not be required by application of some principle of contract (or other) law, then it shall be set aside in the specific case.

a. US law

In the United States, the third-party problem in arbitration is solved, as a general matter, by application of 'ordinary principles of contract law'.[62] This is conceptually based on the notion that '[a]rbitration agreements are to be treated like other contracts, subject to the policy favoring arbitration'.[63]

Principles of contract law that would usually apply in a group of companies context include agency, third-party beneficiary, universal succession, *estoppel*, equitable *estoppel*, *alter ego* and veil piercing. Principles of good faith and fraud may also come to apply.

b. National contract principles in continental case law

The application of national contract law to extension in group settings does not characterize French solutions – quite the opposite. French contract law is normally hostile to admit exceptions to *privity*. To be able to formulate their arsenal of *règles matérielles* of extension that are less reliant on consent, including those that were extrapolated from the group of companies doctrine, French courts needed to exclude the application of the *droit commun*. Similarly, Swiss and German courts, unlike their US counterparts, generally admit piercing of the corporate veil only in limited circumstances that amount to fraud or abuse of rights.[64]

Nevertheless, the application of national contract law seems to be regaining interest on the continent. In particular, French courts have compelled non-signatories to arbitrate based on the *principe de l'apparence*,[65] the theory of *contrat de fait*[66] and fraud.[67]

c. Consent *indifferent*

Contrary to first impressions, the application of national contract law is ambivalent in its effect on consent. Typically, it would result in a determination of jurisdiction by interpretation of the parties' intentions. However, a significant measure of objectivity is built into most of these contract principles, which brings about a less consensual – or sometimes even non-consensual – obligation to arbitrate. For example, the principles of veil piercing and *alter ego* usually aim to redress an unjust situation or give effect to apparent positions. A finding of implied consent is neither necessary nor, indeed, sufficient to operate extension. In addition, equitable considerations are not only latent in the rationale of many of these principles but also seem to underlie the decision-making process of courts. 'This contractual approach seems to focus as much on equitable considerations after the conclusion of the contract as on discerning the intent of the parties *ex ante*.'[68]

The fundamental point here is that extension by application of national contract law is a domain where the jurisdictional exercise is largely *indifferent* to consent. The applicable principle applies in its own right when its conditions are met. Systematic consensual analysis is not undertaken. This does not mean that consent is simply flushed out of the basis of jurisdiction.

The application of third-party principles results in a basis of jurisdiction embodying a 'spectrum' of degrees of consent,[69] depending on the extent of objectivity built into the principle of extension. The actual degree of *ex ante* consent associated with the application of a particular third-party principle would also depend on contextual factors, such as the factual and procedural setting.[70] Regardless of the actual degree of assent one might *impute* to the non-signatory in a given case, consent is simply *not required*. It is not part of the intellectual process of decision making, except in so far as it may indicate the existence of an objective element necessary for the application of the principle of contract law in question, such as characterizing a contradictory behaviour for the purpose of *estoppel*.

Finally, the methods of decision-making in certain jurisdictions may obscure the degree of consent involved in the application of contract principles:

> *"[...] One also finds instances of sweeping and fact-intensive application of such principles as equitable estoppel and piercing the corporate veil, that are beyond the normal reach of those doctrines. Indeed, sometimes even where consent is insufficiently manifested to permit 'extension' of the agreement to bind the non-signatory, procedural mechanisms are employed to achieve the same result."*[71]

The initial limit on consent – *context* – brings out another one: equity.

5. EQUITY

a. '[T]o remedy a grievance there without changing the general legal arrangement'

Considerations of equity and jurisdictional efficiency are more likely to arise in complicated factual settings, such as economic groups and the involvement of entities in the performance of contracts that they did not sign, than in *simple* settings for which arbitration law was originally designed. Arbitration law is concerned primarily with guaranteeing the *ab initio* validity of arbitration agreements. It is less concerned with their ongoing efficacy in cases where the circle of parties involved in the underlying transaction is altered. In these cases, the application of arbitration law may deprive the arbitration agreement of effect or yield unjust outcomes. The role of 'equitable' arrangements, as explained by Professor Michael Reisman in the quote cited at the beginning of this article, would be 'to remedy a grievance there without changing the general legal arrangement'.

b. Ruling on jurisdiction *ex aequo et bono*

Analysis of case law suggests that, not infrequently, arbitrators and courts take equity and efficiency considerations into account when ruling on jurisdiction in complex settings. Arbitrators do not always restrict their mission to the application of a set of legal rules to conclude whether or not extension should take place. They also rule by reference to whether extension is 'appropriate', 'fair' or even 'wise' in the specific case. This more realist process of decision-making is not mere speculation. It has been identified by a number of imminent commentators. 'Concerns of equity often underlie the reasoning of courts and, even more, of arbitral tribunals.'[72] Furthermore, these considerations seem to *compete* in the minds of arbitrators and courts with well-established principles of arbitration law – the writing, consent and *privity* requirements – and are often given prevalence over a formalist or even purely consensual approach to jurisdiction. '[T]he equities that appear from the underlying facts are likely to be far more important to the outcome than which theory of law is advanced.'[73]

Prevailing patterns of decision making also confirm the emerging importance of equity and the changing nature of ruling on jurisdiction in complex settings. Indeed, where arbitrators proceed with a global assessment of jurisdiction, which is a frequent practice in groups of companies due to the significant weight of contextual elements, the process of decision making, based on *the convergence of a multitude of elements*, would necessarily involve a measure of equitable thinking that is hard to ignore. The purely legal no longer occupies the forefront of jurisdictional assessment. Interestingly, when courts and tribunals exclude the normal application of arbitration law and uphold jurisdiction notwithstanding consent, in order to accommodate economic realities or in pursuit of considerations that are deemed more just, they do so without spending much effort to justify, on the level of *legal technique*, the exclusion of consent. Classic analysis is simply excluded, spontaneously and *comme si de rien n'etait*. Furthermore, when the 'equities' of the case are taken into account by courts and tribunals, they are not mere *dicta*. They can also be made part of the determinative reasons of the award.

In the United States, consensual analysis is predominant. However, one still finds references to considerations of practicality and efficiency of arbitration agreements.[74] The arbitration agreement 'would be of little value if it did not extend to [the non-signatory].'[75] In some cases, practical considerations are invoked in conjunction with the federal policy in favour of arbitration in order to justify extension. 'If the parent corporation was forced to try the case, the arbitration proceedings would be rendered meaningless and the federal policy in favor of arbitration effectively thwarted.[76] The Fifth Circuit has even applied veil-piercing and *alter ego* theories 'in the name of equity'.[77] Nevertheless, US courts seem to be less responsive to equitable arguments as a basis for extending arbitral jurisdiction in the absence of consent, when no general principles of contract or corporate law are applicable.

Equitable considerations also seem to play a role in jurisdictional settings involving non-signatory states.[78] Interestingly, the *Westland tribunal* noted: 'Finally, mention must be made of the practical reasons and considerations of equity which have motivated the arbitrators in this matter, *quite apart from the legal ground.*'[79]

The pursuit of efficiency is more explicit in French case law on involvement in performance. In Sté V 2000 v. Sté Project XJ 220 ITD et autre,[80] the Paris Court of Appeal referred explicitly to considerations of good administration of justice as part of the legal argument that justified the decision to extend jurisdiction to a non-signatory involved in the performance of the contract containing the arbitration clause. V 2000 (Jaguar) was entitled to arbitrate 'so that all legal and economic aspects of the dispute are brought before the arbitrator.'[81]

c. Realism in decision making as a limit on the rigorous search for consent

This *post-modernist* methodology, which favours arbitration beyond international standards and internalizes justice into arbitration law, involves more than flushing out the search for consent: it involves marginalizing rigorous legal reasoning altogether in favour of decisions made in a more pragmatic and realist environment. Evidence of *ex ante* consent or *ex post* assumption of the obligation to arbitrate may be part of the equitable weighting of different elements. However, ruling on jurisdiction typically involves a setting where requiring consent would yield injustice and a decision on whether justice should prevail notwithstanding the absence of consent. The extent to which equity would materialize in an actual decision to extend is also influenced by other practical considerations that would, or at least should, occupy the minds of tribunals. These include how much support there is in the facts and the law for the arbitrators' equitable conclusions and, hence, the extent to which they would need to depart from their duty to render an enforceable award in order to implement extension.

6. RELEVANCE OF THE INQUIRY INTO THE LIMITS OF CONSENT IN EMERGING JURISDICTIONS

It has been noted that the practice of extending arbitration agreements to non-parties 'appears to have little impact on the strict formal approach maintained in many civil jurisdictions'.[82] It is also true that, with the exception of scenarios involving the application of contract law principles, such as assignment, formalist approaches remain the rule in jurisdictional assessment in the developing world. Thus, *a priori*, there is little room to discuss extension in a group setting, whether by application of the group of companies doctrine or even by consensual analysis. In other words, in most cases, the debate on extension to non-signatories is situated in a different sphere: between formalism and consent rather than between consent and the criteria that minimize consent. The main question is a question de principe: Is extension possible in the first place or is it excluded by mandatory form requirements under national laws? The answer is usually negative.

On occasion, emerging jurisdictions show signs of significant openness, by reason of regulatory competition or the process of global pollination built in a universal practice of arbitration. The situation may be changing, and the question of the limits of consent is likely to arise in broader terms in the future. The question will even arise in more fateful terms for emerging jurisdictions that recently adopted international standards protecting consent and that have a basic right to follow a gradual path of arbitral development.

In a decision of 22 June 2004,[83] the Court of Cassation of Egypt dealt at length with the question of the outer limits of consent as a basis to compel non-signatories in a group of companies. The court confirmed the annulment of an award rendered in *ad hoc* proceedings administered by the Cairo Regional Centre (Award No. 212 of 2001), which had compelled non-signatories based solely on the existence of an economic group.

However, while the court dismissed the mere existence of a group as a sufficient basis for extension, it did not exclude this possibility and in fact omitted any reference to the writing requirement, which is mandatory under UNCITRAL-inspired Egyptian arbitration law. The court formulated a principle of extension that is not even entirely consensual:

> "[A]rbitration agreements are of relative effect, and may not be invoked except against the parties who have consented thereto. Therefore, the mere fact that one of the parties to the arbitration proceedings is a company member of a corporate group, in which a parent company holds in the capital of its member entities, is not by itself sufficient basis to hold the parent company bound by the contracts concluded by other companies of the group, and which may contain arbitration clauses; unless evidence is submitted that the parent company was involved in the performance of these contracts, or has caused by its conduct, confusion as to the identity of the member of the corporate group contracting with the third party, in such a way that it has become difficult to distinguish the wills of the companies involved."[84] *[Emphasis added]*

The passage starts by reciting the basic canon of consent. However, the Court then goes on to formulate a composite basis of jurisdiction using a dual criterion: (1) involvement in performance (possibly as evidence of consent, if the requirement of involvement in performance is interpreted in conjunction with the earlier reference to consent); and (2) the confusion or false appearance such involvement or other conduct has created in the mind of the third party claimant. Using language that refers to the parties' intentions less than the *Dow award* itself, the court not only excluded formalist criteria but also explored what may exist beyond consent: objective notions such as the creation of confusion, legitimate expectations and appearances, some of which are explicit in the court's reasoning.

7. RATIONALIZING THE DECLINING RELEVANCE OF THE REQUIREMENT OF CONSENT

a. Sophistication of jurisdictional assessment

To say that consent depends on the factual context and equitable *calculus* is a deceptively simple phrase. It connotes a dramatic sophistication of jurisdictional assessment *vis-à-vis* non-signatories and the corrosion of the simple and unitary rule of consent. In principle, arbitration law ignores the economic structure of different plaintiffs and defendants or the equities that may underlie the decision to extend arbitral jurisdiction to a non-signatory in the case concerned. It is premised on consent (and on formalism in most cases) as a *per se* and *abstract* rule. Its application induces a jurisdictional inquiry that is in most cases *simple*. This traditional simplicity has faded, and the jurisdictional exercise is *sophisticated* beyond consensual habits in a variety of ways. First, the rule of consent applies less *in abstracto* and more in context. Second, jurisdictional assessment is no longer limited to contractual interpretation and even less so to a yes/no question regarding whether 'writing' exists. Instead, a multitude of approaches are available, and a number of criteria and principles come into play, besides a simple search for consent. Third, ruling on jurisdiction is not even limited to pure *legal* analysis. A more practical methodology is noted in case law, based not only on the legal permissibility but also on the *utility* and *fairness* of extension beyond consent in the specific case.

The changing nature of decisions on jurisdiction may be understood as a fundamental challenge to two paradigms of arbitration law, namely legal rigour and the notion that the source of the right or obligation to arbitration is necessarily a contract.

b. From consent *per se* to a rule of reason

The rise of realism in decision-making methods suggests that the per se rule of consent has been replaced by a *rule of reason*, to borrow vocabulary akin to competition law. When ruling on extension, courts and tribunals reason less in terms of norms (consent and formalism) and more in term of effects of extension (or its absence) in the specific case. Extension may be ordered, notwithstanding the fact that consent has not been found or has not been searched for, in order to honour considerations that are deemed worthy of prevailing, in the specific case, over a simple, automated and abstract search for *ex ante* consent.

Indeed, it has been suggested that the decision to extend or not to extend is frequently made under a 'what if not' scenario. Hanotiau explains: 'It seems that at least in a great number of cases, a good test to decide whether an "extension" of the clause is appropriate is to determine whether the same solution would be justified if the situation were reversed.'[85] It has also been suggested that the intellectual process of ruling on jurisdiction in these cases involves some form of *reverse reasoning*. A decision on extension is taken, at least prima facie, based on considerations of equity and jurisdictional efficiency, with the decision then being confirmed by reference to applicable legal principles or simply being clothed in legal reasons *a posteriori*. 'One is occasionally tempted to wonder whether equity is not in some cases the paramount consideration and all the legal theories advanced to justify the final decision, *ex post facto* creation.'[86]

c. Diversification of the sources of the right or obligation to arbitrate

i. 'Extension' and jurisdiction beyond consent: an inaccurate concept

The term 'extension' is conceptually problematic, whether or not the jurisdictional inquiry *vis-à-vis* the non-signatory is based on consent. In the first case, it overstates the jurisdictional exercise, which merely attempts to identify the true parties to the arbitration agreement.[87] Where non-signatories are compelled to arbitrate notwithstanding the absence of their consent, the term 'extension' understates the nature of the jurisdictional assessment. Describing what happens as merely extending an existing consensual arbitration conceals in the minds of tribunals and courts the fact that jurisdiction *vis-à-vis* non-parties often rests on *an independent legal basis, itself more or less consensual*.

ii. Multiplicity of norms competing to govern jurisdiction

The once exclusive rule of consent has given way to a number of principles and norms that coexist today and compete to govern jurisdiction. In comparative law, a non-signatory in a group context may be compelled or entitled to arbitrate based on one or more of the following grounds: consent (explicit or implicit, proven or presumed), national contract law principles (third-party beneficiary, agency, *alter ego* and veil piercing), general principles of law (estoppel, good faith, fraud or the principe de l'apparence), context-specific judicial doctrines (such as the group of companies doctrine) which bear the distinctive mark of particular legal systems or are part of the *lex mercatoria* and, finally, involvement in performance (either *per se* or combined with the notion of knowledge of the existence of the arbitration agreement).

In many cases, the applicable principle would simply reveal that the non-signatory has either consented (for example, involvement in performance as evidence of consent) or should otherwise be considered a party to the arbitration agreement (for example, veil piercing). In other cases, the 'ground' of extension conceals or constitutes a self-standing source of the right or obligation to arbitrate that is *distinct from consent*. These emerging sources include objective notions such as involvement in performance (per se and not as evidence of consent). They also include a notion of justice lato sensu that is built into most general principles of law, such as *estoppel* or good faith, and is sometimes explicit in the reasons of awards.

In addition, the factual context of a group not only matters but often also is outcome-determinative. It commands, at least in part, why a particular non-signatory is entitled or compelled to arbitrate. That is to say, the facts constitute an integral part of the basis of jurisdiction vis-à-vis non-signatories. On the one hand, many of the principles or grounds of extension characteristic of group settings are highly fact-specific (such as veil piercing or involvement in performance). On the other hand, where tribunals base their decision to extend or not to extend on a global factual evaluation of subjective and objective elements, an amalgam of legal principles, intent to be bound, equitable notions and determinant elements of facts (such as specific conduct or appearances) form the basis of jurisdiction vis-à-vis the non-signatory entity.

iii. Sources other than contract

The development of a multitude of norms and principles that govern jurisdiction in addition to consent also means that the sources of the right or obligation to arbitrate have diversified beyond contracts. Such a development may be rationalized by reference to the universal practice of arbitration. Without much audacity, one could suggest that, as a result of the banalization of arbitration agreements and their increasing treatment as ordinary contracts (including the loss of autonomy for purposes of assessing the scope of jurisdiction), the sources of the right or obligation to arbitrate may be falling back into the *droit commun*, specifically the théorie générale des obligations. For example, the source of the right or obligation to arbitrate may be, and often is, directly the law (national contract law or general principles of law) or trade usages (jurisdictional principles that are said to belong to the *lex mercatoria*, such as the obligation of subsidiaries to arbitrate with the parent entity).

The source of the obligation to arbitrate may also be some form of delict, lato sensu. A non-signatory may be compelled to arbitrate, or a signatory may be compelled to arbitrate with a stranger, if its conduct was inconsistent with the principle of good faith in the performance of obligations or amounted to fraud. In such cases, a finding of consent is neither part of the jurisdictional exercise nor even attempted by the tribunal. Consent and *châtiment* do not usually go hand in hand. ICC case No. 7245 offers an interesting example.[88] The tribunal considered that, by causing the dissolution of the signatory state entity, the non-signatory state – Libya *en l'occurrence* – must be deemed to have become a party to the arbitral proceedings. Extension seems to have taken place here as a measure of responsibility. In fact, the tribunal unanimously held the Libyan state liable for ending the existence of the party to the arbitration agreement.

8. LEGALISM *REDUX*

a. Complexity of the tasks of arbitrators and courts

i. The decline in legal rigour and the constraints of law

The retreat of the *per se* rule of consent (or of its *per se* application), the rise of equity and of global assessment of jurisdiction, and the resulting general sophistication of jurisdiction may create the impression that arbitrators and courts, faced with questions of considerable complexity, rule on jurisdiction, as a matter of fact, *ex aequo et bono*. However, this more sophisticated and less-rigorous decision-making environment should not be taken as an excuse to authorize arbitrators to do as they please with respect to compelling non-consenting parties. Similarly, the predominant context by reference to which the effect of the decision to extend or not to extend is assessed should not be a domain of pure fact-based inquiry, which gives arbitrators unlimited discretion. Even if empowered to act as *amiables compositeurs*, arbitrators are always bound to render a decision on jurisdiction justified in law. This is inherent in the nature of arbitration as a limited delegation of power. This tension between the decline in legal rigour and the necessity of a decision justified in law imbues the process of ruling on jurisdiction with unique complexity.

ii. Uncertainty of applicable rules

The uncertainty of applicable rules adds to the complexity of the task of arbitrators to render an award that is enforceable jurisdiction-wise and the task of courts to exercise control. Because a multitude of approaches and criteria coexist, there is often not one 'right' answer but only 'safer', 'efficient', 'just' or above all 'wise'[89] answers. In addition, national laws provide very divergent solutions to questions of extension, and applicable law methodology is often bypassed. Tribunals also often decide on the basis of rules that are different from those by reference to which courts exercise control, since courts usually apply their *lex*, even to supersede previous findings under the otherwise applicable law. Finally, national solutions are also volatile (for example, the frequent judicial restatements of the principle of extension in groups of companies under French law), and the rules of the game change during the game.

Devising approaches that are neither dismissive of consent nor indifferent to the complexities of the factual context or the equities of the case is a complicated matter. Solutions should be sought in a spirit of 'back to basics': (1) effective control of consent and the arbitrators' duty to give reasons to jurisdictional findings; (2) revival of applicable law methodology; and (3) recourse to general principles of law.

b. General principles of law

Often, the departure from consensual analysis is made by application of some national law (of contract). When this is not the case, the presumably *equitable* decision-making process identified earlier usually revolves around basic notions of common sense justice and basic functionality of arbitration. It may find legalistic expression in the fundamental principle of good faith and can usually be rooted in general principles of law such as the punishment of fraud and bad faith, the prohibition to contradict oneself to the detriment of others,[90] the doctrine of unclean hands, the protection of legitimate expectations and reliance on apparent positions. Blessing provides the basic insight: 'Again the "heart" of all the above notions or doctrines clearly is the *bona fides* principle, respectively the requirement to act in good faith and the notion that positions or defenses which stand in contradiction to the exigencies to act in good faith will not deserve legal (or arbitral) protection.'[91] General principles of law in the sense of Article 38 of the Statute of the ICJ thus have a decisive role to play in absorbing the rising complexity of jurisdictional assessment and in permitting equitable considerations to affect decision making, while maintaining legal rigour and simplicity of applicable rules. The application of general principles of law to the particular case should not pose a problem, since they also constitute basic principles of law in most legal systems.

c. Essentialism of effective control

i. Giving reasons

Advancing economic, equitable or pragmatic reasons for extension is not necessarily exclusive of judicial control. It nevertheless induces a unique difficulty in the task of giving *legal* reasons for jurisdictional findings. In discharging their duty to render an enforceable award, arbitrators must make explicit the *necessity* of compelling non-consenting parties, that is to say, their reasoning must lay out the contextual elements that would render the exclusion of the consent requirement *compelling* and the opposite solution grossly unjust. When possible, the tribunal should verify whether the equitable outcome could also be rooted in some applicable principle of law. As mentioned above, it usually will be.

ii. Controlling the genuineness of consent

On the other hand, the attraction (and danger) of using a language of consent, even if none can be derived from the facts, is clear and present. It would enhance the chances of enforcement of the award, if enforcement were attempted outside the most refined jurisdictions. Courts, exercising control, should not give tribunals an additional incentive to call 'consent' that which is not. Consensual analysis, reducing the jurisdictional function to a matter of contractual interpretation, could undermine in the minds of courts the need to exercise control. When confirming the *Dow* award, the Paris Court of Appeal noted: 'The arbitrators [...] are exclusively empowered to interpret the aforementioned contracts [...]'.[92] Therefore, their interpretation, correct or incorrect, is tenable. Obviously, this approach is fundamentally flawed. Exclusion of control of jurisdiction gives arbitrators final say over their jurisdiction, which is something they can never have. It also confuses jurisdiction and substance. The arbitrators' interpretation of the contract(s) is final only when it is part of the decision on the merits. When it is part of the jurisdictional inquiry, it should be subject to a full de novo control. In another case (in which arbitrators rendered a negative decision on their jurisdiction), the Paris Court of Appeal held that: 'To exercise its control, the court must find all the elements of law and fact to appreciate the scope of the arbitration agreement.'[93]

In order to be deemed to have discharged their duty to render an enforceable award, tribunals need to do more than conduct a *prima facie* verification of consent. In the final award in ICC case No. 7453, the sole arbitrator noted that: 'the consent of each party must be unambiguously demonstrable if any resulting Award is to be safely enforceable.'[94] The tribunal would need to state the factual basis upon which a finding of tacit consent is made, the elements indicating the extent of involvement in performance or, when extension is decided by application of veil piercing, *alter ego*, or *apparence*, the extent of control, confusion of assets or the basis for legitimate reliance.

d. Applicable law

The application of national contract law and domestic judicial theories of extension brings back to centre stage questions of applicable law. The question of the law governing the extension of the arbitration agreement in groups of companies, or in general, is particularly complex.[95] An analysis of the case law reveals two prevailing trends in addressing this question. On one hand, the issue of applicable law is often simply omitted in the reasoning of tribunals. In particular, when extension is decided by consensual analysis, the nature of the jurisdictional exercise, which boils down to the interpretation of the parties' intentions, usually conceals in the minds of arbitrators the need to proceed with a conflict approach to determine an applicable law by reference to which interpretation is made. On the other hand, a somewhat uniform position exists, as far as national courts are concerned. In ruling on or in controlling the decision on jurisdiction, courts tend to simply apply their *lex*, not as the outcome of a conflict method, but *as is*. They apply it either under the sophistication of the method of substantive norms (France) or *tel quel* (the United States and the United Kingdom). The *lex fori* also applies in general, not only when the courts are acting as courts of the place of arbitration but also when ruling on enforcement of awards rendered elsewhere.[96]

The following critical observations may be made. First, consensual analysis should not dispense with or short-circuit the process of identifying an applicable law. Contractual interpretation should be made by reference to a set of norms. National contract laws differ, sometimes substantially, with respect to the acceptable forms of expression of consent, the principles of interpretation and the conditions and scope of application of third-party principles.

Second, in group contexts, applicable national law does not only include contract law. Fundamentally, it also encompasses the law of corporate groups, or the body of rules that govern, substantively and procedurally, the inter-entity attribution of rights and obligations. Thus, ideally, the jurisdictional inquiry would start with (or at least involve) the identification of this law. This is not how courts usually proceed. For instance, US courts invariably apply domestic standards of veil piercing, sometimes even when they are acting as enforcing courts, to reassess findings of arbitral awards rendered under foreign law.[97]

Eurosteel Ltd v. Stinnes AG [98] provides a model for identifying the applicable law in a merger scenario. The English court held that the arbitration agreement was transmitted by universal succession to the non-signatory entity in which the signatory entity merged. The court distinguished between German law, which governed the conditions and regime of the merger as the law of the place of incorporation, and English law, which governed the assignment of the arbitration agreement as the law of the place of arbitration; and applied each in its own domain.

9. CONSENT *REDUX?*

a. The decline of consent

For the first time in modern times, consent is not the sole criterion that is allowed to govern the validity of the waiver of judicial jurisdiction in favour of private justice. The decline of consent within a broader context of sophistication of jurisdictional assessment epitomizes a major breakthrough in solutions to problems of jurisdiction in international commerce. Tribunals and courts have ventured to accommodate complex commercial settings beyond the arbitration system's final frontier and *logical* limit: consent.

International arbitral practice has developed limits on a pure and simple search for consent in assessing jurisdiction vis-à-vis non-signatories. These limits are contextual (derived from the distorting effect of the existence of an economic group), *intrinsic* (ensuing from the retrieved nature of the arbitration agreement as an ordinary contract, which brings about the application of contract law principles and reduces the autonomy of the arbitration clause from the main contract), *pragmatic* (when the pursuit of consent is inconsistent with equity or the efficacy of the jurisdictional construct) and *functional* (derived from the universal development of arbitration and hence the growing treatment of the right or obligation to arbitrate as the accessory of the substantive rights and obligations themselves). Today, the jurisdictional fate of non-signatories is often decided at the intersection of subjective intent and objective context, of legal principles and subjacent equity.

b. Is it good?

Undermining consent is, in most cases, inevitable. More often than not, the judicial trends that depart from classic consensual analysis or consecrate forms of objective jurisdiction are not luxury exercises in judicial or arbitral lawmaking. They simply reflect the complexity of the context of jurisdictional assessment in groups of companies and constitute a necessary adaptation of a living law to the necessities of practice. The decline of the requirement of consent may be rationalized by reference to the emergence of arbitration as the *juge naturel* of disputes arising under international contracts. One consequence of this is the reduced conceptual necessity of consent as a technique of opting out of the default jurisdiction of national courts.

Nevertheless, the development of limits on consent tests the limits of the legitimacy of the arbitration system. Arbitral practice should be geared, insofar as possible, towards ways to restore consent to its previous empire. In this respect, the fate of non-signatories (and to a certain extent of the arbitral system) also depends on the parties themselves and, above all, on the wisdom of those who decide.

c. Contractual management of jurisdictional exposure

i. Exclusion-of-extension clauses

With the development of practices of extension, the parties' focus will shift from which jurisdictional option to choose (i.e. whether to arbitrate) to how to contractually or factually manage the scope of possible exposure to arbitral jurisdiction. *A priori*, parties may re-exercise their partially expropriated autonomy in ways that would defeat or restrict prevailing extension practices. Signatory entities (of a group or of the state) may wish to restrict the scope of a particular transaction from reaching non-signatory corporate entities or the state itself. They may do so via a restrictive interpretation clause, which would require the tribunal, in case of doubt, to exclude an economic or expansive interpretation of the scope of the arbitration agreement. They may also simply exclude the application of particular doctrines or principles of extension under the applicable law.

ii. Express choice of the law governing jurisdiction

An often forgotten yet important option is a choice of law clause. The parties may revive their dormant party autonomy and choose the law applicable to the arbitration agreement with respect to the *scope* of jurisdiction. They may extend the application of the law governing the merits to govern jurisdiction as well, choose a different law to apply or refer to a-national [non-national] norms. The choice of a national law with restrictive views on the particular question of extension that is likely to arise avoids surprise attempts on non-signatories by third parties. However, it could also tie the hands of the group entities when the need to bring claims against the third party contracting with the group arises. The selection of a governing law that provides for liberal solutions gives broader discretion to the tribunal but increases the exposure of both non-signatory entities and the third party contracting with the group to a possible expansive assertion of jurisdiction.

iii. Regime

Despite their usefulness, aspects of these 'management of jurisdiction clauses' are uncertain, and it is the task of future case law to clarify their operation. As agreements between signatory entities and the third party contracting with them, it is likely that these clauses would not bind non-signatories that may still be able to bring a claim against the third party signatory. If this were the case, these clauses would provide more protection to non-signatory entities than to third parties contracting with the group. In principle, management of jurisdiction clauses would bind the tribunal, since they relate to the exercise of its mandate in ruling on jurisdiction. However, the extent to which such contractual arrangements will be given effect to the detriment of objective considerations that justified the exclusion of consent in the first place is also an open question. Finally, the development of management of jurisdiction clauses also involves a risk of entrenching current extension practices. It would enshrine the notion that, if parties do not manage exposure to arbitration in groups of companies, i.e. if they do not opt out of rules expanding jurisdiction, they may be deemed to have implicitly consented to the application of these rules.[99] As a general matter, courts should give maximum effect to these arrangements, in a spirit of giving back to the parties what belongs to them.

10. THE FUTURE: CONSENT AS A *DEFAULT* CRITERION

Experts on international arbitration should take notice of the significant effacement of consent in jurisdictional assessment *vis-à-vis* non-signatories and should fully understand the practical, normative and conceptual consequences of this major phenomenon. They should also take notice of the richness of and significant potential for creative advocacy in the field, permitted by the transition towards a more sophisticated decisional environment and less certain rules.

Tribunals asserting jurisdiction *vis-à-vis* non-consenting parties should pay special attention not only to jurisdictional but also to *procedural* issues. Extension of jurisdiction entails an extension of procedural safeguards to non-signatories. Non-consenting parties, attending or absent, must be kept informed of all procedural steps and communications. Equality of treatment is of the essence.

Fundamentally, decision-makers should not forget that consent remains, and is likely to remain, the *default* rule in assessing jurisdiction, even though practice permits the usage of a number of approaches, criteria and norms that are less or even non-consensual. Blessing affirms that: '[…] such fundamental principles cannot easily be removed […] unless very specific circumstances demand such a removal.'[100] Similarly, Hanotiau recalls that: 'However far one is ready to stretch the concept of consent (and it may go as far as considering certain specific conduct as a substitute for consent), one should not forget that consent is the fundamental pillar of international arbitration.'[101] Looking at 'The Future', one can hear Leonard Cohen humming: 'Give me back [consent, consent, consent].'

END NOTES

* Associate Professor of Law, Cairo University; Associate, Cleary Gottlieb Steen & Hamilton LL.P.

1   A.S. Rau, 'Arbitral Jurisdiction and the Dimensions of "Consent"', Arb. Int'l 24(2) (2008) p. 199.

2   J. Hosking, 'Non-Signatories and International Arbitration in the United States: The Quest for Consent', Arb. Int'l 20(3) (2004) p. 289.

3   J. Hosking, 'The Third Party Non-Signatory's Ability to Compel International Commercial Arbitration: Doing Justice Without Destroying Consent', Pepp. Disp. Resol. L.J. 4 (2004) p. 469.

4   D. Cohen, 'Arbitrage et Groupes de Contrats', Rev. Arb. (1997) pp. 477-478.

4   J. Fouret, 'Denunciation of the Washington Convention and Non-Contractual Investment Arbitration: "Manufacturing Consent" to ICSID Arbitration', J. Int'l Arb. 25(1) (2008) p. 71.

6   See K. Youssef, 'The Decline of Consent in International Commercial Arbitration: The Disintegration of the Arbitration Agreement and the Construction of a World Commercial Justice', JSD thesis, Yale University, 2007.

7   V. Dominique, 'Extension of Arbitration Agreements Within Groups of Companies: The Alter Ego Doctrine in Arbitral and Court Decisions', ICC Bulletin 16(2) (2005) p. 63.

8   See supra n. 4.

9   See supra n. 5.

10 C.P.R. Romano, 'The Shift from the Consensual to the Compulsory Paradigm in International Adjudication: Elements for a Theory of Consent', 39 N.Y.U. J. Int'l L. & Pol. (2006-2007) p. 791.

11 The term is classic in US federal case law.

12 Compelling a non-signatory to arbitrate does not per se violate the right to a fair trial. Nisshin Shipping Co. Ltd v. Cleaves & Company Ltd [2003] EWHC 2602 (Comm). (Compelling a third party to arbitrate under the UK 1999 Contracts (Rights of Third Parties) Act does not violate Article 6(1) of the European Human Rights Convention).

13 Even under very liberal French law, an arbitral award can be challenged 'if the arbitrator has rendered his decision in the absence of an arbitration agreement or on the basis of an arbitration agreement that is invalid or that has expired' (Article 1502(1) French NCPC).

14 Adams v. Cape Industries plc., English Court of Appeal [1990], 1st Ch. 433, p. 544: 'We do not accept as a matter of law that the court is entitled to lift the corporate veil as against a defendant company which is the member of a corporate group merely because the corporate structure has been used so as to ensure that the legal liability (if any) in respect of particular future activities of the group [...] will fall on another member of the group rather than the defendant company. Whether or not this is desirable, the right to use a corporate structure in this manner in inherent in our corporate law.'

15 According to Otto Sandrock: '[I]t is the very purpose of the group of companies-concept that each member of such group maintains its legal independence to the effect that its own legal actions bind only itself and do not bind the other members of its group, and that the

other members of its group also cannot avail themselves of the rights accruing out of its actions. To decide otherwise, would mean to give up the group of companies-concept itself. The notion of the separate entity of each juristic person would also have to be sacrificed. This would be unacceptable.' See O. Sandrock, 'Extending the Scope of Arbitration Agreements to Non-Signatories', in The Arbitration Agreement – Its Multifold Critical Aspects, ASA Special Series No. 8 (1994) pp. 165-180 at p. 167.

16 See B. Hanotiau, Complex Arbitrations (Kluwer, 2005).

17 See Working Group on 'Jurisdiction over Non-Signatories: National Contract Law or International Arbitral Practice?', in A.J. van den Berg (ed.), International Arbitration – Back to Basics?, ICCA Congress Series No. 13 (2006).

18 See K. Youssef, Consent in Context, Fulfilling the Promise of International Arbitration: Multiparty, Multi-Contract and Non-Contract Arbitration (West, 2009).

19 I am very indebted to Jan Paulsson for suggesting this expression.

20 Dow Chemical France and others v. Isover Saint Gobain ('Dow'), Interim Award, ICC case No. 4131 of September 1982; ICCA YB 9 (1984) p. 131; Coll. ICC Arbitral Awards 1974-1985 (1990) p. 150.

21 ICCA YB 9 (1984) pp. 131, 136.

22 In this sense, see B. Hanotiau, 'Non-signatories in International Arbitration: Lessons from Thirty Years of Case Law', in A.J. van den Berg (ed.), International Arbitration – Back to Basics?, ICCA Congress Series No. 13 (2006) pp. 341-358 at pp. 343-344.

23 E. Gaillard and J. Savage (eds.), Fouchard, Gaillard, Goldman on International Commercial Arbitration (Kluwer, 1999) at para. 500.

24 ICC cases Nos. 7604 and 7610, J.D.I. (1998) p. 1029.

25 See, for example, ICC case No. 1434, J.D.I. 103 (1976) pp. 978, 979-980, obs. Y. Derains.

26 Hanotiau, supra n. 22, at p. 343.

27 Ibid.

28 ICC case No. 6519 (1991), J.D.I. (1991) p. 1065: '[W]ithout denying the economic reality of a "group of companies", the scope of an arbitration clause may be extended to non-signatory companies with separate legal significance only if they played an active role in the negotiations leading to the agreement containing the arbitration clause, or if they are directly implicated in the agreement.' See also the cases cited in Vidal [INSERT FULL REFERENCE], p. 73, n. 61.

29 The Paris Court of Appeal extended the arbitration agreement contained in a charterparty to the non-signatory carrier who took part in the performance of the charterparty. Cotunav, 28 November 1989, Rev. Arb. (1990) p. 675.

30 The group of companies doctrine has been applied to economic structures as varied as joint ventures and consortiums. A variation of the doctrine has been applied, by analogy, to extend the arbitration agreement signed by a state entity to the non-signatory state itself, or to non-signatory states of a signatory organization (e.g. the Westland award).

31 Sandrock, supra n. 15, at p. 180.

32 '[A] first conclusion may be drawn from the awards and court decisions to the effect that the determination of whether an arbitral clause should be extended to other companies of the group or its directors or shareholders is "fact specific" and may differ depending upon the circumstances of the case.' Hanotiau, supra n. 22, at p. 351.

33 Ibid., at p. 344.

34 Ibid.

35 Under general principles of contract interpretation, the circumstances that accompanied the conclusion of the contract should be taken into account. Joseph M. Perillo (ed.), Corbin On Contracts – Interpretation of Contracts (1998) § 24.21.

36 N. Rubins, 'Group of Companies Doctrine and the New York Convention', in E. Gaillard and D. Di Pietro (eds.), Enforcement of Arbitration Agreements and International Arbitral Awards: The New York Convention in Practice (Cameron May, 2008) pp. 449-479 at p. 457 (emphasis added).

37 30 November 1998 (unpublished), cited in Hanotiau, supra n. 22, at pp. 351-352.

38 Ibid.

39 See infra section 2.b: Global assessment of jurisdiction.

40 See infra section 5: Equity.

41 M. Blessing, 'Extension of the Arbitration Clause to Non-Signatories', in The Arbitration Agreement – Its Multifold Critical Aspects, ASA Special Series No. 8 (1994) pp. 151-164 at p. 160.

42 Fouchard, Gaillard and Goldman, supra n. 23, at paras. 500-501.

43 Dow, ICCA YB 9 (1984) pp. 131, 136 (emphasis added).

44 For the application of the principe de l'apparence as basis for extension in French case law, see infra n. 65,

45 See, for example, ICC cases Nos. 7604 and 7610, J.D.I. (1998) p. 1029: 'It is necessary to look for the actual and common intention of the parties at the time of the facts, or, at the very least, that of the non-signatory third party.'

46 Dow, ICCA YB 9 (1984) pp. 131, 136.

47 Pau Court of Appeal, 26 November 1986, Rev. Arb. (1988) p. 154.

48 ICC case No. 6519 (1991), J.D.I. (1991) p. 1065: '[W]ithout denying the economic reality of a "group of companies", the scope of an arbitration clause may be extended to non-signatory companies with separate legal significance only if they played an active role in the negotiations leading to the agreement containing the arbitration clause, or if they are directly implicated in the agreement.'

49 Involvement was 'an insufficient showing of complete domination or extensive control' for purposes of assessing veil piercing (and not for implying consent). Bridas II, 447 F.3d 411, 415 (5th Circuit, 2006), citing the District Court decision of 2004 before reversing it and holding the non-signatory state entity liable on alter ego grounds.

50 Hanotiau, supra n. 22, at p. 352 (footnote omitted).

51 ICC ICA Bull. 2(2) (1991) pp. 31, 34 (emphasis added).

52 M.J. Mustill, 'The New Lex Mercatoria', in M. Bos and I. Brownlie (eds.), Liber Amicorum for Lord Wilberforce (Clarendon Press, 1987) p. 176, Principle No. 8.

53 Sté Ofer Brothers v. The Tokyo Marine and Fire Insurance Co. Ltd. et autres, Paris Court of Appeal (1re Ch. Suppl.), 14 February 1989, Rev. Arb. (1989) p. 691. For almost identical language, see Orri v. Sté des Lubrifiants Elf Aquitaine, Paris Court of Appeal (1re Ch. Suppl. D), 11 January 1990, Rev. Arb. 2 (1992) pp. 95-98; and Sté Jaguar (V 2000) v. Sté Project XJ 220, Paris Court of Appeal (1re Ch.) 7 December 1994, Rev. Arb. (1996) p. 250.

54 Rev. Arb. (1989) p. 694.

55 J.F. Poudret, 'L'extension de la clause d'arbitrage: approches française et suisse', J.D.I. (1995) at p. 901.

56 Sté Jaguar (V 2000) v. Sté Project XJ 220, Paris CA Court of Appeal (1re Ch.) 7 December 1994, Rev. Arb. (1996) op. 254, obs. C. Jarrosson.

57 Poudret, supra n. 55, at p. 901.

58 B. Hanotiau, 'Problems Raised by Complex Arbitrations Involving Multiple Contracts – Parties – Issues: An Analysis', J. Int'l. Arb. 18(3) (2001) pp. 253, 273.

59 ICC case No. 3879, Interim Award of 5 March 1984, YBCA 11 (1986) p. 130.

60 "The issue of who is party to the arbitration clause is therefore mainly viewed as an issue of consent, but 'extension' may nevertheless be achieved by recourse to other theories such as agency, trust or piercing the corporate veil." Hanotiau, supra n. 22, at p. 351.

61 Sandrock, supra n. 15, at p. 168.

62 'Arbitration is contractual by nature [...]. It does not follow, however, that under the [Federal Arbitration] Act an obligation to arbitrate attaches only to one who has personally signed the written arbitration provision. This court has made clear that a non-signatory party may be bound to an arbitration agreement if so dictated by the ordinary principles of contract and agency.' Thomson-CSF, S.A. v. American Arbitration Ass'n, 64 F.3d 773, 776 (2d Cir. 1995).

63 MacNeil, Speidel and Stipanowich, Federal Arbitration Law: Agreements, Awards and Remedies Under the Federal Arbitration Act (1994) § 18.7.1.1.

64 Poudret, supra n. 55, at p. 913.

65 Paris Court of Appeal, 7 October 1999, Rev. Arb. (2000) p. 288 (D. Bureau): 'Les circonstances de la négociation, de la conclusion et de l'exécution du contrat ayant créé pour l'un des contractants la croyance légitime qu'une société, avec qui elle avait delà traite dans le passe, était également partie à ce contrat bien qu'étant pas signataire, la convention d'arbitrage a un effet obligatoire pour cette dernière conformément au principe de l'apparence applicable aux relations du commerce international.'

66 See, for example, Cass. com., 20 November 1990, Bull. inf. stés (1991) p. 99.

67 See Cass. civ. 1re, 11 June 1991 (Orri), Rev. Arb. (1992) pp. 74-75 (non-signatory owner of a group of companies compelled to arbitrate based on the creation of confusion among different entities and his attempt to avoid being personally bound).

68 Rubins, supra n. 36, at p. 460.

69 See Hosking, supra n. 3, at pp. 469, 486.

70 Ibid., at p. 487.

71 Hosking, supra n. 2, at pp. 289, 303.

72 Hanotiau, supra n. 58, at p. 278.

73 J. Townsend, 'Non-signatories and Arbitration', ADR Currents 3 (1998) p. 19 at p. 23.

74 'While the case law generally shows a deference to consent, especially in the United States, one finds that it sometimes takes a backseat to such notions as "the need for efficiency" or upholding the "presumption of arbitrability".' Hosking, supra n. 2, at pp. 289, 303.

75 Pritzker v. Merrill Lynch, Pierce, Fenner & Smith, 7 F.3d 1110, 1122 (3d Cir.1993).

76 Sam Reisfeld & Son Import Co. v. S.A. Eteco, 530 F.2d 679, 681, 1976-1 Trade Cas. (CCH) para. 60851 (5th Cir. 1976); Burlington Ins. Co. v. Trygg-Hansa Ins. Co. AB, 9 Fed. Appx. 196 (4th Cir. 2001) (compelling a parent non-signatory to arbitrate disputes under reinsurance agreements signed by its subsidiary).

77 'Courts will apply the alter ego doctrine and hold a parent corporation liable for the actions of its instrumentality in the name of equity when the corporate form is used as a sham to perpetrate a fraud.' Bridas S.A.P.I.C. v. Government of Turkmenistan, 447 F.3d 411, 416 (5th Cir. 2006).

78 George Rosenberg seems to suggest that jurisdictional assessment in these cases depends more on the balance of policy considerations at stake than on strict application of general contract law and the interpretation of the will of the parties. G. Rosenberg, 'State as Party to Arbitration', Arb. Int'l 20(4) (2004) pp. 387, 398.

79 ICC case No. 3879, Interim Award, 5 March 1984, YBCA 11 (1986) pp. 127, 132.

80 Paris Court of Appeal (1re Ch.), 7 December 1994, Rev. Arb. 2 (1996) pp. 245-249 and case note of C. Jarrosson at pp. 250-258.

81 Ibid., at p. 250.

82 Rubins, supra n. 36, at p. 466 (referring inter alia to the position of Dutch and German law).

83 Khatib Petroleum Services International Co. v. Care Construction Co. and Care Services Co., Case No. 4729 of Judicial Year No. 72, 22 June 2004. For the full text and commentary, see K. Youssef, 'The Group of Companies Doctrine in Egyptian Law', SIAR 3 (2007) pp. 103-113.

84 Ibid., at pp. 105-106.

85 Hanotiau, supra n. 22, at p. 353.

86 Hanotiau, supra n. 16, at pp. 8-9.

87 Ibid., at p. 5.

88 Interim Award of 28 January 1994. See M. Blessing, 'State Arbitrations: Predictably Unpredictable Solutions?' J. Int'l Arb. 22(6) (2005) pp. 435, 440, n. 17.

89 We owe the clairvoyant association of 'wisdom' and jurisdictional assessment to Marc Blessing.

90 E. Gaillard, 'L'interdiction de se contredire au détriment d'autrui comme principe général du droit du commerce international', Rev. Arb. (1985) p. 241. For the reception of the principle in French law, see Cass. civ. 1re6 July 2005, Rev. Arb. (2005) p. 993 et seq.

91 Blessing, supra n. 41, at p. 162.

92 Paris Court of Appeal, 21 October 1983, Rev. Arb. (1984) p. 98 (the decision that rejected the annulment of Dow).

93 SNCFT v. Sté Voith, Paris Court of Appeal (1re Ch. C), 26 October 1995, Rev. Arb. (1997) p. 555.

94 Final Award in ICC case No. 7453 (1994), A.J. van den Berg (ed.), YBCA, Vol. XXII (1997) pp. 107-124, at para. 10.

95 See 'The Law Applicable to the Question of Extension', in Youssef, supra n. 18, at § 9:1 et seq.

96 J.F. Poudret, 'L'originalité du droit français de l'arbitrage au regard du droit comparé', Bull. cass., No. 589, 15 December 2003.

97 See Sarhank Group v. Oracle Corp., 404 F.3d 657 (2d Cir., 2005) (rejecting the enforcement of an award rendered against a non-signatory US parent by application of Egyptian law).

98 Com Ct [1999] All ER (D) 1394.

99 Blessing, supra n. 41, at p. 164.

100 Ibid., at p. 160.

101 Hanotiau, supra n. 22, at p. 348.

CHAPTER 5

EXTENDING AN ARBITRATION CLAUSE TO A NON-SIGNATORY CLAIMANT OR NON-SIGNATORY DEFENDANT: DOES IT MAKE A DIFFERENCE?

JOHN M. TOWNSEND*

1. INTRODUCTION

Some questions should simply be answered 'yes', and this is true of the question that appears in the title. It would have the virtue of being a complete sentence and an accurate answer.
Before tackling the reasons for this answer, some clarifications are needed, because the terminology in this field provides significant opportunities for confusion.

First, I use non-signatory in the sense of a party that is not a signatory to the agreement containing the arbitration clause under which an arbitration is conducted. A non-signatory thus may be, but need not be, an affiliate of a signatory. But it may equally have another relationship to one or more signatories, or to the transaction, that has been recognized by some legal authority as conferring the right, or imposing the obligation, to participate in the arbitration.

Some relationships that have been so recognized are:

- parent-subsidiary
- principal-agent
- third-party beneficiary
- employer-employee
- predecessor-successor.

Alternatively, the non-signatory's relationship to the contract or the transaction may be characterized by some theory of law, such as:

- assumption
- incorporation by reference
- equitable estoppel.

Second, the question whether a non-signatory may insert itself into an arbitration (usually as a claimant) or may be compelled to participate in an arbitration (usually as a defendant) often arises, at least in the United States, in the context of another proceeding, usually litigation in court, in which the roles may be reversed. Thus, for example, a defendant in a court proceeding may seek an order from the court compelling the plaintiff in the court proceeding to take the claim to arbitration, rather than to court. If, as often happens, the plaintiff is a non-signatory to the contract containing the arbitration clause, it becomes a claimant in an arbitration, but involuntarily.

That was the case, for example, in *Azhar Ali Khan v. Parsons Global Services*.[1] The wife of a company employee who had been kidnapped abroad sued her husband's employer in court. The husband's employment contract contained an arbitration clause. The court required the claim to go to arbitration, because the non-signatory wife's claim derived from the husband's contract, which contained an arbitration clause.

If it was the defendant in the court proceeding that was the non-signatory, that defendant would become the defendant in an arbitration, but a voluntary one. For example, in *Birmingham Associates v. Abbott Labs.*,[2] Birmingham had contracted with a subsidiary of Abbott to fund various medical technologies. Birmingham later sued the non-signatory parent company, Abbott, in court for alleged breach of a 'keep well' obligation. The court granted Abbott's motion to compel arbitration, because Abbott's relationship to its subsidiary that was the signatory was close enough to permit the non-signatory parent to rely upon the arbitration agreement.

It is probably therefore better to reframe the question to distinguish between:

- a non-signatory that wishes to participate in an arbitration under an arbitration clause to which it is not a signatory, which will be called a '**willing non-signatory**'; and
- a non-signatory that is compelled against its will to participate in such an arbitration, which will be called an '**unwilling non-signatory**'.

It makes considerable practical difference to the non-signatory and to the other parties to the arbitration which of those positions the non-signatory is in.

2. WILLING SIGNATORIES

One way to approach this difference is to look at why a willing non-signatory would wish to become a party to an arbitration under a contract it did not sign. The most common reason, at least in the United States, is to escape a proceeding in court. Much otherwise inexplicable behaviour can be explained by the imperative need, felt by nearly all defendants, to escape from an American court proceeding.

This arises in many contexts. For example, an employee, such as a stockbroker, may be sued in court by an unhappy customer who has lost all his money by following the broker's advice. Judging from the law reports, this happens with appalling frequency. In any event, this was the case in *Pritzker v. Merrill Lynch*.[3] A broker in such a position will have a strong motive to invoke the arbitration clause in the customer's agreement with his employer, in order to be able to move the dispute from court to arbitration.

As another example, a franchisor that has granted its franchisees the right to sub-franchise might be sued in court by a sub-franchisee for alleged violations of competition law. That was the situation in *Sunkist Soft Drinks, Inc. v. Sunkist Growers, Inc.*[4] Depending on the wording of the arbitration clause in the contract between the franchisee and the sub-franchisee, to which the franchisor is not a party, the franchisor may be able to persuade the court to order the dispute to arbitration under that clause.

As yet another example, the parent of a subsidiary that was a party to a contract may be sued in court (perhaps in tort) by the other party to that contract, or its parent, and may wish to insist that disputes be resolved under the arbitration procedures agreed to between its subsidiary and the other party. An example of this configuration is *J.J. Ryan & Sons v. Rhone Poulenc Textile, S.A.*[5]

A different reason why a willing non-signatory might wish to become a party to an arbitration under a contract it did not sign would be if it felt that some subject in which it had a vital interest was going to be decided in an arbitration between two other parties. For example, the owner of a trademark might wish to intervene in an arbitration between a company to which it had licensed the trademark and another company that the licensee had engaged to manufacture the trademarked item, in order to protect its mark or to take a position on the quality of the goods sold under it. Similarly, a guarantor of a contract containing an arbitration clause, to which the guarantor is not a signatory, may wish to intervene in a dispute between the parties to that contract.

3. Unwilling signatories

It is also worthwhile to look at why one or more of the parties to an arbitration might wish to require an *unwilling* non-signatory to the contract containing the arbitration clause to participate in the arbitration.

Most often, one of the parties fears that the other party lacks either the financial means to pay a monetary award or the necessary authority to carry out a non-monetary award (such as an order to cease using a licensed technology) and seeks to bring in a more solvent affiliate (usually a parent company) or the affiliate in control of the subject of the non-monetary relief sought.

Sometimes the impetus to bring an unwilling non-signatory into an arbitration arises from the need to reconcile multiple agreements among parties, each of which has not signed every agreement. For example, a party seeking to enforce a contract may wish to require a non-signatory to that contract to participate on the grounds that the non-signatory was a party to a separate guaranty or indemnity agreement (which may or may not contain its own arbitration clause), in order to avoid the expense of two proceedings or the risk of inconsistent results in separate proceedings against the guarantor. An example of this is *General Electric Co. v. Deutz AG.*[6]

4. consent

Other contributors to this volume discuss the importance of consent when it comes to extending the reach of an arbitration clause to a non-signatory. Consent seems to me to provide the key distinction between extending the reach of such a clause to a willing non-signatory and extending the reach of such a clause to an unwilling non-signatory.

In the case of the willing non-signatory, all the proposed participants in the arbitration have consented to arbitrate with someone. Each party may not have consented to arbitrate with all the parties involved, but at least all parties will have crossed the initial threshold of having agreed in principle to arbitration:

- The signatories to the arbitration clause have consented to arbitrate with each other.
- Presumably, all of them will have consented to arbitrate the subject matter in question, by virtue of having signed the same contract.
- Finally, the willing non-signatory has consented to arbitrate with the other parties and to arbitrate the subject matter in question by seeking to participate in the proceeding.

The signatories may not wish to arbitrate the dispute in question with the willing non-signatory – indeed, they may well be seeking to take the willing non-signatory to court. But whether they can be compelled to add another party to the circle of parties with which they have consented to arbitrate seems to me to be qualitatively different from seeking to compel a party that has never consented to arbitration in any form to arbitrate.

The analysis simply becomes a question of contract law: Do the provisions of the contract concerned support the inclusion of the additional party over the objections of those already bound by the contract?

This reference to the underlying contract law may be seen in a very recent decision of the United States Supreme Court, *Arthur Anderson v. Carlisle*,[7] which is noteworthy for three reasons. First, the Arthur Anderson case is the first one in which the Supreme Court has directly addressed the rights and obligations of a non-signatory to an arbitration agreement. We have had many court of appeals decisions, but no Supreme Court decision on the subject.

Second, the Supreme Court recognized not only that a non-signatory may have rights under an arbitration agreement but also that a non-signatory has the same right as a signatory to take an appeal from a decision of a district court refusing an application to stay a proceeding in court in favour of arbitration.

More significant for the purpose of this discussion is the fact that the Supreme Court held that whether the non-signatory has rights under the contract containing the arbitration clause was a question not of federal arbitration law but of state contract law. Thus, for the purpose of deciding whether a contract may be enforced by or against a non-signatory, federal courts are now instructed to look to principles of state contract law. As the Supreme Court put it: 'where state law permits it, a third-party claim is "referable to arbitration under an agreement in writing".'[8] As I am indebted to Paul Friedland for pointing out, this reference to state law is likely to have significant consequences for American arbitration law.

In the parallel case, where an attempt is made to bring into an arbitration an unwilling non-signatory, the consent question seems to me to be different. It may be that ordinary principles of state contract or agency law permit the consent of a signatory to be imputed to the non-signatory. For example, the consent of an agent may be imputed to a principal, or vice versa. Or the consent of a subsidiary may be imputed to a parent, in cases where the law would otherwise permit the corporate veil to be pierced. Or the non-signatory may be deemed, by seeking to take advantage of one clause of a contract, to have accepted other provisions of that contract, including the arbitration clause – what American courts call equitable estoppels. In all of these cases, it seems to me, consent is present, even if it is provided by operation of law rather than by a simple signature.[9]

However, where no principle of law permits the consent of one party to a contract to be imputed to a stranger to that contract, I do not know of any legal system that will permit an unwilling non-signatory to be forced to arbitrate a dispute under the arbitration clause in that contract if it does not wish to do so. As the Second Circuit Court of Appeals put it in *Merrill Lynch Investment Managers v. Optibase, Ltd.:* [10]

> "[I]t matters whether the party resisting arbitration is a signatory or not. '[A] court should be wary of imposing a contractual duty to arbitrate on a non-contracting party.'"

That, fundamentally, is the difference between extending an arbitration clause to a willing non-signatory and an unwilling non-signatory. Whether the non-signatory is the claimant or defendant in the arbitration concerned seems relatively insignificant compared to whether it wishes to become a party.

5. CONCLUSION

In the case of the willing non-signatory, the element of consent is present in some form on the part of all parties. The inquiry should then become, I submit, whether one or more of the signatories that is resisting inclusion of the willing non-signatory in the proceeding can demonstrate either: (1) that the contract in which the agreement to arbitrate is found does not countenance the addition of the non-signatory; or (2) that the signatories would in some significant way be prejudiced by the addition of the non-signatory to the arbitration.

In the case of the unwilling non-signatory, however, consent must be found somewhere, in some form, or there will be no proper basis for requiring the non-signatory to arbitrate. If the applicable law permits the attribution to the unwilling non-signatory of someone else's consent – as a matter of agency, piercing the corporate veil, succession or assumption, or incorporation by reference – the element of consent is supplied by attribution and the unwilling non-signatory should be compelled to arbitrate. Similarly, if the unwilling non-signatory has sought to take advantage of other elements of the contract in which the arbitration clause appears, it would be unseemly to permit it to do so without also holding it to the arbitration clause. That also seems an acceptable form of consent.

Absent one form of consent or another, however, it would seem to be bad law and bad policy to compel an unwilling non-signatory to participate in an arbitration, whether as a claimant or as a defendant.

END NOTES

* John M. Townsend is a partner in the Washington office of Hughes Hubbard & Reed LLP and chairs that firm's Arbitration and ADR Practice Group. He is also the Chairman of the Board of Directors of the American Arbitration Association.

1 480 F. Supp.2d 327 (D.D.C. 2007).

2 547 F. Supp2d 295 (S.D.N.Y. 2008).

3 7 F.3d 1110 (3rd Cir. 1993

4 10 F.3d 753 (11th Cir. 1993).

5 863 F.2d 315 (4th Cir. 1988). Another example, InterGen N.V. v. Grina, 344 F.3d 134 (1st Cir. 2003), was discussed by the present author in 'Non-Signatories in International Arbitration – An American Perspective', *International Arbitration 2006: Back to Basics*, International Council for Commercial Arbitration Congress Series No. 13 (2007).

6 270 F.3d 144 (3rd Cir. 2001)

7 129 S.Ct. 1896 (2009),

8 129 S.Ct. at 1902, note 6. I am indebted to Paul Friedland for pointing out that this reference to state law is likely to have significant consequences for US arbitration law.

9 The implications of this sort of attribution of consent are learnedly discussed by Professor W.W. Park in 'Non-signatories and International Contracts: An Arbitrator's Dilemma', in Multiple *Party Actions in International Arbitration 3* (2009), adapted from 'Non-Signatories and International Arbitration', *Leading Arbitrators' Guide to International Arbitration*, 2nd edn. (L. Newman & R. Hill, 2008) p. 553; reprinted in *Dispute Res.* Int'l 2 (2008) p. 84.

10 337 F.3d 125, 131 (2d Cir. 2003).

CHAPTER 6

EXTENSION OF THE ARBITRATION CLAUSE TO NON-SIGNATORY STATES OR STATE ENTITIES: DOES IT RAISE A DIFFERENCE?

GEORGIOS PETROCHILOS**

Just as other contributors to this volume, this author proceeds from the basic premise that the extension of the effect of an arbitration agreement to a non-signatory party does not mean that it is possible to dispense with the need for consent to arbitration. Rather, it means that in certain circumstances the necessary consent can derive from circumstances other than the signature of an arbitration agreement. Another way to put this is to say that the binding force of an arbitration agreement can extend beyond its signatories.

When states or state entities of any sort are involved, are the rules about non-signatories different – or ought they to be different? In my submission, the answer is yes and no. For the most part, the answer is no: the rules for non-signatory states and state entities are the same as for all parties. But in part the answer is yes: there is a discrete spectrum of circumstances calling for the application of different or modified rules.

There are a number of reasons for which states and their entities may be thought to raise special issues and be treated as a case apart:

1. In the first place, the state – any state – is a conglomerate by definition. It is an aggregation of a multitude of bodies: some with legal personality, some without; some more autonomous and some less; some having a public-law status and some the legal cloth of a private law corporation, foundation or other entity. It is in such expanded formation that all states exist and act.

2. The state is a unitary concept only for the purposes of public international law, which approaches states as monoliths. That is a conception, however, of public international law and only for the purposes of public international law. Indeed, some states (e.g. Poland) do not have legal personality at all in terms of their domestic 'corporate' law: they are simply the sum total of a number of discrete bodies with separate legal personalities.

3. Accordingly, public international law has a number of rules, called 'rules of attribution', which operate to impute to the state the acts of the multitude of discrete bodies that make up the apparatus of the state. These rules are designed precisely to determine for which separate entities the state can be answerable.

4. The rules of attribution acknowledge that, if an entity with a separate legal personality that is not formally an organ of the state has acted (a) under the direction or control of the state or (b) in the furtherance of governmental powers given to it, then that entity's acts may be attributed to the state. [1]

In the light of these considerations, it is tempting to think that in reality a state-owned or state-controlled entity ultimately acts for the benefit of the state. When an entity, notwithstanding its discrete and distinct legal personality,

- can be dissolved at will by the state;
- is managed by government appointees;
- is charged with functions for the broader good of the community;
- is subject to special rules different from those that apply to private entities; or
- produces income that is consolidated in a line in the state's budget,

can it not be said that ultimately the benefit and burden of an arbitration agreement with such an entity should be extended to the state?

The answer, in principle, is no.

The reason for this answer is that the rules of attribution operate in the field of international responsibility for breaches of public international law. These rules do not operate on the plane of contract or private law, which is the legal environment in which an arbitration agreement typically produces its effects.

1. PERSONAL SCOPE OF ARBITRATION AGREEMENTS CO-EXTENSIVE WITH SUBSTANTIVE LAW OBLIGATIONS

The principle is, as it should be, that an arbitration agreement will extend to non-signatories when the substantive law rights and obligations in the main agreement also extend to those same non-signatories.[2] In other words, the extension of an arbitration agreement to non-signatories is the jurisdictional aspect or consequence of a substantive law legal bond that extends to non-signatories of the relevant agreement. The substantive law and jurisdictional aspects are in principle co-extensive: one is hard-pressed to see any legal basis for a person to be a party to an arbitration if that person has no rights or obligations in the substantive dispute. Special cases of *amici curiae* apart, innocent bystanders have no place in arbitration proceedings.[3]

Naturally, not all legal bonds creating rights and obligations for non-signatories can also create a jurisdictional bond with those persons. A principal can be bound by the agreement concluded by its agent, and this can also be the case for a successor in title, the beneficiary of a cession or subrogation, and so forth. But a guarantor may or may not be bound by an arbitration agreement between the primary debtor and the creditor; and an insurer will in principle not be bound by an arbitration agreement between the insured and its counter-party. The principle is that having substantive law rights and obligations under the main agreement will be a necessary – though not always sufficient – condition for extending the effect of an arbitration agreement to a non-signatory. That principle applies to states as it applies to all other entities.

One does not always see this kind of analytical clarity in the decided cases. In *Zeevi v. Bulgaria*,[4] the basis of the tribunal's jurisdiction was to be found in a privatization agreement concluded between Zeevi and Bulgaria's privatization agency. The tribunal held that both the Republic of Bulgaria and the privatization agency were proper respondents to the claim. As for the Republic, the tribunal's reasoning was that it was bound by the arbitration agreement that had been signed by the privatization agency as a 'mere agent' of the Republic.[5] It is difficult to see a compelling ground for regarding both the principal (the Republic) and its 'mere agent' (the privatization agency) as being parties to the arbitration agreement and respondents in the arbitration. Ordinary principles of contract law would suggest that the privatization agency ought to fall out of the picture.

No more light is shed on this point by the tribunal's conclusion on the question of liability on the merits, where the tribunal held:

> "[T]he Tribunal concludes that, on one hand, the actions of both Respondents have to be taken into account in evaluating the conclusion and performance of the contract, because [the privatization agency] acted on behalf and with the authorization of [Bulgaria]. But, on the other hand, should the Tribunal come to conclude a liability in its Award, only [Bulgaria] shall be liable." [6]

From the tribunal's reasoning and terminology, it is difficult to say whether it characterized the relationship between Bulgaria and the privatization agency as one of private law agency rather than an administrative law delegation of functions. Yet this is an important distinction. In principle, administrative law delegation of functions does not create a contractual relationship with the state, for the simple reason that such delegation does not operate on the private law plane. Rather, it concerns matters wholly unrelated to contract, such as supervision by administrative bodies, court jurisdiction, form and procedure prescribed for various kinds of decisions.

The position has recently been stated as follows by the English Court of Appeal:

> "A government is not to be taken to be a party to an agreement or to have submitted to arbitration simply as a result of the fact that it has put forward a state organisation to contract with a foreign investor. In a case where the state organisation enjoys separate legal personality and the government is not named as a party to the agreement and has not signed it in the capacity of a party, we think it would be difficult to reach any other conclusion." [7]

The Court's reasoning is difficult to fault on orthodox contractual principles of privity. Nevertheless, there are some decisions in the opposite direction. ICC case No. 9762 concerned claims under a suite of contracts of the Ministry of Agriculture and Food of state Z. This ministry was later 'liquidated' by law, its debts transferred to a fund specially created for this purpose and a new Ministry of Agriculture was established as a different legal entity. (A few years later, the new Ministry of Agriculture was merged with another ministry to form the Ministry of Agriculture and Water Management.) The claimant brought suit under the contracts against the latest incarnation of the ministry, the fund, and state Z itself. A primary question in the arbitration was whether state Z was liable for the original ministry's debt – i.e. whether Z was bound, as a non-signatory, by the relevant contracts and by the arbitration agreements therein.[8] The tribunal held that 'the mandatory force of the arbitration clause (or arbitration agreement) cannot be dissociated from that of the substantive contractual commitments'.[9] That conclusion is of course entirely uncontroversial. The tribunal went on to hold that 'no distinction can be made between the [contractual] liability of [the Ministry of Agriculture and Water Management] and [state Z] (if any)'.[10]

These two conclusions, both of which are based on ordinary principles of private law, would appear to form a sufficient basis for the tribunal's jurisdictional holding, but the tribunal did not seem to think so. It went on to draw on theories of attribution under public international law, holding that:

"What is important in our case is that the contracts [...] were not signed by an entity separate from the State of Z, but by a Ministry, i.e., by an organ of the State, whose acts are undoubtedly performed on behalf and in the interest of the State. [...]

[A]s is obvious for any Ministry, particularly in a country where the power is highly centralized in the hand, under the directions, and under the control of the President, [the Ministry of Agriculture and Water Management] was and is in charge of carrying out the agrarian policy of the government of Z. It represents the State, within its competence, and the State is bound by its acts. [...]" [11]

In its conclusion, the tribunal merged the private law concept of agency/representation with notions of attribution in public international law. It formulated the end-result as follows:

"[T]he tribunal decides that it has jurisdiction vis-à-vis [the Ministry of Agriculture and Water Management] as validly representing [state Z] and as far as need be vis-à-vis [state Z] as validly represented by the [same ministry]." [12]

There are two sets of circumstances where the effects of an arbitration agreement may be extended to a non-signatory state or state entity in the absence of substantive liability on the basis of ordinary private law principles. These circumstances are discussed separately below.

2. IMPLICIT INTENT TO BE BOUND: CONTRACT DISTINGUISHED FROM ADMINISTRATIVE SUPERVISION

There is considerable authority for the proposition that an arbitration agreement can be extended to a non-signatory on the basis of an implicit intent to be bound. Such intent may be inferred from the agreement itself or from the specific circumstances surrounding the performance of the contract containing the arbitration agreement. In all cases of this nature, the question will be whether the *indicia* available are sufficient evidence of an intent to be bound. Where states or state entities are concerned, the salient point will be whether the indicia demonstrate a *contractual* intent rather than being part of the process of administrative supervision as a matter of public law.

In the *Pyramids* case, an ICC tribunal extended an arbitration agreement concluded between a foreign investor (SPP) and an Egyptian state-owned entity for hotel management (EGOTH) to the Tourism Ministry that supervised EGOTH. The ministry's intent to be bound was inferred from the notation 'approved, agreed and ratified' under the ministry's seal, which had been affixed next to the parties' signatures on the contract. The Paris Court of Appeal disagreed with the tribunal on the proper meaning and effect of the notation. The Court set aside the award, stressing the difference between consent to arbitration as a matter of private law and the 'ratification' that had been conferred on the contract as a matter of administrative law:

> "[C]ompte tenu des mots employés, de leur place après l'acte et du rapprochement qui s'impose avec la déclaration annexe, il est démontré que la ratification portée après les signatures de la société SPP et de EGOTH constitue, non un engagement solennel de l'Etat de souscrire au contrat, mais précisément la matérialisation de l'approbation de l'autorité de tutelle dont fait état le «statement» [du Ministère];
>
> Que l'existence de cette déclaration permet donc de confirmer sans ambigüité que, si le ministre du Tourisme a bien donné son agrément, l'Etat égyptien n'était pas lui-même partie au contrat." [13]

Another case where the *indicia* of putative consent were not sufficient was *Dallah v. Pakistan*.[14] A contract was concluded between Dallah and a trust created by ordinance of the Pakistan government. The trust was an entity managed by a board of trustees. The secretary of the board was the official holding at any time the post of Secretary of the Ministry of Religious Affairs. A few months after the contract was concluded the trust ceased to exist because the government failed to republish the ordinance, which it had to do at regular intervals for the trust to remain in existence. (It was unclear whether the failure to republish the ordinance was by choice or due to oversight.) The government was not described as a party in the contract between Dallah and the trust, nor was it a signatory to that contract.

Shortly after the contract was concluded, there was a change of government in Pakistan. It was not long before relations soured between Dallah, the trust and the government. There then followed a letter, on ministry stationery but signed by the secretary of the board of the trust, giving notice to Dallah that the trust would treat the contract as discharged, on the basis that Dallah had repudiated it. At the time of this letter, the trust had already legally ceased to exist. Ultimately, the dispute that ensued from these events was referred to an ICC tribunal sitting in Paris. The tribunal held that the government of Pakistan was a party to the contract with Dallah; that the government, not Dallah, had repudiated the contract; and that the government was to pay damages to Dallah. Pakistan objected to the tribunal's jurisdiction. It reiterated its objections in enforcement proceedings in the English courts. The courts agreed with Pakistan, refusing enforcement of the award. There were on any view *indicia* of government involvement in the Dallah-trust contract. But the question was whether involvement amounted to consent to be bound by the contract. In material part, the Court of Appeal reasoned as follows:[15]

> *"Prior to the establishment of the Trust the Government was the only party with whom Dallah could negotiate and its position was made clear in the Memorandum of Understanding, a document which was drafted in formal terms and clearly intended to be legally binding. In my view, however, the establishment of the Trust and, most importantly, the execution of an Agreement between the Trust and Dallah represented a fundamental change in the position and must have been recognised as such by all parties. Indeed, correspondence which preceded the Agreement shows that Dallah was well aware that it would be contracting with the Trust rather than the Government. The Government was not expressed to be a party to the Agreement, nor did it sign the Agreement in any capacity. It is difficult, therefore, to infer that Dallah, the Trust and the Government each intended (and knew that each of the others intended) that the Government was to be a party to it. If that had been their common intention the Government would surely have been named as a party to the Agreement, or would at least have added its signature in a way that reflected that fact. Other aspects of the Agreement, to which the judge referred, tend to bear out that conclusion. The fact that the Agreement contemplated that the*

> *Government would guarantee the Trust's obligations in respect of a loan required to enable it to finance the project is certainly evidence of its continued involvement and support, but the fact that the Agreement does not purport to impose any such obligation on the Government directly is telling when it comes to deciding whether it was intended that it should be a party to it. [...]*
>
> *The fact that the letter was written on the headed stationery of the Ministry of Religious Affairs also loses much of its significance when it is appreciated that the Trust did not possess its own headed stationery. Equally, the fact that the letter was written by a Government official counts for little when one realises that the Ministry of Religious Affairs had routinely dealt with correspondence and carried out similar functions on behalf of the Trust and that the writer was (or had been) its secretary. Such evidence no doubt demonstrates that the Government continued to be closely involved in the project and was behind the scenes pulling the strings, but it is not evidence that the Government, the Trust and Dallah shared a common intention that the Government was to be a party to the Agreement. [...]"*

One of the points raised by *Dallah* is the scope of the enforcement forum's review of an arbitral tribunal's jurisdictional findings. (An appeal is pending before the Supreme Court.) Here, however, the point is that at the very least as a matter of English law it will be almost impossible to overturn the presumption that an entity with separate legal personality – though owned, controlled or supervised by the state – will be taken to have concluded an arbitration agreement for its own account and not for the state. That, it seems, will be the case whenever the arbitration agreement has been concluded in a formal document bearing the signatures of the parties: the non-inclusion of a party will be regarded as a deliberate, emphatic choice to exclude that party from the contractual relationship.

On that basis, it seems that nothing short of explicit evidence of an intent to be bound will suffice to extend the arbitration agreement to a non-signatory state. One case where such evidence did exist was *Svenska*. There, the relevant contract was concluded by a Swedish company and a Lithuanian state-owned company, Geonafta. The contract concerned a joint venture between the two signatories to develop hydrocarbons resources. Nevertheless, there were two important factors which led to the conclusion that Lithuania was to be regarded as being party to the contract with Svenska. Firstly, the contract specifically dealt with the rights and obligations of the state (in addition to those of Geonafta); and, secondly, it explicitly provided that '[t]he Government of the Republic of Lithuania hereby approves the above agreement and acknowledges itself to be legally and contractually bound as if the Government were a signatory to the Agreement'.[16] The High Court had little difficulty concluding that Lithuania was a party to the arbitration agreement.

Based on the first of the two considerations in Svenska, a similar result obtained in the first of the two parallel *Bridas* arbitrations involving Turkmenistan in the late 1990s.[17] Bridas, an Argentine hydrocarbons company, had concluded agreements with a state-owned entity in Turkmenistan, Turkmenneft, to exploit oil and gas resources in the country. The tribunal held Turkmenistan to be bound by the Bridas-Turkmenneft joint venture agreement on the ground that the agreement set forth obligations that could be fulfilled only by the state itself – such as tax arrangements, stabilization clauses and terms regarding the use of state infrastructure. These provisions demonstrate the 'significant involvement of government powers and interests in the contractual relationship. [...] [They] are integral to the effective operation of the project. They all reflect the direct hand of the Government.' The tribunal concluded on this basis that Bridas had a legitimate expectation that these obligations in the joint venture agreement would be fulfilled by Turkmenistan, this legitimate expectation meant that there were representations by Turkmenistan embedded in the agreement, and '[t]he legitimate expectation of a party can translate into intention'.[18]

There is no question that the tribunal's assessment of the relevant *indicia* called for delicate judgement. As is well-known, only days earlier a different tribunal had reached the opposite conclusion in the second *Bridas* case, namely that there was no intention on Turkmenistan's part to be bound by joint venture agreements concluded by a state-owned entity in similar circumstances.[19]

These notions of legitimate expectation and justified reliance bring us to the second special case that falls to be examined here.

3. PIERCING THE VEIL: ABUSE OF LEGAL PERSONALITY

The doctrine of corporate-veil piercing can work as an exception to privity of contract, but it covers a broader ground than the personal scope of contractual relations. In matters of contract, the doctrine operates to prevent a non-signatory from relying on privity when permitting it to do so would work out intolerable injustice, frustrate justified reliance or – worse – amount to toleration of fraud. There is no reason to suppose that those basic notions operate in a different way, or call for different standards, where state entities are concerned. Nevertheless, the context may well be different from a straightforward manipulation of corporate personality by private law entities.

The US court cases that dealt with the setting-aside of the first Bridas award (which was rendered by a tribunal sitting in Texas) illustrate the exceptional circumstances in which veil-piercing (or the *alter ego* doctrine) operate. Bridas obtained a favourable award against Turkmenistan (*inter alios*) in 2001. The District Court upheld the award but the Court of Appeals remanded the case for further consideration.[20] The District Court confirmed again, and the matter went up to the Court of Appeals for a second time. In a 2006 decision, the Court confirmed the award on the basis that Turkmenneft was indeed the alter ego of Turkmenistan and that, in the circumstances, the corporate veil should be lifted. The Court found that 'the Government "did not really deal with Turkmenneft at arm's length"',[21] as it had 'manipulated Turkmenneft legally and economically to repudiate the contract with Bridas and then render it impossible for Bridas to collect damages'.[22] The Court stressed Turkmenneft's lack of financial independence and the government's manipulation of this lack of financial separateness to 'commit a fraud or another wrong on [Bridas]'. The central holding of the Court was as follows:

> "[T]he reality was that when the Government's export ban forced Bridas out of the joint venture, the Government then exercised its power as a parent entity to deprive Bridas of a contractual remedy. Intentionally bleeding a subsidiary to thwart creditors is a classic ground for piercing the corporate veil. It is true that the standard for this equitable remedy should be more stringent in breach of contract cases, because the creditor has willingly transacted business with a subsidiary and, as here, forewent the opportunity to obtain a guarantee of Turkmenneft's debts by the Government. The standard is met in this case, however, because [...] [t]he Government, as Turkmenneft's owner, made it impossible for the objectives of the joint venture to be carried out [...]. In this rare case we [...] conclude that the Government acted as the alter ego of Turkmenneft in regard to this Joint Venture Agreement with Bridas."[23]

END NOTES

* Slightly edited version of a speech delivered on 8 December 2009.

** Freshfields Bruckhaus Deringer LLP, Paris.

1 On these matters, see generally G. Petrochilos, 'Attribution', in K. Yannaca-Small (ed.), *Arbitration under International Investment Agreements*: A Guide to the Key Issues (2010) Ch 13.

2 See *Westland Helicopters Ltd v. Arab Organization for Industrialization*, ICC case No. 3879, Interim Award (1984), YCA 11 (1986) p. 127, para. 7.

3 For a critical view on this point, see Mourre, 'L'intervention des tiers à l'arbitrage', 1 *Cahiers de l'Arbitrage* (2001) p. 100.

4 *Zeevi Holdings v. Bulgaria and the Privatization Agency of Bulgaria*, Final Award, 25 October 2006, available at <http://www.investmentclaims.com>.

5 Ibid., at para. 169.

6 Ibid., at para. 172.

7 *Svenska Petroleum Exploration AB v. Lithuania* [2006] EWCA Civ. 755, para. 81.

8 *Cf. Société des Grands Travaux de Marseille v. République populaire du Bangladesh et Bangladesh Industrial Development Corporation* (1976) ATF 102 Ia 574, YCA 5 (1980) p. 217; and see the critical case note by Lalive, 34 *Annuaire Suisse de Droit International* (1978) p. 387.

9 Final Award in ICC case No. 9762, YCA 29 (2004) p. 26, para. 49.

10 Ibid., at para. 57.

11 Ibid., at paras. 50-51.

12 Ibid., at para. 56.

13 CA Paris, 12 July 1984, *République Arabe d'Egypte v. Southern Pacific Properties* (SPP) [1986] Rev. Arb. 75.

14 *Dallah Estate and Tourism Holding co. v. Ministry of Religious Affairs, Pakistan* [2009] EWCA Civ. 1529.

15 Ibid., at paras. 32 and 36.

16 *Svenska*, see above n. 7, at para. 4.

17 See *Bridas SAPIC and ors v. Turkmenistan and ors*, ICC case no. 9058, Partial Award, 24 June 1999, Mealey Publications Doc. No. 05-011026-012A.

18 Ibid., at pp. 17-19.

19 See *Joint Venture Yashlar and Bridas SAPIC v. Turkmenistan*, ICC case No. 9151, Interim Award, 8 June 1999, Mealey Publications Doc. No. 05-011026-020A. On the two Bridas cases, see Derains and Schwartz, *A Guide to the ICC Rules of Arbitration*, 2nd edn. (2005) p. 96 et seq.

20 See *Bridas v. Turkmenistan* (Bridas I), 345 F.3d 347 (5th Cir., 2003).
21 *Bridas SAPIC et al. v. Turkmenistan et al (Bridas II)*, 447 F.3d 411 (5th Cir., 2006) para. 26.
22 Ibid., at para. 27.
23 Ibid., at paras. 29-30.

CHAPTER 7

IS THERE A GROUP OF COMPANIES DOCTRINE?

YVES DERAINS*

1. INTRODUCTION

Chapter II of the now classic book by Bernard Hanotiau on complex arbitrations tries to answer the following question: 'May an Arbitration Clause be Extended to Non-Signatories: Individuals, States or Other Companies of the Group?'. However, the title of the chapter is immediately followed by the title of its first section, which refers doubtfully to 'The so-called group of companies doctrine'.[1] The implication is that such a doctrine is either wrongly named or does not exist. Thus, the question whether a group of companies doctrine is able to provide a solution to the problem of the extension of the effects of an arbitration clause to parties that have not signed the contract concerned appears to be a legitimate one. Beyond the issue of jurisdiction, it is also legitimate to wonder whether a group of companies doctrine may play a role in strictly procedural matters, such as joinders of parties in existing arbitral proceedings or the consolidation of two or more arbitral proceedings.

The concept of a group of companies is well known in financial law and even more so in tax law. Although it is referred to in several arbitration awards and court decisions, few of them give a general definition of this concept, as discussed below. They prefer to affirm the existence of a group of companies on a case-by-case basis and to justify such affirmation by mentioning a number of factual elements, such as one company's control over the other and/or a common management.[2] However, as correctly summarized by Dominique Hascher[3], a group of companies may be defined as an economic unit with an integrated management, beyond the legal personalities of the companies that belong to it. The economic reality is preferred to the legal organization, but only up to a point. There is no group of companies in the absence of distinct legal entities. This means that, if a branch of a company without legal personality signs an arbitration agreement, the party to that agreement will be the parent company and not the branch, whatever their respective economic size [4]. It takes at least two companies to have a group of companies!

Boosted by a number of arbitration awards and court decisions rendered mainly in France, the group of companies doctrine had its moment of glory in the three last decades of the twentieth century, which also witnessed the beginning of its decline (see section 2). Today, there is little doubt that the existence of a group of companies plays a limited role in the decisions of arbitrators and courts dealing with arbitration issues (see section 3).

2. THE REFERENCE TO A GROUP OF COMPANIES IN ARBITRATION CASE LAW

In the 1970s, several arbitral awards were at the origin of the group of companies doctrine. One, issued in Paris in the ICC case No. 2375 in 1975,[5] was bold enough to state that '[t]he autonomy of the international community of businessmen, governed in their mutual relations by specific rules must be acknowledged', and further that 'international commercial companies are beyond the realm of State law'. The award adds that 'the concept of group is defined, beyond the formal independence resulting from the creation of discreet legal persons, by a single economic orientation depending on a common power'. On the basis of this doctrine, the arbitral tribunal found that companies belonging to two groups of companies were bound by or could take advantage of an arbitration clause signed by others companies of their respective group.

In the same year, another ICC award, issued in Geneva in Case No. 1434,[6] came to similar conclusions, stressing that the leader of a multinational group had negotiated an agreement with a state on behalf of a group of companies. The award pointed out that '[...] it is customary in international industrial agreements of that size [that] the State [...] deals with a group or a big "multinational" company which, for internal reasons of organization or of opportunity will entrust the performance of the operation to one or several subsidiaries, existing or to be created on an ad hoc basis'. It concluded that, in line with 'economic reality', neither the group nor its chairman or any of its member companies could avoid the extension of the effect of the arbitration agreement to them, unless it was established that such had been the parties' intent.

However, although it was not the first award using the concept of a group of companies as a basis for deciding that non-signatories to an arbitration agreement were nevertheless a party to that agreement, the *Dow Chemical award,*[7] issued in Paris in 1982 in the ICC case No. 4131, remains the most famous one. Indeed, it introduced the three constitutive elements of the group of companies doctrine and for this reason deserves to be extensively quoted here:

"[...] irrespective of the distinct juridical identity of each of its members, a group of companies constitutes one and the same economic reality of which the Arbitral tribunal should take account when it rules on its own jurisdiction [...].

Considering that the tribunal shall, accordingly, determine the scope and effects of the arbitration clauses in question, and thereby reach its decision regarding jurisdiction, by reference to the common intent of the parties to these proceedings, such as it appears from the circumstances that surround the conclusion and characterize the performance and later the termination of the contracts in which they appear. In doing so, the tribunal, following, in particular, French case law relating to international arbitration should also take into account usages conforming to the needs of international trade, in particular, in the presence of a group of companies [...].

Considering, in particular, that the arbitration clause expressly accepted by certain of the companies of the group should bind the other companies which, by virtue of their role in the conclusion, performance, or termination of the contracts containing said clauses, and in accordance with the mutual intention of all parties to the proceedings, appear to have been veritable parties to these contracts or to have been principally concerned by them and the disputes to which they may give rise."

In this award, issued by prominent scholars and arbitrators (Professors Pieter Sanders, Berthold Goldman and Michel Vasseur), the arbitral tribunal states firmly at the beginning of its reasoning that a group of companies is an economic factor that must be taken into account by arbitrators when assessing their own jurisdiction, without regard to the respective legal identity of each member of the group. This is the first element of what would become the group of companies doctrine. Then, the award indicates, in the presence of a group of companies, that such an approach is required by the needs of international trade. This is the second constitutive element. The third and most significant one is that the common intent of the parties is to be found in the surrounding circumstances that characterize the conclusion, performance or termination of the contract. The combination of those three elements led to the now well-known principle according to which an arbitration clause signed by certain companies of the group binds the other companies of the group that played a role in the conclusion, performance or termination of the contract containing the clause.

This interim award was the object of a setting-aside procedure before the Paris Court of Appeal,[8] which decided to uphold it. However, it did not grant the concept of a group of companies the importance that the arbitrators had thought it deserved. The main grounds for the decision of the Court of Appeal were:

"The arbitrators for good reasons have observed that the law applicable to determine the scope and effects of an arbitral clause providing for international arbitration does not necessarily coincide with the law applicable to the merits of the dispute.

Following an autonomous interpretation of the agreement and the documents exchanged at the time of their negotiation and termination, the arbitrators have, for pertinent and non-contradicted reasons, decided, in accordance with the intention common to all companies involved, that Dow Chemical France and Dow Chemical Company have been parties to these agreements although they did not actually sign them and that therefore the arbitration clause was applicable to them as well".

The court further noted that: 'The arbitrators have also, by the way, [*accessoirement*] referred to the notice of "group of companies", the existence of which according to the customs of international trade has not been seriously contested by the defendant'. It is clear that the Paris Court of Appeal was not prepared to follow the arbitrators as far as the effect of the existence of a group of companies was concerned. What was important for the court was the intent of the parties, as revealed by their behaviour and the documents they had exchanged between themselves.

In a decision of 26 November 1986 in the *Sponsor A.B.* case,[9] the Court of Appeal of Pau was not as prudent as the Paris court. It almost entirely reproduced the reasoning, if not the wording, of the *Dow Chemical* award:

"It is admitted in law that the arbitration clause expressly accepted by companies of the group must bind the other companies which, because of the role they played in the conclusion, performance and termination of the contracts containing those clauses, appear, pursuant to the common intent of all the parties to the proceedings, to have been actual parties to those contracts or to be primarily concerned by them or by the disputes resulting

therefrom. Indeed, a group of companies has, in spite of the distinct juridical identity of each of them, a single economic reality that Courts should take into account, its existence being recognized by the usages of international trade [...]".

No other French court went that far, with the significant exception of the decision of the Paris Court of Appeal in the Orri case on 11 January 1990, which is discussed below.[10] In subsequent decisions concerning the effect of an arbitration agreement on non-signatories, the Paris Court of Appeal was able to generalize the approach initiated in its judgment in the *Dow Chemical* case by declaring case after case that:

"an arbitration clause in an international contract has a validity and an effectiveness of its own, such that the clause must be extended to parties directly implicated in the performance of the contract and in any dispute arising out of the contract, provided that it has been established that their respective situations and activities raise the presumption that they were aware of the existence and scope of the arbitration clause, and irrespective of the fact that they did not sign the contract containing the arbitration agreement."

This statement may be found, with very few differences in wording, in decisions of the Paris Court of Appeal of 30 November 1988 and 14 February 1989,[11] 28 November 1989[12] and 11 January 1990[13]. However, although the *Cour de cassation* upheld those decisions, it was more prudent in its reasoning, as indicated below.

This consistent case law confirms that the decisive element is the common intent of the parties to be bound by an arbitration agreement. Such a common intent may be implied in the absence of the signature of an arbitration agreement under two conditions: (1) an active role of the non-signatories in the performance of the contract that contains the arbitration agreement and in the disputes arising therefrom; and (2) a presumption that the non-signatory had knowledge of the arbitration agreement. This prominent role given to the common intent of the parties is part of a substantive rule of French law that French courts apply without any regard to any national law that might be applicable to the arbitration clause pursuant to a conflict of laws rule. It was clearly expressed in the *Dalico* case of 1993 by the *Cour de cassation*, which stated that:

"By virtue of a substantive rule of international arbitration, the arbitration agreement is legally independent of the main contract containing or referring to it, and the existence and effectiveness of the arbitration agreement are to be assessed, subject to the mandatory

rules of French law and international public policy, on the basis of the parties' common intention, there being no need to refer to any national law."

The above-mentioned solutions are not specific to groups of companies. For instance, the decision of 14 February 1989 was rendered in the completely different context of a charter party. The existence of a group of companies only strengthens the presumption that the non-signatory party had knowledge.

The position of French law was clearly summarized in an unpublished ICC award of 2001 in the case No.11405, quoted by Bernard Hanotiau:[15]

"[t]here is no general rule, in French international arbitration law, that would provide that non-signatory parties members of a same group of companies would be bound by an arbitration clause, whether always or in determined circumstances. What is relevant is whether all parties intended non-signatory parties to be bound by the arbitration clause. Not only the signatory parties, but also the non-signatory parties should have intended (or led the other parties to reasonably believe that they intended) to be bound by the arbitration clause [...]. The legal literature confirms that what is relevant is whether the non-signatory parties were intended to be bound, rather than a general rule about a group of companies: '[c]learly, however it is not so much the existence of a group that results in the various companies of the group being bound by the agreement signed by only one of them, but rather the fact that such was the true intention of the parties'."

On the basis of the above, one may be tempted to conclude that the group of companies doctrine represented a brief momentum in the evolution of the French case law relating to the application of arbitration clauses to non-signatories. As a matter of fact, this doctrine has been firmly excluded in other jurisdictions with the apparent exception of Spain.[16] Switzerland is a well-known example in this regard as explained by a prominent author:[17]

"In short, Swiss law ignores the concept of group of companies [...] and is resolutely committed to the legal independence of the company in relation to its sole shareholder or of the subsidiary in relation to the parent company. It will only be disregarded in exceptional circumstances, where the fact of resorting to such a subsidiary to escape one's obligations would amount to fraud or to a patent abuse of right."

Likewise, an arbitral tribunal constituted under the auspices of the *Chambre de commerce et d'industrie de Genève*[18] pointed out in 2000 that:

> *"the principle according to which a company may be considered a party to a contractual undertaking made by another company as a consequence of the fact that both companies belong to a group which constitutes one economic reality, does not exist in Switzerland de lege lata. It is therefore not possible to apply here the solutions which were applied in this context by arbitral tribunals in a number of ICC arbitrations."*

This position was clearly confirmed by the Swiss Federal Tribunal in a decision of 29 January 1996[19], which states that the existence of a group of companies, as such, is not a sufficient ground to find that a company of the group that has not signed an arbitration clause is bound by that clause because it was signed by another member company. In reality, the Swiss view today appears to be very flexible and not so different from the present position of the French courts: on the basis of the surrounding circumstances, Swiss lawyers and courts look for the actual intent of the parties revealed by their *'actes concluants'*[20]. No such flexibility exists in England. A striking example of the reluctance of English courts to accept that an arbitration agreement may be binding on non-signatories is provided in the *Dallah* case, where the enforcement in England of an ICC award issued in Paris was refused in 2009, on the grounds that the arbitrators had wrongly applied French law when holding that a non-signatory was party to the arbitration agreement[21]. Even though the case did not involve a group of companies but a state, the decision was based on a strict interpretation of the parties' consent that was at odds with the French tradition in this respect.

In the United States, the existence of a group of companies seems to greatly facilitate the decision to declare an arbitration clause signed by members of the group binding on non-signatory members of the group.[22] However, it would not be correct to try to relate the US approach to the group of companies doctrine as developed in French law. The group of companies doctrine relies on the assumption that the usages of international trade require that all the members of the group that were involved in the negotiation, performance and – where applicable – termination of a contract containing an arbitration clause be bound by this arbitration clause. It is presented as a substantive rule. The concern of the US courts is not substantive but procedural. What matters is the efficiency of the procedure, as illustrated by the decision of the Court of Appeals for the Fourth Circuit in the *Ryan* case:[23]

"When the charges against a parent company and its subsidiary are based on the same facts and are inherently inseparable, a court may refer claims against the parent to arbitration even though the parent is not formally a party to the arbitration agreement. [...] If the parent corporation was forced to try the case, the arbitration proceedings would be rendered meaningless and the federal policy in favour of arbitration effectively thwarted."

That being said, it does not mean that the group of companies doctrine has lost any practical interest, although its effects are far more limited than previously accepted.

3. THE LIMITED EFFECT OF THE EXISTENCE OF A GROUP OF COMPANIES

As already pointed out in the discussion of the French case law, the existence of a group of companies is a circumstance that plays an important role in revealing the intent of parties (see section a). Beyond the specific issue of the scope of the arbitration clause, the existence of a group of companies is a factor that should also be taken into consideration when deciding whether to order the joinder of a party or consolidate procedures (see section b).

a. The group of companies: an element of the factual matrix revealing the intent of the parties

It is largely admitted today that the question whether a party is bound by an arbitration agreement essentially depends on the intent of the parties, whether or not they have signed this agreement. The fact that the law applicable to the arbitration agreement may require that it be made in writing, as most national legislations do, is irrelevant. Indeed, signature and writing are two different things. The signature is just one of several means of expressing consent. In the factual matrix where the group of companies doctrine is discussed, there is an arbitration agreement made in writing. The issue at stake is the determination of the parties that consented to this written agreement. Some of them signed it; others did not, but their consent may be proved in many different ways depending on the circumstances. The existence of a group of companies cannot be a neutral fact in this respect.

The *Kis France* case[24] provides a good example of the role played by the existence of a group of companies in the assessment by arbitrators and courts of the parties' intent to be bound by an arbitration agreement. The dispute was related to several agreements entered into by various members of two groups of companies: Kiss France and its subsidiaries, on the one hand, and Société Générale and its subsidiaries, on the other. There was an ICC arbitration clause in a framework agreement entered into by Kiss France and

Société Générale. Arbitration proceedings were initiated by Société Générale and some of its subsidiaries against Kis France and some of its subsidiaries. The arbitral tribunal retained jurisdiction over all claimants and all respondents and over the various agreements. An action to set aside the award was filed with the Paris Court of Appeal, which upheld the award. Two major grounds for challenging the award were raised. One was that the arbitrators had exceeded their jurisdiction, and the other was that they had not applied French law, as contemplated by the parties' agreement, because they had relied on the usages of international trade to refer to the concept of a group of companies.

As to the second ground for setting aside the award, the Court of Appeal was of the view that, by referring to the usages of international trade to rely on the concept of a group of companies, the arbitrators had respected the scope of their mission. The fact that the court confirmed that the arbitrators could, while applying French law, introduce the usages of international trade in their reasons is not surprising. They are entitled to do so, whatever the applicable law pursuant to Article 1496 of the Code of Civil Procedure. What is more interesting is that the court took for granted that the concept of a group of companies was part of the usages of international trade. The spirit of the decision of the Pau Court of Appeal of 1986 in the Sponsor A.B. case is not very far removed from this! [25] But the main interest of the case is not there. It is in the Court of Appeal's confirmation of the arbitrators' jurisdiction because:

> *"the arbitrators, on the basis of the interpretation of the parties' conventions [...] and considering the domination of the mother companies over their subsidiaries, [...] held that there was a common intention of the parties to consider that Kis France [and subsidiaries] were direct debtors of any amount due by themselves or their subsidiaries."*

The Paris Court of Appeal used the concept of a group of companies as a basis to extend the scope of the arbitration agreement over a group of contracts. This is an example of a cross-fertilization between the concepts of a group of companies and a group of contracts in order to find out the intention of the parties.

However, the decision of the *Cour de cassation* in the *Orri* case in 1991[26] shows that the reference to the concept of a group of companies is not necessary to find that a non-signatory is bound by an arbitration agreement even in a situation where the existence of such group is a fact. In this case, the Paris Court of Appeal[27] refused to set aside an award in which the arbitrators had found that an individual was bound by an arbitration agreement signed by a company of the group he controlled. To reach that decision, the court had used its classical argument that:

"[...] an arbitration clause in an international contract has a validity and an effectiveness of its own, such that the clause must be extended to parties directly implicated in the performance of the contract and in any dispute arising out of the contract, provided that it has been established that their respective situations and activities raise the presumption that they were aware of the existence and scope of the arbitration clause, and irrespective of the fact that they did not sign the contract containing the arbitration agreement",

adding that this was 'according to the usages of international trade'. The Court of Appeal also found that the non-signatory individual was guilty of fraud, since he had hidden that he was the true contracting party, and that, as a result, the arbitrators had been right to declare that he was bound by the arbitration agreement. However, the court decided to add that this solution was further grounded in

"the concept of group of companies since it appeared that the respondent [the beneficiary of the award] had always had business relations with an individual presiding over a group of companies having a formal legal existence and independence, while being linked within an economic unit dominated by a single power."

This decision of the Paris Court of Appeal was confirmed by the Cour de cassation, but the Supreme Court did not follow the Paris Court on the grounds of usages of international trade and the concept of a group of companies. It retained the fraud as the sole reason to declare that the individual was bound by the arbitration agreement.

The prudence of the *Cour de Cassation* is to be approved. It is true that the existence of a group of companies is an important fact to be taken into consideration in order to decide whether non-signatories are party to an arbitration agreement. However, it is a circumstance that does not command any specific conclusion. On the contrary, the existence of a group of companies is an ambiguous indicator of the intent of the parties. It may mean that in the mind of the parties, the whole group was involved and not just the member of the group that signed the contract. However, it may also mean that the parties were aware of the existence of the group but only wanted to involve one of its members in the transaction, namely the signatory of the contract.

In the *Dow Chemical* case, the Paris Court of Appeal showed that the existence of a group of companies was not a determining factor, as it was not an essential element of the decision to uphold the award that had found that non-signatory members of the group were party to the arbitration agreement. Besides the existence of a group of companies, the decisive element is the intent of the parties, which must be assessed on a case-by-case basis. The active participation of the non-signatories in the negotiation, performance and, where applicable, termination of the agreement containing the arbitration clause are the true factual elements that reveal the true intent of the parties. The existence of a group of companies often explains such active participation, just like it explains that the non-signatories were aware of the arbitration clause. However, finding out that there is a group of companies does not reveal the intent of its members to be party to an arbitration agreement that they did not sign nor does it reveal the intent of the other parties to the contract to arbitrate with the non-signatories.

b. The role of a group of companies in the case of a joinder or consolidation

In 1992, in the *Dutco* case,[28] the French Court of Cassation decided that 'the principle of the equality of the parties in the appointment of the arbitrators is a matter of public policy; one cannot therefore waive it until after the dispute has arisen'. This decision led the ICC to introduce new provisions in its Rules relating to multiple parties cases in 1998. As a result, Article 10 of the Rules reads as follows:

"1. Where there are multiple parties, whether as Claimant or as Respondent, and where the dispute is to be referred to three arbitrators, the multiple Claimants, jointly, and the multiple Respondents, jointly, shall nominate an arbitrator for confirmation pursuant to Article 9.

2. In the absence of such a joint nomination and where all parties are unable to agree to a method for the constitution of the Arbitral Tribunal, the Court may appoint each member of the Arbitral Tribunal and shall designate one of them to act as chairman. In such case, the Court shall be at liberty to choose any person it regards as suitable to act as arbitrator, applying Article 9 when it considers this appropriate."

It is likely that this article will be amended as a result of the revision of the ICC Arbitration Rules, but its application is interesting insofar as groups of companies are concerned.

Indeed, there are many cases with multiple parties that are not necessarily true multiparty arbitrations. This is true, for example, in cases where multiple respondents are part of a group of companies under common control. It is obvious in such cases that they have identical interests in the outcome of the arbitration. Consequently, the multiple entities concerned might more properly be seen as forming, in reality, a single respondent party, and there would not seem to be any legitimate reason why they should not normally be expected to agree upon an arbitrator.

By the same token, the existence of a group of companies may also play an important role in the case of the joinder of a party to an existing procedure or the consolidation of different procedures. Among the various difficulties resulting from a request to join a party to an arbitral procedure, the fact that the arbitral tribunal may have already been constituted is a serious one. Even if the party to be joined is also a party to the arbitration agreement, it may object that it was deprived of the opportunity to participate in the constitution of the arbitral tribunal. Such an objection should not be accepted when the party concerned belongs to the same group as a party that participated in the constitution of the arbitral tribunal and actually appointed an arbitrator. Under that hypothesis, there is a strong presumption that the party to be joined was aware of the nomination of an arbitrator by the other member of the group and had no objection to this nomination.

The same remark can be made in the case of the consolidation of two procedures. When consolidation is theoretically possible in law, one potential problem is that a party that objects to the consolidation may be tempted to block it by appointing an arbitrator who has not been appointed so far. To be more precise, let us imagine that, in a dispute concerning a contract between three parties (A, B and C), A has different claims towards B and C. B and C both nominate different arbitrators and require that two different procedures be organized. This will not be acceptable if B and C belong to the same group of companies. Having identical interests, they may be obliged to nominate the same arbitrator and participate in the same proceedings.

4. CONCLUSION

The impact of the existence of a group of companies on an arbitration procedure is very limited today. Contrary to what was briefly believed and/or desired in the last part of the twentieth century, the group of companies doctrine does not provide an objective rule to solve the difficulties relating to the determination of the parties to an arbitration agreement. The existence of a group of companies is nothing more than a factor to be taken into consideration to assess the intent of the parties. Moreover, it is an ambiguous factor, as opposite conclusions may be drawn from its existence, depending on the circumstances of the case concerned. However, it may play a more significant role when the intent of the parties is a decisive factor in a decision concerning a joinder or the consolidation of procedures, as the economic reality must prevail and members of the same group should not be allowed to abuse their discreet legal personalities in such cases.

END NOTES

* Founding partner of Derains Gharavi; Vice Chairman of the ICC Institute for World Business Law.

1 B. Hanotiau, Complex Arbitrations, Multiparty, Multicontract, Multi-issue and Class Actions (2005) p. 49.

2 See, for instance, the ICC award of 1988 in case No. 8910, Collection of ICC Awards 1996-2000, p. 569, note by Dominique Hascher.

3 Hascher, supra n. 2.

4 See the ICC award of 1990 in case No. 5721, Collection of ICC Awards 1986-1990, p. 400, note by Jean-Jacques Arnaldez.

5 Collection of ICC Awards 1974-1985, p. 257, note by Yves Derains.

6 Collection of ICC Awards 1974-1985, p. 263, note by Yves Derains.

7 ICC interim award of 1982 in case No. 4131, Collection of ICC Awards 1974-1985, pp. 146 and 464, note by Yves Derains.

8 Paris Court of Appeal, 21 October 1983, Revue de l'arbitrage (1984) p. 98, note by A. Chapelle.

9 Pau Court of Appeal, 26 November 1986, Revue de l'arbitrage (1988) p. 153, note by A. Chapelle.

10 See infra n. 27.

11 Paris Court of Appeal, 30 November 1988 and 14 February 1989, Revue de l'arbitrage (1989) p. 691, note by P.Y. Tschanz.

12 Paris Court of Appeal, 28 November 1989, Revue de l'arbitrage (1990) p. 675, note by P. Mayer.

13 Paris Court of Appeal, 11 January 1990, Revue de l'arbitrage (1992) p. 95, note by D. Cohen.

14 French Cour de cassation, 1993, Revue de l'arbitrage (1994) p. 116, note by H. Gaudemet-Tallon.

15 Hanotiau, supra n. 1 at p. 50, n. 142.

16 I. Quinata and E. de Nadal, 'Spain', in The International Comparative Legal Guide to: International Arbitration 2006, p. 392, section 3.4.

17 J.F. Poudret, 'L'extension de la clause d'arbitrage: approches française et suisse', Journal du droit international (1995) p. 813 especially at p. 912.

18 Award of 24 March 2000, ASA Bulletin (2003) p. 781.

19 ASA Bulletin (1996) p. 496.

20 Swiss Federal Tribunal, 16 October 2003, Revue de l'arbitrage (2004) p. 695, note by L. Lévy and B. Stucky.

21 Dallah Real Estate and Tourism Holding Co. v. The Ministry of Religious Affairs, Government of Pakistan [2009] EWCA Civ. 755.

22 Hanotiau, supra n. 1, at p. 59 et seq.

23 863 F. 2d (4th Cir. 1988).
24 Paris Court of Appeal, 31 October 1989, Revue de l'arbitrage (1992) p. 90, note by L. Aynès.
25 See supra n. 9.
26 Cour de cassation, 11 June 1991, Revue de l'arbitrage (1992) p. 73, note by D. Cohen.
27 Paris Court of Appeal, 11 January 1990, Revue de l'arbitrage (1992) p. 106, note by D. Cohen.
28 Cour de cassation, 7 January 1992, Revue de l'arbitrage (1992) p. 470, note by P. Bellet.

CHAPTER 8

PIERCING THE CORPORATE VEIL: BACK ON THE RIGHT TRACK

SÉBASTIEN BESSON *

1. INTRODUCTION

Contrary to its title, this article does not pretend to know the 'right' track, even less to be able to guide readers 'back' on to the right track. It is an attempt to present the doctrine of piercing the corporate veil in the context of arbitration and to distinguish it from other legal theories, in particular the group of companies doctrine.

The doctrine of piercing the corporate veil, also known as *Durchgriff* in German or levée du *voile social* in French is difficult to define because it has been developed in different jurisdictions and varies in the different legal systems.

However, the following interesting elements can be found in Garry Born's book on international commercial arbitration:

> *"the essential theory is that one party so dominates the affairs of another party, and has sufficiently misused such control, that it is appropriate to disregard the two companies' separate legal forms and to treat them as a single entity."* [1]

The doctrine is hence an exception to the principle that corporations generally benefit from limited liability and separate legal identity.

The exception is justified by elements of fairness, or, to put it differently, the doctrine is an expression of the general principle that substance should prevail over form when adherence to form would be abusive. As one arbitrator has put it:

> "la question qui se pose à la fin est celle de savoir dans quelle mesure la fiction juridique de la personnalité morale doit céder le pas devant les réalités du comportement des hommes et cesser de protéger ceux qui se cachent derrière le voile social." [2]

Along similar lines, the US Court of Appeals for the Second Circuit has stated the following:

> "Ultimately, the question in any particular case is whether, in light of the circumstances, 'the policy behind the presumption of corporate independence and limited shareholder liability – encouragement of business development – is outweighed by the policy justifying disregarding the corporate form – the need to protect those who deal with the corporation." [3]

2. PIERCING THE CORPORATE VEIL IN THE CONTEXT OF ARBITRATION

The doctrine can be used in different contexts and serve different purposes. Most commonly, it is used to hold a shareholder liable for the liabilities of its corporation. In that respect, one commentator has referred to the concept of 'piercing for liability'. [4]

In arbitration, the doctrine has also – or essentially – been used to extend the arbitration agreement to non-signatories.

In that respect, piercing the corporate veil is one of many other theories permitting, under certain circumstances, the extension of the arbitration agreement to non-signatory third parties. [5]

The 'extension' can be based on other theories, in particular contract law theories. It is likely that the different theories will overlap to some extent or at least that they will be invoked in the same cases. This is simply because the same factual scenario is likely to support arguments based on contract as well as on the doctrine of piercing the corporate veil. [6]

There is a broad variety of contract law concepts that may be used to extend an arbitration agreement, such as agency, including apparent or ostensible authority, 'assumption of debt', tacit ratification of the contract, third-party beneficiary doctrine or estoppel and the abuse of right doctrine. [7]

I will not enter into such concepts, but it is important to stress the primary role of these classic contract law theories in resolving questions relating to the extension of the arbitration agreement. As Redfern et al. put it, in relation to the doctrine of piercing the corporate veil, '[m]ore established principles of private law – such as assignment, agency and succession – thus remain the surest way in which to bind a third party to an arbitration agreement'. [8]

In practice, one sometimes notes the opposite, namely parties writing pages on piercing the corporate veil and not a word on apparent authority arguments.

3. PIERCING THE CORPORATE VEIL AND THE GROUP OF COMPANIES DOCTRINE

The 'extension' of the arbitration agreement can also be based on the group of companies doctrine, which leads us to the relationship between the corporate veil-piercing doctrine and the group of companies doctrine. The group of companies doctrine has been dealt with in detail by Yves Derains, but it is important for our purposes to distinguish it from the doctrine of piercing the corporate veil.

Although they are different, these two theories are too often treated according to the same standards or mixed up.

Piercing the corporate veil doctrine focuses on the fraud or the abuse of right resulting from the use or abuse of a corporate form in order to limit the liability of the real party.

The group of companies doctrine focuses on the determination of the intention – or the presumed intention – to arbitrate. The fact that the non-signatory belongs to a group of companies is merely one factor to take into account in order to determine such presumed intention.

The differences between the two theories are convincingly highlighted by Gary Born, who states that there is a 'fundamental difference between the *alter ego* doctrine and the group of companies doctrine'. He further states:

> *"The alter ego theory is a rule of law that is invoked to disregard or nullify the otherwise applicable effects of incorporation of separate legal personality. The outcome of this analysis is that one entity is deemed either non-existent or merely an unincorporated part of another entity. [...] In contrast, the group of companies doctrine is ordinarily a means of identifying the parties' intentions, which does not disturb or affect the legal personality of the entities in question."* [9]

The doctrine of piercing the corporate veil therefore pertains to company law, whereas the group of companies doctrine is predominantly a contract law theory.[10] This characterization has an impact on the identification of the applicable laws (see below).

The group of companies doctrine is also broader in the sense that it casts a wider net to catch non-signatories. It is also more controversial and, according to some authors, not necessarily in line with the expectations of the business community.

Finally, the group of companies doctrine is essentially a French doctrine that has not been recognized in other jurisdictions and is specific to arbitration, whereas the doctrine of piercing the corporate veil is much more widespread, if not universal.

In summary, the two doctrines are specific and must be distinguished, although this is not always done. As an example, an – otherwise excellent – book contains the following subtitle 'piercing the corporate veil within groups of companies'.[11] In my opinion, this is a perfect illustration of the confusion between the two theories.

4. PIERCING THE CORPORATE VEIL IN ARBITRAL AWARDS

For the purposes of the present analysis, I have examined published arbitral awards that applied the doctrine of piercing of corporate veil or the group of companies doctrine.

This review is not meant to be exhaustive and is limited to publicly available awards. It obviously has no statistical value.[12]

Nevertheless, some interesting conclusions can be drawn from these arbitral awards:

1. The two doctrines are effectively mixed up in practice.[13] Sometimes, one does not really know which doctrine is being applied by the arbitrators. By contrast, one can mention ICC award No. 10818, which clearly distinguished the two theories.[14]

2. The doctrine of piercing the corporate veil, when properly distinguished, is often based on: (i) a conflict of law analysis; and (ii) the application of a specific domestic law,[15] whereas the group of companies doctrine is often based on trade usages.[16]

3. Cases involving the extension of an arbitration agreement based exclusively on piercing the corporate veil are rare and show the reluctance of arbitrators to rely only on this theory.[17]

5. PIERCING THE CORPORATE VEIL IN SOME JURISDICTIONS

It is outside the scope of this article to examine in detail the doctrine of piercing the corporate veil as it has been applied by national courts in the context of arbitration.

It is sufficient to note that this doctrine has been widely recognized as a means of extending the scope of arbitration agreements in exceptional circumstances.[18] The following examples from US, French and Swiss case law serve as an illustration of this principle.

In the United States, several decisions have applied the doctrine of piercing the corporate veil in relation to the extension of an arbitration agreement.[19]

The corporate veil is pierced only in exceptional circumstances, generally when an 'element of fraud or other wrong' can be demonstrated.

In *Fisser v. International Bank*, the US Court of Appeals for the Second Circuit adopted a three-pronged test for disregarding the separate entity of a corporation:

> "(1) Control, not mere majority or complete stock control, but complete domination, not only of finances, but of policy and business practice in respect to the transaction attacked so that the corporate entity as to this transaction had at the time no separate mind, will or existence of its own; and (2) Such control must have been used by the

defendant to commit fraud or worse, to perpetrate the violation of a statutory or other positive legal duty, or a dishonest and unjust act in contravention of plaintiff's legal rights; and (3) The aforesaid control and breach of duty must proximately cause the injury or unjust loss complained of. (247 App. Div. 144, 287 N.Y.S. 76)." [20]

This test has frequently been referred to in subsequent decisions.[21]

The courts apparently refer to the same standards as those that apply for holding a corporation responsible for the contractual obligations of another entity. The US District Court for the Southern District of New York stressed this point in the following terms:

"Under appropriate circumstances, a corporation which was not such a signatory may be held bound to arbitrate a dispute in which it is involved. However, the principles utilized to determine whether in such cases, arbitration is appropriate are merely those which are employed in other contractual disputes to ascertain whether, on some theory, it is just to disregard independent corporate existence and hold one corporation responsible for the contractual obligations of another."[22]

In France, the courts do not seem to have applied the theory of the levée du voile social specifically in relation to the extension of the arbitration agreement. This can be explained by the prevalence of the group of companies doctrine before French courts.[23]

The group of companies doctrine was sufficient to address those situations that, in other jurisdictions, could have led to an analysis based upon the doctrine of piercing the corporate veil.

However, the concept of fraud is not unknown in French case law. In the *Orri case*, the Paris Court of Appeal and the French Cour de cassation relied upon this concept to extend the arbitration agreement.[24] This notion of fraud was even the only basis for extension in the decision of the French *Cour de cassation*, which ruled as follows:

"*[...] attendu que par divers éléments qu'elle a caractérisés, la Cour d'appel, a relevé que 'Saudi-Europe Lines' n'était que l'appellation sous couvert de laquelle M. Orri exerçait personnellement le commerce maritime et que ce n'est que par un subterfuge, constitutif de fraude, destiné à dissimuler le véritable contractant, que celui-ci s'est effacé pour laisser place au signataire déclaré; qu'ainsi et par ce seul motif, la Cour d'appel a, justement décidé, à la suite des arbitres, que la clause compromissoire engageait M. Orri."*

In Switzerland, the doctrine of piercing the corporate veil is possible in cases of 'abuse of right', but the case law has traditionally been very reluctant to disregard the legal entity of a corporation. [25]

In addition, Swiss case law has clearly distinguished between piercing the corporate veil for liability and piercing the corporate veil for extending arbitration agreements.[26]

Following a judgment delivered in 1996, it was even doubtful whether the latter was available, at least in situations where the piercing of the corporate veil was based on insufficient capitalization of the subsidiary. In such a case, the Swiss Federal Tribunal stated that the parent company would not be held jointly liable with the subsidiary, but only after it has been established that the subsidiary was insolvent and that the liability of the parent company would be not covered by the arbitration agreement.[27]

More recently, however, the Swiss Federal Tribunal has issued a judgment confirming that the doctrine of piercing the corporate veil can be used to extend the arbitration agreement.[28] Federal Judge Bernard Corboz has recently expressed the same opinion. [29]

However, some scholars stress that, in case of *echte Durchgriff*, the arbitration agreement would not be extended but that the non-signatory would replace the signatory. [30]

6. AN ATTEMPT TO DEFINE THE RIGHT TRACK AND TO HIGHLIGHT POSSIBLE ISSUES FOR REFLECTION

The starting point of the analysis is always the legal independence of the signatory (to the extent that it is a legal entity). Piercing the corporate veil is and should remain an exception that is based on fairness.

Control of the signatory by the non-signatory party is necessary but not sufficient for applying the doctrine.[31] Control must have been used to commit fraud or an abuse of right. In fact, the essence of the doctrine lies in the abuse of right of the corporate form.[32] One arbitral tribunal expressed this idea in the following terms:

> *"En résumé, l'appartenance de deux sociétés à un même groupe ou la domination d'un actionnaire ne sont jamais, à elles seules, des raisons suffisantes justifiant de plein droit la levée du voile social. Cependant, lorsqu'une société ou une personne individuelle apparaît comme étant le pivot des rapports contractuels intervenus dans une affaire particulière, il convient d'examiner avec soin si l'indépendance juridique des parties ne doit pas, exceptionnellement, être écartée au profit d'un jugement global. On acceptera une telle exception lorsqu'apparaît une confusion entretenue par le groupe ou l'actionnaire majoritaire."* [33]

Such abuses can be very diverse, and it is not possible to enter into all possible scenarios. In any event, the analysis is very much fact-oriented, and it is therefore difficult to compare one case to another.

With respect to the effect of the doctrine, the doctrine may or may not result in the extension of the arbitration agreement itself. This point is in fact very delicate and deserves greater attention.

It is important to realize the difference between piercing for liability and piercing for jurisdiction.

It is also important to realize that the effects of the doctrine may vary depending upon the applicable law or even upon the specific circumstances of the case.

If a parent company is liable as a result of the piercing of the corporate veil, will it be solely responsible, jointly responsible (together with the affiliate) responsible only if the affiliate cannot pay? The answer to this question is not obvious and in fact not uniform.

It is also worth noting that, if the parent company is liable, this does not necessarily imply that it is also bound by the arbitration agreement. It is crucial to distinguish between the jurisdictional issue and the liability on the merits.[34]

These issues are too complex to be addressed here in detail with regard to the different domestic laws. My aim is simply to draw attention to these questions and to note that it is too often assumed, without real justification, that the doctrine of piercing the corporate veil entails joint liability and the extension of the arbitration agreement.

Piercing the corporate veil does not require that the intention of the non-signatory third party be expressed in writing. There was an important debate in Switzerland on this question. The Swiss Federal Tribunal has now clearly taken a position by holding that there is no formal requirement to extend the arbitration agreement. [35]

As long as there is an arbitration agreement in writing, it can be interpreted and extended to third parties even if the third parties did not express their intention in writing. I consider that this case law is not wrong, given the fact that the doctrine is based on an abuse of right.

The question regarding the applicable law is difficult and has apparently not been dealt with extensively. If the theory pertains to company law, the place of incorporation of the company should be the starting point of the reasoning.[36] But which company: the signatory or the non-signatory? In addition, since the doctrine is designed to correct the effect of the law based on good faith, the place of residence of the contracting party, which invokes the abuse, could also play a role. I do not pretend to have exhausted the topic of the applicable law, but would merely like to point out the difficulty – and importance – of this issue.

When the issue of the applicable law is difficult or uncertain, one can be tempted to refer to 'transnational' or 'uniform' rules or standards, which avoid such difficulties. This approach is advocated by Born, who states as follows:

> *"As with the doctrines of apparent authority and estoppel, it is artificial to select the law of any particular national jurisdiction to define those circumstances in which basic principles of fairness and good faith in international business dealings require disregarding a corporate identity conferred by national law and subjecting a party to an international arbitration agreement. Rather, uniform international principles better achieve the purposes of the veil piercing doctrine, without materially interfering with the parties' expectations."* [37]

However, it appears that, with respect to the doctrine of piercing the corporate veil, such a 'transnational' approach does not find great support in the case law or in arbitral awards. As pointed out above, courts and arbitrators usually base the doctrine on national law standards. In fact, I have found only one award that expresses a preference for the use of transnational standards for piercing the corporate veil.

7. CONCLUSIONS

In conclusion, based on my review of the case law and awards, I would say that the doctrine of piercing the corporate veil, when correctly identified and applied independently and not in conjunction with the group of companies doctrine, seems to be rather on the right track.

It is applied seriously, not too extensively and consistently by both courts and arbitral tribunals. In particular, I did not find inconsistent standards depending upon whether the doctrine was applied by arbitrators or by courts.

What is missing, however, is a more detailed analysis of the effects of this doctrine. This is a topic that would benefit from further investigation.

END NOTES

* Partner, Python & Peter, Geneva.

1   G.B. Born, *International Commercial Arbitration* (Kluwer Law International, 2009) p. 1154.

2   ICC case No. 8385, JDI (1997) pp. 1061 et seq., 1067.

3   *Carte Blance Pte v. Diners Club International, Inc. et al.*, 2 F.3d 24 (2d Cir., 1993) at 26, citing W*m Passalacqua Builder, Inc. v. Resnick Developers South, Inc.*, 933 F.2d 131 (2d Cir., 1991) at 139.

4   See generally K. Vandekerckhove, *Piercing the Corporate Veil* (Kluwer Law International, 2007).

5   It has been often noted that the terms 'extension' of the arbitration agreement to 'non-signatories' are not only awkward in English but also not absolutely accurate. First, because the issue is not to extend the arbitration agreement but to determine who are the real parties to it, irrespective of the language that was used in the clause. Secondly, because the signature is not the decisive criterion for deciding who is a real party. Nevertheless, I will comply with the apparently dominant terminology and refer to the extension of the arbitration agreement to non-signatories in this article.

6   W.W. Park, 'Non-Signatories and International Contracts: An Arbitrator's Dilemma', in *Multiple Party Actions in International Arbitration* (Oxford University Press, 2009) p. 4, para. 1.17.

7   Ibid., at p. 18, para. 1.64; A. Redfern et al., *Law and Practice of International Commercial Arbitration*, 4th edn. (London, 2004) p. 148, para. 3-30 and p. 150, para. 3-32; Y. Derains and E. A. Schwarz, *A Guide to the ICC Rules of Arbitration* (Kluwer Law International, 2005) p. 89; B. Hanotiau, 'Problems Raised by Complex Arbitrations Involving Multiple Contracts – Parties – Issues: An Analysis', *Jnl. Int. Arb.* 3 (2001) p. 253 et seq.

8   Redfern et al., *supra* n. 7, at p. 151, para. 3-33.

9   Born, *supra* n. 1, at p. 1171.

10 See D. Cohen, 'L'engagement des sociétés à l'arbitrage', Rev. arb. (2006) pp. 35 et seq., 60-63.

11 Redfern et al., *supra* n. 7, at p. 148.

12 See the useful summaries and comparative chart in Park, *supra* n. 6, at pp. 26-31.

13 ICC case No. 5721, JDI (1990) pp. 1020, 1023-1024; ICC case No. 9873, ICC Ct. *Bull.* 16(2) (2005) pp. 89-90; ICC case No. 10758, ICC Ct. *Bull.* 16(2) (2005) p. 91 = JDI (2001) p. 1171.

14 ICC case No. 10818, ICC Ct. *Bull.* 16(2) (2005) pp. 98, 100-101.

15 Ad hoc arbitration 1989, ASA *Bul.* (1990) p. 270 (applying Swiss and Italian laws); Ad hoc arbitration 1991, ASA Bul. (1992) p. 202 (applying Swiss law); ICC case No. 7626, YCA (1997) p. 132 (applying English law); ICC case No. 8163, ICC Ct. Bull. 16(2) (2005) p. 81 (applying German law); ICC case No. 11160, ICC Ct. Bull. 16(2) (2005) p. 103 (applying Venezuelan law); but see ICC case No. 8385, JDI (1997) p. 1061 (manifesting preference for international standards, but noting that New York and Belgian law would lead to the same result).

16 ICC case No. 4131, *Dow Chemical, JDI* (1983) p. 899; ICC case No. 6000, *ICC Ct. Bull.* 2(2) (1991) p. 31.

17 Among the awards cited above in footnote 15, only two (ICC case No. 8385 and Ad hoc arbitration 1991) accepted the piercing of the corporate veil. See also ICC cases Nos. 9719, 10818 and 11209, ICC Ct. *Bull.* 16(2) (2005) pp. 87, 98 and 106 (refusing to pierce the corporate veil). The Orri award – ICC case No. 5730, *Rev.* arb. (1992) p. 125 – does not, in our opinion, belong to this category, although the arbitral tribunal accepted the extension of the arbitration agreement. The main argument was ostensible authority and ratification rather than, strictly speaking, piercing the corporate veil.

18 B. Hanotiau, *Complex Arbitrations, Multiparty, Multicontract, Multi-issue and Class Arbitrations* (Kluwer Law International, 2005) pp. 43-47; D. Vidal, 'L'extension de l'engagement compromissoire dans un groupe de sociétés: application arbitrale et judiciaire de la théorie de l'alter ego', *ICC Ct. Bull.* 16(2) (2005) pp. 67-80; N. Voser, 'Multi-Party Disputes and Joinder of Third Parties', in A.J. van den Berg (ed.), ICCA: *50 Years of the New York Convention* (Kluwer Law International, 2009) pp. 374-376.

19 *Fisser v. International Bank*, 282 F.2d 231 (2d Cir., 1960); *Coastal States Trading, Inc. v. Zenith Navigation SA,* 446 F.Supp. 330 (S.D.N.Y., 1977); *Farkar Co. v. RA Hanson Disc. Ltd.*, 441 F.Supp. 841 (SDNY 1977); *Laborers' Local Union 472 & 172 v. Interstate Curb & Sidewalk*, 448 A.2d 980 (N.J. 1982); *Federated Title Insurers, Inc. v. Ward*, 538 So.2d 890 (Fla. Dist. Ct. App., 1989); *Freeman v. Complex Computing Company, Inc.*, 979 F.Supp. 257 (S.D.N.Y., 1997); *Freeman v. Complex Computing Company,* Inc., 119 F.3d 1044 (2d Cir., 1997).

20 *Fisser v. International Bank*, 282 F.2d 231 (2d Cir., 1960) at 237, citing *Lowendahl v. Baltimore & Ohio R.R. Co.*, 247 App. Div. 144.

21 *Coastal States Trading, Inc. v. Zenith Navigation* SA, 446 F.Supp. 330 (S.D.N.Y., 1977) at 337; Glenn v. Wagner, 329 S.E.2d 326 (N.C., 1985) at 455; *Federated Title Insurers, Inc. v. Ward,* 538 So.2d 890 (Fla. Dist. Ct. App., 1989) at 891; *Freeman v. Complex Computing Company, Inc.*, 979 F.Supp. 257 (S.D.N.Y., 1997) at 1053.

22 *Coastal States Trading, Inc. v. Zenith Navigation* SA, 446 F.Supp. 330 (S.D.N.Y., 1977) at 336.

23 J.-F. Poudret and S. Besson, *Comparative Law of International Arbitration* (2007) p. 220, para. 257.

24 Rev. arb. (1992) p. 95, with a note by Cohen (Paris); *Rev. arb*. (1992) p. 73, with a note by Cohen (Cas.); Poudret and Besson, *supra* n. 23, at p. 219, para. 255.

25 Berger and Kellerhals, *Internationale und interne Schiedsgerichtsbarkeit in der Schweiz* (2006) p. 184, para. 527; ATF 108 II 213; ATF 113 II 31.

26 ATF 120 II 155, c. 6d; Poudret and Besson, *supra* n. 23, at pp. 222-223, para. 258.

27 *ASA Bul.* (1996) p. 496, c. 5-7; Poudret and Besson, *supra* n. 23, at pp. 223-224, para. 258.

28 Decision of 25 August 2009, 4A_160/2009.

29 B. Corboz, in *Commentaire de la LTF* (Berne, 2009) p. 639, para. 105 ad Art. 77.

30 Berger and Kellerhals, *supra* n. 25, at pp. 184-185, para. 528; Voser, *supra* n. 18, at p. 378.

31 ICC case No. 5721, *JDI* (1990) p. 1020, 1024; ICC case No. 9873, *ICC Ct. Bull.* 16(2) (2005) pp. 89-90.

32 Hanotiau, *supra* n. 7, at p. 277; Born, *supra* n. 1, at pp. 1153-1154; Poudret and Besson, supra n. 23, at p. 228, para. 264; ICC case No. 11209, *ICC Ct. Bull.* 16(2) (2005) pp. 106, 107.

33 ICC case No. 5721, *JDI* (1990) pp. 1020, 1024.

34 ATF 120 II 155, c. 6d; Poudret and Besson, *supra* n. 23, at para. 258; L. Lévy and B. Stucki, 'Note concernant l'arrêt du Tribunal fédéral suisse du 16 octobre 2003', *Rev. arb.* (2004) pp. 716-717.

35 ATF 129 III 727, c. 5.3.1; see J.-F. Poudret, ASA Bul. (2004) pp. 390-397.

36 Park, *supra* n. 6, at p. 18, para. 1.64; J.D.M. Lew, L.A. Mistelis and S.M. Kröll, *Comparative International Commercial Arbitration* (Kluwer Law International, 2003) p. 147 (referring to the 'applicable company law'); but see Born, *supra* n. 1, at pp. 1163-1164 (advocating the application of 'uniform international principles').

37 Born, *supra* n. 1, at p. 1164.

CHAPTER 9

CONSOLIDATION, JOINDER, CROSS-CLAIMS, MULTIPARTY AND MULTICONTRACT ARBITRATIONS: RECENT ICC EXPERIENCE

SIMON GREENBERG, JOSÉ RICARDO FERIS AND CHRISTIAN ALBANESI[*]

1. INTRODUCTION

Numerous interesting issues relating to multiparty and multicontract arbitrations arise within the ICC International Court of Arbitration (hereinafter, the 'Court') and its Secretariat (hereinafter, the 'Secretariat') in the process of constituting ICC arbitral tribunals and preparing files for transfer to those arbitral tribunals.

In 'setting in motion'[1] an arbitration, the Court may take *prima facie* decisions on whether a case can proceed, fix the place of arbitration, decide on the number of arbitrators, confirm or appoint arbitrators and/or consolidate arbitration proceedings. The Court's supervisory role in these initial stages of arbitrations goes further than most arbitral institutions. Using the expertise of its members and guided by the experience of the Secretariat, the Court is able to be pro-active in identifying and taking steps to eliminate procedural irregularities that could, at worst, frustrate the enforceability of arbitrations or, at least, cause inefficiency, delays and wasted costs.

The need for a somewhat pro-active approach has been amplified in recent years by the ever-increasing complexity of the transactions behind the disputes that are submitted to ICC arbitration.[2] The complexity of the underlying transactions is, in turn, reflected in the arbitrations administered by the Court. For instance, in each year from 2001-2009, at least 28.5% of ICC arbitrations involved more than two parties. In 2009, 233 out of the 817 cases filed involved more than two parties; six of them involved more than ten parties. Where an arbitration involves multiple parties or multiple contracts, it could be the case that (i) one of the respondents or the claimants has not signed the agreement on the basis of which the request for arbitration has been filed; (ii) the arbitration clauses contained in the different contracts may not be compatible; and/or (iii) the contracts may concern different, potentially unrelated economic transactions. Furthermore, a respondent could file cross-claims against another respondent or even request the joinder of an additional party, which could subsequently also file jurisdictional objections, cross-claims or make other requests.

When entering into the quagmire of procedural mechanisms such as consolidation, joinder of new parties and the compatibility of multicontract arbitrations, the Court exercises extreme caution. It is cautious primarily by virtue of the limitations on its role: it is an administrative body that does not settle disputes.[3] It is not the Court's role to decide disputed issues that can be submitted to fully-briefed arbitral tribunals.

That said, the Court must perform its functions to constitute arbitral tribunals in a manner that is effective in all respects. It is primarily in the performance of those functions that the Court has been faced with particular challenges in relation to the issues that are the subject of the present article. We have selected some of the most complex and captivating of the Court's recent decisions in relation to consolidation, multicontract arbitration, joinder and cross-claims.[4] Each of those concepts is explained before the examples are provided. It should not be assumed, however, that the examples below are representative of the Court's daily work. The vast majority of ICC arbitrations proceed to arbitral tribunal constitution with limited input from the Court.

As will be seen below, in the more complex cases, the combined flexibility of the 1998 ICC Rules of Arbitration (hereinafter, the 'Rules') and the expertise of the Court and the Secretariat have produced solutions to unimaginable situations. Nonetheless, as the proportion of complex cases grows, it makes sense to reflect some of the Court's practices in its Rules. Until the last amendment of the Rules, which took place before 1998, multiparty arbitration was still relatively rare, and there thus appeared to be no particular need at the time to include special multiparty provisions. Since the ICC Commission on Arbitration (hereinafter, the 'Commission') is drawing towards the end of its rules revision process, we also comment below on possible approaches towards consolidation, multicontract arbitration, joinder and cross-claims in the forthcoming ICC Rules of Arbitration (hereinafter, the 'New Rules').

2. CONSOLIDATION

There are various interpretations of the meaning of the procedural mechanism 'consolidation', as it is known in international commercial arbitration. At its broadest, some practitioners include in this definition any arbitration where slightly unrelated claims are heard together. Others include any situation where there are claims arising from more than one contract, for example where: (i) a single arbitration is commenced on the basis of more than one contract; or (ii) a party to an existing arbitration makes a claim against another party based on a different contract from the one that forms the jurisdictional foundation for the arbitration.

While those are possible definitions of consolidation, for ICC purposes consolidation in the strict sense covers only one procedural situation. In this situation, there are at least two separate ICC arbitrations pending (i.e. with separate ICC case numbers) and one or more parties to one of the arbitrations wants them to be consolidated into a single proceeding. Under the Rules, consolidation is dealt with in Article 4(6) as follows:

> *'When a party submits a Request in connection with a legal relationship in respect of which arbitration proceedings between the same parties are already pending under these Rules, the Court may, at the request of a party, decide to include the claims contained in the Request in the pending proceedings provided that the Terms of Reference have not been signed or approved by the Court. Once the Terms of Reference have been signed or approved by the Court, claims may only be included in the pending proceedings subject to the provisions of Article 19.'* (emphasis added)

The Court's practice under this article has been to follow its language strictly. This means that in order to consolidate two or more pending ICC arbitrations:

- the legal relationships underlying the arbitrations must be connected;[5]
- the parties to each arbitration must be the same;
- a party to one of the arbitrations must request consolidation;[6] and
- the terms of reference must not have been signed or approved.[7]

When the cases that are to be consolidated involve more than one contract, the Court will, in addition to the conditions set out in Article 4(6), apply the conditions derived from its practice with respect to multicontract arbitrations. Those conditions are described in section 3 below.

In the three years from 1 January 2007 to 31 December 2009, the Court dealt with 24 contested requests for consolidation, eight of which were accepted and the remainder rejected. These figures exclude those cases where all parties agreed to consolidate. In those instances, a decision of the Court is unnecessary and the Secretariat proceeds to consolidate the matters administratively.

By far the most common reason for the Court to reject an application for consolidation is non-satisfaction of the second element listed above, i.e. the parties are no identical. That requirement can sometimes appear restrictive in situations where two parties are intricately related but not identical, for example members of the same corporate group with exactly the same management and the same address.

Exceptionally, on one occasion the Court decided to consolidate two arbitrations involving parties that were not identical at the time the arbitrations were commenced. In that case, the claimant simultaneously submitted two requests for arbitration, the first against respondents 1, 2 and 3 and the second against respondents 1 and 2, and requested consolidation. Respondents 1 and 2 agreed to consolidation and informed the Secretariat that respondent 3 had merged into respondent 2 and would thus no longer participate in the proceedings. However, the claimant refused to exclude respondent 3 from the proceedings. In view of the agreement between the claimant and respondents 1 and 2 to consolidate the cases, and since respondent 3 did not object to consolidation, the Court decided to consolidate the two cases. The Court took the view that the merger of respondents 2 and 3 allowed the case to meet the 'same parties' requirement. Accordingly, this should not be seen as an exception to the strict application of the requirements of Article 4(6) of the Rules.

For instance, the Court was recently requested to consolidate three arbitrations where (i) all of the parties to the first two arbitrations were involved in the third arbitration; (ii) the claims brought under the first two cases were all technically raised in the third case; and (iii) the two contracts on the basis of which the different claims were raised formed part of a two-prong single economic transaction. However, given that the parties in the first two cases were not identical, a condition of Article 4(6) was not satisfied and consolidation, even if desirable, could not be effected without the agreement of all parties.

The Court has not been indifferent to the difficulties posed by the strict language of Article 4(6), particularly regarding inefficiency and potentially conflicting outcomes where consolidation is impossible. In the case described in the previous paragraph, the Court, before deciding that it could not consolidate the cases, encouraged the parties to agree on consolidation and drew their attention to the financial consequences of conducting the three arbitrations separately. On other occasions, the Court has been pro-active by appointing the same arbitral tribunal in the related cases. Where identical arbitral tribunals are possible, the arbitrations can be run in parallel, thus achieving most of the benefits of consolidation without actually consolidating the matters.

For example, in two arbitrations filed in 2008, the parties were very similar but not identical. Both arbitrations were brought by a single claimant against two respondents. While the respondents were identical in both cases, the claimants were slightly different. The claimants were members of the same group of companies with the same corporate address but had different names and different company identification numbers. The contracts underlying each request for arbitration were separate, but almost identical word for word except that each called for the delivery of a different commodity. The identical arbitration agreements in these contracts called for a three-member arbitral tribunal.

Since the two respondents were unable to jointly nominate a co-arbitrator, the entire arbitral tribunal was to be appointed by the Court under Article 10(2) of the Rules.[8] Using its discretion to select all of the arbitrators, the Court appointed the same arbitral tribunal for both matters. The claimant subsequently challenged the entire arbitral tribunal in the second arbitration on the basis that the arbitrators might form views about the claims in that case based on their detailed knowledge of the first case. Prior to the appointment of the arbitrators, the claimant had also objected to consolidation. The Court rejected the challenge, noting, among other factors, that it had already considered the issue whether to appoint the same arbitral tribunal at the stage of constituting the arbitral tribunals in the first place.

The language of Article 4(6) of the Rules is being assessed by the Commission in the context of the rules revision process. Some members of the Commission's Rules Revision Task Force are content with the restrictive nature of the current language, considering that any change could create a risk of consolidation where the relationship between the parties and disputes is insufficiently proximate. Although it is too early to tell, the Commission may seek a formula that represents some kind of middle ground, providing the Court with some flexibility to allow more consolidations without reducing predictability in this regard.

3. MULTICONTRACT ARBITRATIONS

As a matter of ICC internal practice, 'multicontract' arbitration means a single arbitration where claims have been brought on the basis of more than one contract. As noted above, some practitioners consider this a form of consolidation. It is true that there is a close conceptual link between a request to consolidate two pending arbitrations that have been filed on the basis of different contracts, on the one hand, and a single arbitration that has been filed on the basis of more than one contract, on the other. For ICC purposes, however, the two situations are considered procedurally distinct.

Multicontract arbitrations can raise the most complex of all the multiparty/multicontract issues facing the Court. The main reason for this is that, in order for an arbitration to proceed on the basis of multiple contracts, the Court must take what can be a delicate decision regarding the compatibility of the dispute resolution mechanisms in the different contracts and make a *prima facie* assumption about whether all the parties may have consented to the claims being heard together. Put analogously to the concept of consolidation, that last element could be seen as examining whether there is *prima facie* implicit consent to effective consolidation.

The Rules are silent as to the setting in motion of multicontract arbitrations. As a matter of practice, when a party objects to multicontract claims proceeding in a single arbitration, the objection is dealt with under Article 6(2) of the Rules,[9] although some may consider that a multicontract scenario does not necessarily concern the 'existence, validity or scope of an arbitration agreement'. The evolution of the Court's practice in relation to multicontract arbitrations is a good example of how the Court's experience and expertise equips it to deal with the dynamic nature of international arbitration and the changing needs of its users.

From 1 January 2007 to 31 December 2009, the Court took 35 decisions under Article 6(2) of the Rules in cases involving multiple contracts. That figure includes contested cases only and does not include cases where all the parties to a multicontract arbitration agreed on the case going forward as such.

The Court has developed a relatively well-established practice for determining whether a multicontract arbitration can proceed on a *prima facie* basis. This means that, like all the Court's decisions under Article 6(2) of the Rules, it is for the arbitral tribunal to make a final decision on its jurisdiction. In relation to multicontract disputes, an arbitral tribunal may take into account the criteria set forth by the Court's practice, but is not necessarily required to do so. For instance, in a recent case filed under two contracts, the Court was *prima facie* satisfied that an arbitration agreement may exist between the parties and decided to set the case in motion. However, the arbitral tribunal subsequently decided in a partial award on jurisdiction that, although it had jurisdiction to hear all claims, the arbitrations arising from each contract would proceed separately given that the respondents were slightly different parties. Therefore, where the Court has decided that a multicontract arbitration can proceed, a party dissatisfied with that decision may have recourse to the arbitral tribunal, as for any Article 6(2) decision.

According to the Court's practice, a multicontract arbitration can proceed where the following three conditions are satisfied:

- all contracts are signed by all of the parties;
- the dispute resolution mechanisms in the different contracts are compatible; and
- all contracts are related to the same economic transaction.

It can be quickly observed here that the elements required for a multicontract arbitration to proceed are not dissimilar to the above-mentioned conditions for consolidation. Unlike consolidation, however, the Court's practice for multicontract arbitrations includes limited exceptions to the element concerning the identity of the parties.

With respect to this *first element* of the multicontract test set out above, the Court has, exceptionally, decided to allow a single arbitration on the basis of multiple contracts not signed by all of the parties in situations where:

- the signatory parties belong to the same group of companies; or
- at least one of the arbitration agreements has been signed by all of the parties.

The first of these exceptions, the 'group of companies' exception, is satisfied when it is clear that the signatory parties belong to the same group of companies. A classic situation usually covered by this exception would be a transaction where a framework contract is signed by a parent company and additional implementing contracts are signed by its affiliates.

In a 2009 example, the request for arbitration had been filed on the basis of three contracts. There were slightly different parties to the different contracts: contract 1 was signed by the claimant and all three respondents; contract 2 was signed by the claimant and respondent 1 only; and contract 3 was signed by the claimant and respondents 2 and 3 only. The Court accordingly considered the above-mentioned 'group of companies' exception. Here, the relationship between the respondents was such that the first respondent owned 100% of the second respondent and the second respondent owned 53% of the third. The Court found that this ownership relationship was insufficient to satisfy the 'group of companies' exception and that the case could therefore not proceed.

On this occasion, the Court took a pro-active approach rather than simply terminating the arbitration and fixing the costs. It decided to inform the claimant that the case could not proceed under all three contracts and that the claimant should indicate whether it wanted to proceed with the arbitration under one of the contracts. The claimant did elect to single out one of the contracts (the above-mentioned contract 1), and, after an ordinary Article 6(2) procedure, the arbitration continued between the claimant and all three respondents.

In another recent example of the application of the 'group of companies' exception to the first element of the multicontract test, one of the respondents had not signed all of the contracts. The Court nonetheless decided to allow the case to proceed, taking into account that this respondent had (i) allegedly induced the claimant to invest in the project that was the subject matter of the arbitration; (ii) participated in the negotiation and financing of the project; (iii) made critical decisions with regard to the project; and (iv) took the decision to dissolve and liquidate the joint venture that was created to carry out the project.

As noted above, the second exception to the first element of the multicontract test applies where at least one of the contracts containing an arbitration agreement has been signed by all of the parties. This has been applied by the Court in cases where the claims are so intimately connected and interdependent, because of the nature of the overall transaction, that an arbitral tribunal would have great difficulty handling them separately.

In a recent example of this exception, the claimant had commenced arbitration against three respondents on the basis of two contracts, the first one signed by all the parties and the second one signed only by the claimant and one of the respondents. Given that the outcome of the claims raised under the second contract would depend on the outcome of the claims raised under the first contract, the Court decided that the case could proceed.

As noted above, the *second element* of the multicontract test is that the arbitration agreements in all of the contracts must be compatible. Classic examples of incompatibility include cases where the arbitration agreements provide for different places of arbitration, different numbers of arbitrators or different methods for the constitution of the arbitral tribunal. Unless such an incompatibility is rectified by subsequent party agreement, it will ordinarily prevent the matter from going forward. There may also be incompatibilities in relation to procedural matters, such as the language of the arbitration or time limits, after the constitution of the arbitral tribunal. These incompatibilities might or might not make it impossible for the Court to allow the arbitration to proceed, depending on all the circumstances.

In a recent example, the Court decided that a single arbitration could not proceed on the basis of two arbitration agreements, one of which referred to Paris and the other to Geneva as the place of arbitration. Similarly, the Court has decided not to set in motion a case on the basis of two arbitration agreements where one provided for a three-member arbitral tribunal with the chairman to be nominated by the co-arbitrators and the other was silent as to the number of arbitrators. In that case, even if the Court had decided to appoint a three-member arbitral tribunal in order to harmonize the number of arbitrators, an incompatibility would have remained. Indeed, whereas under the first arbitration agreement the chairman was to be nominated jointly by the co-arbitrators, there was no such provision in the other arbitration agreement meaning that, pursuant to the Rules, the chairman would have been appointed by the Court. In an attempt to overcome this incompatibility, the claimant indicated that it would agree to any reasonable proposal from the respondent as to the method for the appointment of the chairman. However, the claimant's offer alone was insufficient, because it would require both parties' agreement to change the method for constituting the arbitral tribunal.

There are circumstances where the incompatibility between arbitration agreements becomes moot through a decision of the Court or otherwise. For instance, an arbitration was recently filed on the basis of two arbitration agreements, one of which was silent as to the number of arbitrators and the other provided for a three-member arbitral tribunal. The Court decided that the case could proceed and, in order to overcome the apparent incompatibility in the number of arbitrators, decided to submit the case to a three-member arbitral tribunal.

Similarly, the Court was recently faced with an arbitration in which the principal claims were based on an arbitration agreement that was silent as to the number of arbitrators. The parties subsequently agreed to submit the case to a three-member arbitral tribunal and to grant the co-arbitrators 15 days to jointly nominate the chairman. However, the respondent then filed counterclaims based on a different arbitration agreement, which provided that the co-arbitrators be granted 30 days to jointly nominate the chairman. As such, the parties' subsequent agreement had the effect of making the arbitration agreements incompatible, as there was a discrepancy regarding the time limit for the co-arbitrators to nominate the chairman. Despite this incompatibility, the co-arbitrators jointly nominated the chairman even before they were confirmed, thus rendering the issue of incompatibility moot. Given that technically the co-arbitrators' nomination could not be made until after their confirmation by the Court or Secretary General, they confirmed their nomination immediately after they were confirmed.

As noted above, the *third element* of the multicontract test is that all contracts must be related to the same economic transaction. Very few cases have failed to meet this threshold. One example of such a failure was when the Court decided that a case could not proceed because the claimant based it claims on different contracts which, despite having similar objectives and terms (relating to hotel construction), clearly related to different projects (i.e. the hotels were to be constructed in different cities in North Africa). The contracts were therefore considered not to relate to the same economic transaction.

In borderline cases in relation to this third element, the Court generally allows the case to proceed as long as the arbitration agreements are compatible, so that the Court is able to constitute the arbitral tribunal. The issue of whether the parties intended to permit multicontract arbitration is thereby left to the arbitral tribunal. This occurred in a recent arbitration involving claims arising from two different contracts for the construction and installation of transmission lines that were part of the same project according to one of the parties.

Two final comments must be made with respect to multicontract arbitration under the Rules.

First, a mere reference to multiple contracts by a party, or even the filing of claims arising from different contracts, may not necessarily prompt the Court to conduct its multicontract test. It can happen that a party filing claims related to more than one contract invokes only the arbitration clause contained in one of them. The question in such a case may be whether the arbitration clause relied upon is broad enough to encapsulate the claims as raised, but this is normally an issue that would be decided by the arbitral tribunal. A similar situation may also arise when a party commences arbitration based on one contract but later raises claims arising out of another contract.

Second, the most common multicontract situation is when a claimant files principal claims on the basis of more than one contract. However, the Court has recently faced multicontract scenarios that were created either by the filing of counterclaims arising from a contract other than that upon which the claimant had based its claims or by virtue of a request for consolidation of two or more arbitrations involving different but related contracts. This situation could also potentially arise with respect to cross-claims (see section 6 below).

A 2010 example of this situation featured a case in which the multicontract scenario arose when the respondent filed counterclaims against the claimant. In that case, the claimant filed its principal claims against the respondents on the basis of a private concession agreement, pursuant to which the respondents granted the claimant the use of a building for the claimant to exploit as a hotel for 15 years. The respondents then filed counterclaims on the basis of a sale option agreement, pursuant to which the claimant was granted the option to purchase, by a certain date, the building that was the subject of the private concession agreement. The private concession agreement contained an arbitration clause designating Paris as the place of arbitration whereas the sale option agreement provided for Buenos Aires as the place of arbitration.

This kind of situation may require the Court, pursuant to Article 6(2) of the Rules and its multicontract test, to decide that the case should proceed only with respect to the claims arising from the private concession agreement. In this case, the decision was taken only upon both parties' express acknowledgement of the existence of two different and incompatible arbitration agreements. It was *prima facie* clear that one single arbitral tribunal would not have jurisdiction to entertain both principal claims and counterclaims.

Another example arose from a request for the consolidation of three separate arbitrations. Leaving aside the test for consolidation under Article 4(6) of the Rules, the Court was not able to consolidate the three pending arbitrations because in the first case (filed before the other two) the parties had agreed that the chairman would be nominated by the co-arbitrators, whereas in the other two cases the chairman was to be appointed by the Court. Therefore, the parties' agreement in the first case rendered the arbitration agreement of the first case incompatible with the arbitration agreements in the other cases, thus preventing consolidation.

Multicontract scenarios are perhaps the most complex that the Commission will face when revising the Rules. On the one hand, concerns of transparency may call for addressing the issue squarely in the Rules, or at least drawing the users' attention to the issues that such circumstances can generate. On the other hand, it may be burdensome to attempt to provide Rules that cover all possible scenarios. It might be best to leave the issue of multicontract arbitration in the flexible hands of the Court, which is extraordinarily well equipped to deal with any yet unforeseen variations that may arise.

4. JOINDER AND THIRD-PARTY INTERVENTION

a. Joinder

Once again, there is some variation in the way that practitioners understand the procedural mechanism of 'joinder'. For ICC purposes, it means the situation where there is an arbitration underway and a party to that arbitration seeks to add a new party, that is to say, a party that was not named as such in the original request for arbitration. In practice, it is almost always the respondent side in an arbitration that seeks to name new parties, because the claimant side had the opportunity to do so in the request for arbitration. The Court has, however, occasionally heard applications from a claimant to name an additional party at some stage after filing its request for arbitration.

The current Rules are silent as to whether a respondent can name additional parties, whether as claimants, respondents or counter-claim respondents. This silence follows the traditional principle in international arbitration that it is exclusively for the claimant to identify the parties.[10] While it could be said that the Rules imply (in Article 4(3)(a)) that it is for the claimant alone to determine the parties, the Court's practice was clarified in the early years of the Rules so as to allow a respondent to apply to join a new party in certain limited circumstances. This development recognized that the traditional approach could create perceived procedural inequality by denying one side (i.e. the respondent side) the opportunity to name parties. The new practice also recognized that multiple arbitrations concerning closely related matters could lead to inefficiency, increased costs and potentially conflicting outcomes.

The practice that evolved does not put the claimant and the respondent entirely on an equal footing in relation to naming parties. When a claimant names one or more respondents in the request for arbitration, the request for arbitration will be notified to the respondent(s) immediately upon compliance with the filing requirements. On the other hand, when a respondent wishes to join an additional party not named in the request for arbitration, the Court will take a decision on whether to allow the joinder after consulting the other parties. This creates a hurdle for the respondent that does not exist for the claimant.

An inaugural paper on the evolution in the Court's joinder practice was published in the spring 2003 edition of the *ICC Court of Arbitration Bulletin*.[11] The authors noted that, in three then-recent cases, the Court had joined a new party upon the respondent side's request. Since then – perhaps to some extent encouraged by that paper – a number of joinder requests have been filed with the Court. For example, between 1 January 2007 and 31 December 2009, the Court considered 21 contested requests for joinder. It allowed the joinder in 13 of those cases and rejected the rest.

The above-cited statistic excludes cases where all parties agreed to the joinder. In those instances, a decision of the Court is unnecessary, and the Secretariat proceeds to effect the joinder. Such party agreements even occasionally occur where the party to be joined was not a party to the arbitration agreement, such that it would never have been joined via the court's joinder practice (which is discussed below). For example, in one case in 2009, the potential new party was one of the respondent's commercial partners and had nothing to do with the contract between the claimant and the respondent. It was the claimant's position in the arbitration that the respondent had breached the contract by failing to pay the claimant's invoices relating to deliveries made by (among others) the new party upon the respondent's instructions. Upon the respondent's joinder application, the parties agreed to the joinder on the condition that the new party:

'- joins the procedure as a party on the Defendant's side;
- accepts this arbitration procedure as it is in its current status; and
- accepts that the [relevant arbitration agreement] is binding on it.'

It is more common for one side (normally the claimant) to resist the joinder of a new party rather than agreeing to it. According to the Court's joinder practice, the Court may nonetheless allow the joinder where these three conditions are met:

- the third party must have signed the relevant arbitration agreement;
- there must be claims raised against the new party; and
- no steps have been taken towards the constitution of the arbitral tribunal.

With respect to the *first element*, the signature requirement, the practice was in principle strict, i.e. the Court would not join a party unless it had actually signed the contract containing the relevant arbitration agreement. It was therefore sometimes felt that the signature requirement of the joinder test was inconsistent with the Court's practice under Article 6(2) of the Rules and gave rise to inequality. In applying Article 6(2), the Court does not require all parties to have signed the arbitration agreement, provided that the Court is prima facie satisfied that any non-signatory may be a party to the arbitration agreement. Classic non-signatory scenarios include, inter alia, parent companies,[12] guarantors[13] and subrogates.[14] Furthermore, the Court takes a slightly different approach where the respondent is an individual rather than a company.[15] Thus, a claimant could simply name any respondent as a party (subject only to passing the Court's Article 6(2) test), whereas a respondent's request to join a new party would be subjected to the strict signature requirement.

This difference in standards is illustrated by a recent case initiated by two claimants against four respondents. The respondents requested the joinder of the parent company of one of the claimants on the ground that it had participated in the negotiation and performance of the contract at issue. The Court applied its joinder test and, given that the parent company was not a signatory to the contract, decided not to join the parent company. After notification of the Court's decision, the respondents filed a new arbitration against the two claimants and the parent company. The parent company raised jurisdictional objections alleging that it had not signed the contract containing the arbitration clause. The Court decided that the case would proceed against the parent company under Article 6(2) of the Rules, taking into account *prima facie* evidence on the file that it had played an active role in the negotiation and performance of the contract.

The Court has adopted a more flexible case-by-case approach to joinder applications in recent years, albeit always proceeding with great caution. The last few years saw examples of cases where, in certain circumstances, the Court joined a party that had not signed the contract containing the arbitration clause. Some examples are set out below.

The Court allowed the joinder of a third party in a case where it had signed an MOU amending the contract containing the arbitration agreement but had not signed the contract itself. The new party was the claimant's parent company. In addition to the fact that it had signed the MOU, which indisputably related to the contract and incorporated provisions of it, the Court took into account many other factors, including that the parent had closely participated in the performance of the contract and had played a key role in settlement negotiations relating to the dispute.

In another case, the Court joined a third party that was, undisputedly, the legal successor of a party to the contract containing the arbitration clause. The successor had also signed a second, related contract that contained an identical arbitration clause.

In another succession case, the arbitration was commenced by a claimant under a joint venture agreement that had been signed by the respondent and a third party. The respondent sought to join that third party. According to the claimant, the third party had assigned to the claimant all of its rights, interest and obligations under the joint venture agreement. However, the respondent contended that the third party remained separately bound by non-compete obligations in the joint venture agreement and that it therefore remained bound by its arbitration clause. The Court decided that the third party should be joined, leaving to the arbitral tribunal the decision as to whether it had jurisdiction over the new party and, if so, whether that party owed any substantive obligations to the respondent after the assignment.

Another exception to the signature requirement might occur when only the leader of a consortium signs the contract containing the relevant arbitration clause. For instance, in a case where two of three consortium members were claimants (one of them being the consortium leader), the respondent sought to join the third consortium member and raised claims against it. It was argued that the nature of the consortium relationship implied that the leader had signed the main contract on behalf of all consortium members and that its signature was sufficient to satisfy the Court's signature requirement. However persuasive those arguments might have been, the Court decided on that occasion not to join the third consortium member.

In another case, the Court decided to join a third party that, in spite of not having signed the agreement containing the arbitration clause, had (i) signed a letter terminating the agreement; and (ii) referred to itself in that termination letter as being a party to that agreement.

In early 2010, the Court accepted for the first time to join a non-signatory on the basis of a previous state court decision. The case concerned a contract entered into by two parties pursuant to which the claimant acquired from the respondent 100% of the capital stock in a third party. The claimant agreed to pay the respondent a certain amount over a three-year period and to cause the third party to pay the respondent the balance of the purchase price. Before commencing the arbitration, the respondent had filed claims against the third party in a domestic court in Europe. In the course of that action, the third party in its submissions described itself as a party to the agreement on the basis that it had assumed specific obligations under that agreement. The third party relied on the arbitration clause contained in the agreement in support of its application to stay the domestic court proceeding. The domestic court granted the stay, finding that it did not have jurisdiction to hear the dispute due to the existence of the arbitration agreement. The domestic court reasoned that, while the third party was not a signatory to the contract, it had assumed obligations under both that contract and other related agreements. An arbitration was subsequently initiated by the claimant against the respondent. When the respondent sought to join the third party, the claimant objected on the grounds that the third party had not signed the agreement and was not a party thereto. The Court decided to join the third party taking into account the domestic court's decision and the third party's position in that domestic court proceeding.

Another interesting issue arises when the request for joinder is based not only on the agreement on the basis of which the arbitration was initially commenced but also on a different agreement, such as the agreement underlying a counterclaim. The Court was recently faced with this very situation. When examining the joinder request, the Court examined whether the conditions for consolidating the claims arising out of the two agreements had been met. As these conditions had not been met, the Court decided not to join the new party.

The signature requirement may be stricter when it comes to cases involving or potentially involving states or state entities. For instance, in a recent case where the claimant filed its request for arbitration on the basis of a sub-contract it had entered into with the respondents, the respondents sought to join a state, alleging that by virtue of the state's decision to terminate the main contract (the parties to which were the respondents and the state), the state was assigned the respondents' obligations under the sub-contract. The Court decided not to join the state as it had not signed the sub-contract.

With respect to the *second element*, that there are claims made against the new party, it must be noted that merely reserving the right to raise a claim later, or raising a conditional claim, is generally insufficient. The Court has indeed decided not to join a third party in a case where the respondent requesting the joinder merely reserved its right to file claims against the third party at a later stage, in the event that the arbitral tribunal decided against the respondent.

In certain circumstances, the Court has applied this condition more flexibly. Two situations are worth mentioning here.

First, a respondent seeking to join a new party normally files a claim against that party. Therefore, it is ordinarily assumed that the new party is not on the respondent's 'side' in the arbitration. However, in at least one case, the respondent sought to join a third party as an additional respondent, and this third party agreed to be joined as a respondent. Furthermore, the third party expressly agreed to respond to the claimant's claims. In the circumstances, the Court decided to allow the joinder of the new party.

In another case, after the request for arbitration had been filed, the parties agreed that one of the two claimants would no longer be a party to the arbitration. However, a few months later, the remaining claimant requested that the former claimant be reintroduced as a party. The respondent objected. In this case, there were no specific claims raised against the former claimant. However, as this former claimant would be joined on the claimant's side, the Court, rather than assessing whether there were specific claims against the party to be joined, considered whether this party had brought or intended to bring claims against the respondent. The Court decided to join the former claimant.

The *third element* for joinder, that no steps have been taken towards the constitution of the arbitral tribunal, recognizes the *Dutco*[16] principle that all parties to an arbitration should have equal rights with respect to the constitution of the arbitral tribunal. Accordingly, in order for the Court to allow a new party to be joined, no arbitrator may have been confirmed or appointed by Court or Secretary General.

The only case in which the Court decided to join a third party after the arbitral tribunal had been constituted is the one discussed just above, where the new party was a former claimant. When taking the decision to join that party, the Court considered that (i) there was nothing in the file suggesting that the Court would have taken different decisions regarding the constitution of the arbitral tribunal had the third party been present at all times in the proceeding; and (ii) since the third party was initially a party and had commented on the number of arbitrators, all parties had been provided with an opportunity to participate in the constitution of the arbitral tribunal.

An additional note with respect to the constitution of the arbitral tribunal should be made. A positive joinder decision may well change the procedural composition of the case in such a way that there are consequences in terms of the method for constituting the arbitral tribunal. Article 10(1) of the Rules provides that where there are multiple parties, whether as claimants or as respondents, and the dispute is to be referred to three arbitrators, the multiple claimants, jointly, and the multiple respondents, jointly, shall nominate an arbitrator. If either side cannot jointly nominate an arbitrator, the Court is empowered to appoint the entire arbitral tribunal pursuant to Article 10(2) of the Rules. When a newly joined party is neither on the claimant's nor the respondent's side, it would not ordinarily be feasible to expect that party to nominate a co-arbitrator jointly with either of those sides.

Therefore, the Court often has to apply Article 10(2) of the Rules to resolve this situation in cases where a party has been joined but does not fit into either side in the existing arbitration.

Finally, there is now fairly widespread acceptance among arbitration practitioners that all parties to an arbitration should receive equal rights to name parties. It is therefore expected that the revised version of the Rules will address the issue of joinder from that perspective and with a view to crystallizing the joinder practice developed by the Court over the last 10 years.

b. Third-party intervention

A concept somewhat related to joinder is where a non-party to the arbitration learns of the existence of the arbitration and seeks to be joined to it. This is quite rare and, like joinder, not provided for in the Rules.

On those occasions where a potential new party contacts the Secretariat with a request to be joined to an arbitration, the Secretariat informs the person that, due to the confidential nature of the Court and Secretariat's work, the Secretariat is not in a position even to acknowledge the existence of the arbitration, much less entertain a request for intervention.

In 2009, an individual turned up one Friday afternoon at ICC headquarters in Paris and asked to speak to the counsel in charge of one of the case management teams. She had flown from her country with a brief and demanded to be joined to an ICC arbitration underway between a major international petroleum company and the state-run oil company in her country. She claimed that, being a citizen of the state in question, she had an interest in the outcome of the case. After informal consultation between the Secretariat and the arbitral tribunal, the brief was not taken further.

In another case in 2009, the Secretariat received a letter from a non-party requesting to be joined to an existing case. Contrary to the previous situation, the non-party had signed one of the two contracts upon which the arbitration was based. Therefore, after internal discussion at the Secretariat, the Secretariat sent the non-party's letter to the parties in the arbitration and invited their comments. As it happened, one of the parties to the arbitration proposed to allow the joinder upon certain conditions. However, after further discussion, the parties did not reach an agreement on those conditions and the new party could not be joined.

5. CROSS-CLAIMS

For ICC purposes, a cross-claim means a claim filed between parties on the same side of an arbitration, for example a claim made between claimants or between respondents.[17] The Rules are silent as to whether such claims are permitted and, if so, how they are dealt with. While cross-claims are relatively rare, there have been a number of cases where they were introduced.

Typical examples of cross-claims present a multicontract issue. This was the situation in an arbitration filed in 2008 featuring a consortium composed of Z and other companies. The consortium was retained by X to supply, install, start up and commission a blast furnace at X's industrial plant on a turnkey basis. A contract was accordingly entered into between Z as consortium leader and X. Thereafter, Z and Y entered into a subcontract agreement for the performance and execution of the erection works related to the blast furnace. Then, X and Y, as contracting parties, and Z, as intervening party, entered into an additional agreement to govern their respective liabilities and rights with respect to the project. Y initiated arbitration against X and Z for breaches of their contractual obligations under the subcontract agreement and the additional agreement. Both agreements contained arbitration clauses. X further filed counterclaims against Y and cross-claims against Z.

In the past, cross-claims have been a decisive factor for the Court to appoint the whole arbitral tribunal pursuant to Article 10(2) of the Rules, which is what occurred in the case described above. The Court has considered cross-claims as clear evidence that the parties between which such claims exist have opposing interests and thus cannot be expected to jointly nominate an arbitrator as required by Article 10(1) of the Rules.

Another area of ICC arbitration in which cross-claims have an impact is the costs of the arbitration. In that regard, the Rules foresee only the notion of principal claims and counterclaims. As such, the advance on costs is fixed on the basis of the sum of those two types of claims. Furthermore, Article 30(2) of the Rules permits the Court to fix separate advances on costs for the principal claims and counterclaims without reference to possible separate advances on costs for cross-claims. In the past, issues concerning advances on costs in cases where cross-claims were filed have been dealt with by the Secretariat and the Court on a case-by-case basis.

In view of the increasing number of cases involving multiple parties and multiple contracts – and as a consequence the increasing number of potential cross-claims – the revised version of the Rules will probably provide for the notion of cross-claims and regulate the ways in which they can be filed and, in particular, their impact on the advance on costs.

6. Conclusion

The situations covered by the present article are an illustrative sample of the diversity of the Court's caseload. The examples demonstrate that the seemingly infinite number of combinations of factual scenarios that can arise out of that caseload can only be managed under modern yet very flexible arbitration rules and reliable institutional support.

Throughout their existence, the Rules have been able to meet the challenges of the ever-evolving circumstances and demands of their users. This is mainly due to their flexible and universal nature. It is also due in great part to the practices developed by the Court in order to adapt the Rules to the needs of particular circumstances.

In revising the Rules, the Commission is currently facing the challenge of preserving the flexible and universal nature of the Rules while adapting them to the most current needs. The increasing complexity of cases demonstrates that the Rules will probably need to deal head on with the onset of multiparty and multicontract arbitration.

Fortunately, in conducting its revision process, the Commission will have the advantage of drawing from the rich experience and practices developed by the Court as set out in this article.

END NOTES

*   Respectively, Deputy Secretary General, Counsel and Deputy Counsel at the Secretariat of the ICC International Court of Arbitration. Any opinions expressed in this article belong to the authors alone and will not in any circumstances bind the Court or its Secretariat. The section on joinder below draws from a conference paper entitled 'The Practice of the ICC International Court of Arbitration Concerning Multi-Party Contracts and Scrutiny of Awards' prepared by Simon Greenberg and Loretta Malintoppi and distributed to participants at the ICC Young Arbitrators' Forum in Barcelona on 28 June 2008.

1   For ICC internal purposes, a case is 'set in motion' when the Secretariat and Court have dealt with all preliminary procedural issues and the case file is sent to the arbitral tribunal for resolution of the parties' dispute.

2   More than one third of the cases registered between 2005 and 2009 related to the construction, engineering, energy, financing and insurance industries, which normally involve highly sophisticated transactions dealing with highly technical and legal issues and involving multiple and diverse players. As to the types of contracts involved, the number of purchase and sale contracts increased from 120 in 2005 to 262 in 2009, representing 28.1% of the total number of cases registered in 2009. Construction and engineering contracts were involved in around 15% of the cases registered between 2005 and 2009. The third most common type of contracts were shareholders' and share purchase agreements, with a slight increase from 8.7% in 2005 to 9.9% in 2009.

3   Article 1(2) of the ICC Rules of Arbitration provides that '[t]he Court does not itself settle disputes. It has the function of ensuring the application of these Rules.'

4   As the Court takes its decisions on a case-by-case basis, these examples do not represent or constitute in any way precedents or have any binding character as to situations that may arise in the future with a similar fact pattern. Furthermore, the examples we provide are significantly simplified in the interests of confidentiality and concision, whereas the Court takes into account all relevant circumstances in making its decisions.

5   For the purposes of Article 4(6), the Court has interpreted the term '*same legal relationship*' in a broad sense, associating it with the notion of '*same economic transaction*'.

6   The Court does not consolidate arbitrations sua sponte. In practice, however, in cases where the Secretariat notices that two or more arbitrations could be consolidated, it will usually draw the parties' attention to this possibility. This is because consolidated arbitrations are generally more economical and efficient than separate arbitrations concerning related matters and because the latter may lead to the undesirable result of inconsistent outcomes.

7   See Article 18 of the Rules in relation to terms of reference.

8   In brief, Article 10(2) recognizes the right of multiple parties to jointly nominate a member of the arbitral tribunal if *both sides* can agree on such joint nomination. However, unless the parties have agreed on a different method, if *either side* is unable to agree on a nominee, the Court may decide to appoint all three arbitrators and select one to act as chairperson.

9   Article 6(2) of the Rules provides: 'If the Respondent does not file an Answer, as provided by Article 5, or if any party raises one or more pleas concerning the existence, validity or scope of the arbitration agreement, the Court may decide, without prejudice to the admissibility or merits of the plea or pleas that the arbitration shall proceed if it is prima facie satisfied that an arbitration agreement under the Rules may exist. […]'

10 See H.A. Grigera-Naon, 'Conclusions', *ICC Bulletin*, Special Supplement (2003) pp. 83-84, discussing the rationale for the principle that it is for the claimant to designate the parties to an arbitration.

11 A.M. Whitesell and E. Silva-Romero, 'Multiparty and Multicontract Arbitration: Recent ICC Experience', *ICC Bulletin*, Special Supplement (2003).

12 In such cases, the Court normally analyzes whether the parent company may have consented to be bound by the arbitration agreement signed by its subsidiary. For that purpose, it examines the parent company's involvement in the negotiation, performance and/or termination of the agreement containing the arbitration clause. One interesting example of this is a case in which the Court took into account the parent company's claim in a parallel ICSID arbitration relating to the sale contract.

13 The Court has decided to allow arbitrations to proceed under Article 6(2) of the Rules against non-signatory guarantors *inter alia* where: (i) the agreement containing the arbitration clause imposed obligations on the guarantor and those obligations were reiterated in the guarantee; (ii) there were elements in the file suggesting that the guarantor had participated in the negotiation and/or performance of the agreement containing the arbitration clause; (iii) the guarantee was incorporated into the agreement containing the arbitration clause; (iv) the guarantee, although constituting a separate document, specifically referred to the arbitration clause contained in the main agreement; or (v) there were supported allegations that, pursuant to the applicable law, a guarantor was bound by the arbitration clauses contained in the main agreement.

14 The Court has administered a number of cases involving insurance companies that, after having paid the beneficiary, subrogate in the insured's claim under the arbitration agreement. In these cases, the Court ordinarily considers the involvement of the insurance company in the negotiation and/or performance of the agreement as well as the actions taken by the insurer after the termination of the agreement. However, in most cases, the Court considers that the question of whether or not a subrogation is valid is a legal issue that ought to be left for the arbitral tribunal to decide.

15 The Court would normally not allow a case to proceed against an individual that contests jurisdiction unless there are elements in the file suggesting that he or she: (i) signed the contract containing the arbitration clause on his or her own behalf; (ii) assumed individual obligations under the contract; (iii) individually performed the contract; or (iv) exercised absolute control over the signatory entities. For instance, the Court has recently decided that a case could proceed against two individuals who: (i) played significant roles with respect to the transaction in question, because one of them negotiated the agreements on the basis of which the request for arbitration was filed and the other one made the final decision on the business activities of the company that signed the agreements; (ii) assumed basic obligations under one of the agreements; and (iii) fully owned and controlled the company that entered into the agreement.

16 *Sociétés BKMI et Siemens c/ Société Dutco construction*, Cour de Cassation (7 January 1992), Rev. arb. (1992) p. 470.

17 Even if the notion of cross-claims exists in many legal traditions, a direct translation of the term 'cross-claim' as such is not found in other languages or legal systems.

CHAPTER 10

CLASS ARBITRATION OUTSIDE THE UNITED-STATES: READING THE TEA LEAVES

S.I Strong[*]

1. INTRODUCTION

It has been said that class arbitration – also known as 'class action arbitration' – is a '"uniquely American" device'.[1] Certainly the procedure, which combines elements of US-style class actions (i.e., large-scale lawsuits seeking representative relief in court on behalf of hundreds to hundreds of thousands of injured parties) with arbitration, reflects a strong bias towards US conceptions of collective justice.[2]

Class arbitration has had its share of growing pains over the last 20 years, as an ever-increasing body of domestic US case law and commentary suggests, and the United States Supreme Court decision in *Stolt-Nielsen S.A. v. AnimalFeeds International Corp.* has done little to clarify the already muddy waters.[3] However, it is by no means clear that the procedure will either fade from use or remain limited to the United States. Instead, there are at least three good reasons for thinking that the device will expand beyond US borders in one form or another in the not-so-distant future.

First, the global legal community is facing an unprecedented amount of interest in issues involving large-scale group injuries. For years, this debate has focused solely on the merits of US-style class actions as compared to European-style regulatory relief. However, changed social and political circumstances, combined with the rise of new forms of legal injury, have resulted in states considering new means for providing collective redress.

Second, class arbitration is no longer limited to domestic US disputes. For example, at least three different types of international class arbitrations have already been brought in the commercial realm.[4] Collective relief has been sought in other specialized arbitral contexts as well,[5] including an international investment class arbitration filed by 195,000 Italian parties against Argentina and an arbitration filed with the Permanent Court of Arbitration under the Energy Charter Treaty by Yukos Oil Co. shareholders that could involve up to $100 billion.[6]

Third, courts, commentators and legislatures in a variety of jurisdictions have already begun to discuss the merits of allowing some form of class arbitration to develop within their borders. Though no known class arbitration has yet been seated outside the United States, there have been public indications of interest in domestic and international group arbitrations in countries as diverse as Canada, Colombia and Luxembourg. [7]

In some ways, interest in group forms of private dispute resolution makes perfect sense given the current legal and commercial reality. Large-scale cross-border disputes are one of the biggest issues facing the international legal community today,[8] and arbitration is uniquely situated to address two of the more difficult problems with respect to those kinds of claims: identifying a single forum that has jurisdiction over the entire dispute and providing relief that will be easily enforceable in one or more states. [9]

Nevertheless, some might say it is too soon to debate the expansion of class arbitration to other states, either as a matter of probability or propriety. Certainly it is true that no long-term feasibility studies have yet been conducted on class arbitration in either the domestic or international context.[10] Furthermore, existing laws regarding class arbitration are continually in flux, even in the United States, where the Supreme Court's opinion in *Stolt-Nielsen* has made the issue even more of a moving target.[11]

However, lawyers are often called upon to give advice in an uncertain world, and this is no exception. Timely consideration of the issues is particularly important in this situation both to (1) assist any state or institutional reform efforts and (2) help parties determine whether and to what extent their own actions may actually be increasing the likelihood of being brought into a class or other collective arbitration.

Though necessarily limited in scope, this paper addresses three issues relating to the possible development of class arbitration outside the United States. First, section 2 identifies some of the concerns enunciated by opponents to class arbitration so as to set the stage for further discussion. Interestingly, much of the conflict is not about arbitration per se. Instead, the debate involves larger issues – some real, some perceived – about the commercial impact of collective relief and conflicting concepts of individual rights.

Section 3 tackles one of the primary objections to class arbitration, i.e., that it is a '"uniquely American" device'. [13] Critics often appear to assume that any privatized form of collective redress will involve the class arbitration procedures currently in use in the United States. However, it is not only likely that the US approach will change over time; [14] it is also likely that different countries will develop procedures appropriate to their own national systems. Therefore, this section considers what form 'collective arbitration' – a newly coined term used to distinguish these alternative forms of group arbitration from US-style class arbitration – might take if it were to develop outside the United States.

Section 4 considers a second criticism of class arbitration, namely that it will never expand beyond the United States. Thus, this section examines the social, legal and political forces that influence the development of class and collective arbitration. Section 5 concludes the paper with some final observations about how mass claims in arbitration might be addressed in the future.

2. CONFLICTS REGARDING CLASS ARBITRATION – REAL AND PERCEIVED

Opponents to US-style class arbitration typically challenge the procedure on three fronts. Interestingly, only one line of argument involves issues relating to arbitration, with the other two debates focusing on matters that are more commonly raised when discussing collective relief in the judicial context.

Specialists in arbitration are often tempted to focus only on questions related to arbitration *per se*, both as a matter of interest and expertise. However, it has been noted that:

> *"[i]t would be a mistake […] for the international arbitration community to […] avoid discussion of these [other] issues. The participants in the international class arbitration debate will surely be informed by their long-formed, general perspectives on both arbitration and class actions, but the convergence of class actions and international arbitration does shine some new light on old questions and require a further look."* [14]

Thus, this section will outline all three areas of debate to set the stage for further discussion.

a. Economic issues

The most vocal opposition to class arbitration thus far has come from the international commercial community, which claims that US-style class actions (and thus US-style class arbitrations) are bad for business. Interestingly, this argument is to some extent based more on perception than reality. For example, empirical studies have shown that corporate actors' biggest criticism of US-style class actions – i.e., that class claimants routinely file frivolous suits to assert pressure to settle cases for enormous sums of money – is demonstrably incorrect. [15]

In some regards, however, the claims of the business community are correct. Class actions do have an effect on business practices. For example, empirical research shows that that US-style class actions 'tend to increase the frequency and breadth of litigation' against corporate defendants, which 'raises the cost of doing business and makes the legal environment more uncertain; it also has the potential to bring questionable business practices into the media spotlight. In short, the threat of litigation constrains corporations' decision-making freedom.' [16]

However, just because a law or action increases corporate costs or corporate caution does not mean that it harms or costs society as a whole. Indeed, corporations' focus on *ex post* costs of litigation alone fails to recognize the role that class actions play in a deregulated market society and the *ex ante* benefits enjoyed by these same corporations as a result of their having to meet very few regulatory requirements when entering the market.[17] Experts in the field of comparative civil procedure have noted the absence of any detailed empirical evidence regarding the complex cost-benefit analysis of a private system of relief for collective harm (i.e., various forms of private litigation, including class action suits) and a public system (i.e., a comprehensive regulatory regime). [18]

Given the lack of relevant economic data in this area, this paper will move on to the next subject of discussion. However, it is useful to recognize from the outset that the empirical research does not necessarily support that proposition that US-style class suits are inevitably bad for business and thus bad for society. In the absence of any hard data, it would therefore be improper to dismiss class or collective arbitration out of hand as economically unfeasible. This conclusion seems particularly appropriate given that some of the greatest proponents of arguments against class arbitration are those whose financial self-interest augurs against the device.

b. Jurisprudential issues

The second argument against class arbitration involves the long-standing debate about the legitimacy of collective relief, particularly US-style representative relief. Traditionally, civil law jurisdictions have refused to create collective forms of action due to jurisprudential concerns about the nature of individual rights. These states have often used regulatory mechanisms to address the same types of social ills that the United States addresses through litigation brought by 'private attorneys general'.

Experts continue to debate whether private (i.e., judicial) enforcement of public rules, including the recovery of individual damages, is a more 'efficient institutional choice' than government regulation.[19] The approach used in the United States is often set in contradistinction to that used in Europe. However, this black and white, either-or dichotomy ignores the fact that both the US and European models are changing to adapt to new legal and social circumstances. Furthermore, this sort of binary thinking ignores the wide (and growing) diversity of other means of addressing group injuries, which are discussed in more detail below.[20]

Critically, a society's perspective on the nature of individual rights is affected by the public regulatory structure and *vice versa*. Comprehensive regulation allows and leads to restrictive interpretations of individual rights regarding collective relief. Broadly deregulated societies have much more permissive interpretations of individual rights. States that adopt mixed or intermediary positions on regulation – and their number is growing, according to recent empirical research [21]– take an equally moderate view of the scope of individual rights to collective relief.

In all cases, policy choices are based on states' perception of how best to address legal injuries suffered within their territorial borders. These developments will likely affect official state views about the propriety of various forms of collective arbitration as well as the views of private individuals.

c. Arbitral issues

The final argument against class arbitration invokes basic notions of what arbitration is or is not meant to be. Arbitration is routinely described as a relatively informal, inexpensive, business-oriented dispute resolution mechanism. International arbitration carries the additional benefit of being able to meld civil law and common law procedures into a cohesive whole. Class arbitration is viewed by its opponents as expensive, time-consuming, legalistic and closely tied to US civil procedure. Furthermore, the representative nature of US-style class arbitrations violates many people's views about the consensual nature of arbitration. As such, class arbitration is thought by some people not to constitute 'arbitration' at all. [22]

Interestingly, the tension in this area may perhaps arise out of several important historical shifts in the international arbitral community. First, it has been said that, ever since the mid-1980s, the world of international commercial arbitration has been in the process of changing from 'an older system of private informal justice controlled by senior European law professors and judges into a more legalistic form of dispute resolution resembling US style litigation.'[23] The perceived 'Americanization' of international commercial arbitration has led to the spread of 'certain norms, ideas and principles that Anglo-American law expresses', much to some people's dismay.[24] Thus, to some extent, concern about US-style class arbitration may reflect resistance to American commercial imperialism and a real or imagined loss of control over the proper shape of arbitration.

Second, opposition to class arbitration may partially reflect a yearning for 'the good old days' of arbitration, when procedures were allegedly simple, informal and inexpensive. This type of sentiment has been expressed in other mature forms of arbitration.[25] However, like other forms of nostalgia, this view may not be factually correct (arbitration may never have been a truly inexpensive form of dispute resolution) or may draw incorrect conclusions regarding causality.

For example, some may believe that increased legalism in international commercial arbitration was brought about by Americans intent on bringing their domestic litigation techniques into the arbitral context. However, it could also be that arbitrations became more legalistic because international disputes became more complicated at the same time that US parties were becoming more inclined to participate in international arbitration. Certainly, it is well established that there has been an increase in the number of international disputes involving the complex interweaving of multiple contracts between two or more parties and requiring more sophisticated adjudication.[26] These types of transactions are markedly different from the simple bilateral agreements of years past. Thus, to the extent that an arbitral 'paradise' ever existed, it was likely as much a reflection of the types of disputes that were at issue as it was due to the absence or presence of certain parties.

Regardless of which view one holds regarding the reason for the changes in the field, it is impossible to return to arbitration's 'golden age'. One cannot undo the changes that have been made over time, and the concept of class or collective arbitration is here to stay.[27] Evolution, however, is neither bad nor good. The only question is how the relevant communities – commercial, legal and arbitral – will respond to this new challenge.

3. POSSIBLE FORMS OF ARBITRATION-BASED COLLECTIVE RELIEF OUTSIDE THE UNITED STATES

a. Alternative forms of collective arbitration

For years, US judicial class actions appeared to be a particularly virulent form of American exceptionalism. The procedure was maligned, domestically and internationally, for a variety of reasons: abusive discovery practices, outrageous punitive damages awards and entrepreneurial counsel seeking quick settlements based on the suit's nuisance value. However, much of the international criticism focused on the belief that the United States was the only nation in the world that allowed private individuals to use widespread representative litigation to address group or collective injuries.[28]

However, recent empirical research demonstrates that US-style class actions are not as unusual as once believed.[29] Although the broad, trans-substantive approach used in the United States may reflect one end of the spectrum, several other legal systems – including Canada and Australia – have adopted judicial forms of collective relief that are markedly similar to that used in the United States.[30] For this reason, the author has suggested elsewhere that these two nations might be among the first to develop their own forms of class arbitration.[31]

However, Canada and Australia are not the only nations to allow collective relief. As group injuries increase, so, too, has the need to provide for collective redress. Therefore, the global legal community has seen rising interest in 'any procedure (public, private, self-regulatory, or even impromptu) that achieves resolution of a collective problem'.[32] At least 15 countries (in addition to

Australia, Canada and the United States) have legislatively adopted some form of collective redress, with additional nations and regions considering the possibility.[33] Furthermore, some states have embraced judicially developed forms of collective relief in the absence of any formal statutory procedures.[34]

This development is important, because the form of US-style class arbitration reflects the national biases and predilections of its country of origin. In short, the early users of class arbitration adopted procedures that were familiar to them.[35] Indeed, two of the three published rules regarding class arbitration were based explicitly on the class action provisions of the US Federal Rules of Civil Procedure,[36] so as to avoid problems with procedural fairness and take advantage of a large body of case law interpreting the relevant language and legal principles.[37]

If history repeats itself, then it is entirely possible that different states may develop their own unique forms of collective arbitration for domestic disputes using procedures that resemble their own judicial models of collective relief. Indeed, that process may have already begun. For example, both Canada and Colombia, two nations that have enacted legislation permitting collective relief in judicial contexts, appear to have come close to adopting their own domestic forms of collective arbitration.

Thus, in *Valencia v. Bancolombia*, a tribunal based in Bogotá, Colombia, was faced with a class suit initiated by shareholders following the merger of two financial entities.[38] Although the claim was initially filed in court, both the civil circuit judge and the District Superior Court held that they had no jurisdiction over the matter, given the existence of an arbitration agreement in the by-laws of one of the financial entities. The plaintiffs argued that class actions in Colombia are subject to the exclusive jurisdiction of the court, but the Supreme Court of Justice rejected that argument on the grounds that the arbitration agreement did not limit the types of claims that could be submitted to arbitration and thus did not exclude class arbitrations as a matter of law. Furthermore, the Supreme Court held that arbitrators have the same duties and powers as a court and thus have the competence to resolve class claims. Although the Supreme Court did not go so far as to say that class arbitrations are permitted in Colombia in all circumstances, it did appear to state that the arbitrator could find that the existence of an arbitration agreement in a common shareholder agreement could give rise to a collective claim.

Similar circumstances have arisen in Canada. Several different Canadian courts appear to have come close to ruling on the availability of class arbitration, based on domestic Canadian class action legislation, although subsequent legislation in several of the relevant provinces has created some question about the continuing effect of the judicial opinions.[39] Nevertheless, the methods used by the Canadian courts suggest that the development of class arbitration outside the United States will not require reliance on the existence or use of specialized rules on class arbitration or on analogies to US arbitral or judicial procedures. Instead, the analysis will proceed on the basis of domestic legislation and policies.

It is impossible for this paper to discuss all the various forms of collective redress used throughout the world. Each system has its own individual quirks, even among European nations that are responding to European directives ostensibly intended to harmonize national procedures.[40] Furthermore, the situation is in a constant state of flux, given that states have a tendency to expand their ability to provide collective relief once even limited judicial procedures are established.[41] Nevertheless, there are certain trends that might suggest several ways in which collective arbitration might develop outside the United States.

i. Representative relief

The first type of collective redress involves private representative claims for mass injuries. There appears to be an increase in the number of states around the world that offer some form of representative relief for group or collective injuries. Recent studies suggest that approximately half of the legal systems that have adopted a form of representative relief use a trans-substantive model, which is a purely procedural device that is available regardless of the type of substantive claim made. (This is the approach used in the United States.) The remaining states restrict the ability to bring a claim for representative relief to certain limited subject matter areas, such as securities, antitrust (competition), consumer or public law. In these situations, the right to collective action is typically contained in the provisions of the substantive law rather than the code of civil procedure, as is true with the trans-substantive model.[42]

Notably, the representative nature of US class arbitrations has created a number of conceptual problems for those who subscribe to a view of arbitration that requires the parties' explicit consent not only to arbitration of the dispute but to the procedure to be used in the arbitration. A similar debate may arise in other jurisdictions that consider permitting representative claims to be brought in arbitration, at least to the extent such actions are opt-out rather than opt-in.

Other variations exist regarding the type and scope of representative relief to be provided. For example, some states that have recently developed a right to representative relief do not give the right to pursue such claims to private individuals, as is the case in the United States. Instead, these jurisdictions require such claims to be brought by an intermediary entity, such as a trade association, governmental agency or public interest group, which is entitled to seek collective relief on behalf of all injured individuals.

Notably, if an intermediary entity were to bring a claim, many of the existing concerns regarding US-style class arbitration – including issues about notice to the group, opting in versus opting out of the action and the *res judicata* effect of an award – would be eliminated. Furthermore, only allowing intermediary entities to bring claims for representative relief would avoid many of the problems typically associated with multiparty arbitration, such as procedures for naming arbitrators and ensuring the confidentiality and privacy of the proceedings.

Finally, some states have limited the right to representative relief by only allowing injunctive relief (rather than individual damages) to be sought for collective harms. Using this type of approach in collective arbitration would seem unproblematic, given that 'arbitral awards frequently – even routinely – make awards of declaratory or injunctive relief.'[43]

ii. Aggregate relief

Representative relief is not the only means of addressing large-scale group harms. Some countries have decided to deal with collective injuries through judicial aggregation of claims. Two examples of aggregate mechanisms are the group litigation order procedure used in England and the multi-district litigation procedure used in the United States.[44] The English approach involves the creation of a registry of individual claims that arise out of the same fact pattern. These claims are then assigned to the same judge for management purposes. The US approach involves the collection of related claims from different federal districts and the consolidation of those claims during the pre-trial period to ensure efficiencies of scale. However, the cases are subsequently separated for individual trials on liability and/or damages.

Aggregation of claims is relatively uncontroversial in the judicial context, and many states simply apply their pre-existing procedural rules regarding joinder, intervention or consolidation when addressing the needs of mass injuries. However, consolidation, joinder and intervention are nowhere near as simple in arbitration. As with any multiparty procedure, problems may arise if the parties do not all consent to consolidation or aggregation.[45] However, use of a voluntary system of registration (similar to that used with English group litigation orders or certain mass dispute systems set up by the Permanent Court of Arbitration (PCA)) would eliminate virtually all of those concerns.

Once the question of consent has been addressed, the parties need to address procedural matters. Fortunately, those considering large-scale aggregate relief in the arbitral context would likely be able to proceed under existing laws and rules regarding consolidation of arbitrations. Arbitration is equipped to handle large-scale consolidation of claims (such as those involving more than 100 parties)[46] as well as mass claims heard through the creation of special tribunals and commissions, such as those set up through the PCA.[47]

iii. Settlement relief

Finally, collective arbitration could take advantage of recent and proposed legislation that encourages or promotes the settlement of mass claims. Perhaps the most innovative developments in this area come from the Netherlands, which permits parties to a mass dispute to subject a settlement agreement to court approval.[48] Interestingly and somewhat controversially, the Dutch procedure uses an opt-out approach. However, an opt-out procedure can be seen to increase defendants' inclination to sign onto the agreement, since it is often in a defendant's interest to have a broad class for settlement purposes.

Parties might attempt to transform this technique into an arbitral option in situations where Dutch courts do not have jurisdiction or where the parties wish to keep the terms of the settlement itself private. Of course, privacy in mass disputes may not be possible or desirable. For example, some publicity is necessary, particularly in an opt-out regime, so as to ensure the proper identification of the collective. Furthermore, states may need or want to have some public knowledge of the terms or existence of the settlement, either as a deterrent to other potential defendants or as a soft form of precedent.[49]

Parties wishing to adapt this procedure should be cautious, however. In particular, they should take care when attempting to create a collective for arbitral settlement purposes alone. Although some institutional rules appear to allow parties to transform a settlement agreement into an arbitral award,[50] and numerous arbitral rules and arbitration laws permit the entry of a consent award in situations where the parties settle their dispute during the pendency of an arbitration, there are concerns about whether an arbitral award based on a settlement agreement is internationally enforceable if there is not a pre-existing arbitration agreement.[51]

b. Creating or adapting procedures for collective arbitration

i. Reliance on judicial procedures

As the preceding discussion demonstrates, US class actions are not the only form of collective redress available in state courts. Thus, there is no need to conclude that US-style class arbitrations are or should be the only form of collective redress available in arbitration.

In describing the various forms of collective relief now available in courts around the world, this paper is not suggesting that arbitral institutions or individual arbitrators seeking to design new forms of collective arbitration should precisely duplicate existing judicial procedures. Indeed, the international arbitral community has worked long and hard to disabuse newcomers to the process of the notion that they are entitled to the same procedures that would be available in litigation. Furthermore, several critics of class arbitration have noted that the decision for specialized rules on class arbitration to track US civil procedure was 'uninspired and superficial'[52] and that class arbitration would benefit from the implementation of 'innovative procedures that courts have been hesitant to accept'.[53]

However, to the extent that arbitration is considered 'a substitute for State justice, albeit of a private nature, but nevertheless pursuing the same ends', then an arbitrator or arbitral institution may decide that some aspects of arbitral procedure could or should be similar to those used in national courts.[54] Furthermore, those who are designing new arbitral procedures may decide that reflecting certain judicial procedures is a wise course of action, so as to benefit from any judicial opinions or commentary construing certain legal principles or questions of procedure.

Even more to the point, any developments in arbitral procedure – collective or otherwise – should not outpace fundamental principles embodied in the relevant legal systems, lest the resulting arbitral awards be subject to claims that the arbitration in question violates public policy or procedural fairness.[55] For this reason, it will be easier for new forms of collective arbitration to develop domestically, as this will not only allow them to reflect the principles of the arbitral seat but will also ensure that the necessary legal structures are in place to support the arbitral award after it has been issued.

It may be more difficult to come to agreement on procedures for cross-border group arbitrations unless the parties are from states that share a common understanding about the propriety of collective relief. Thus, a group arbitration that involved parties from the United States, Canada and/or Australia might be relatively easy to set up and enforce, since these three states share a common understanding regarding the availability and form of representative relief.[56] A group arbitration involving parties from one of those states and Germany might be more problematic, since German law only allows intermediary entities to bring a collective claim in a limited area of law and only permits injunctive relief in response to a group action.[57] Despite these difficulties, however, it is important that the international arbitral community consider some cross-border issues, since international class arbitrations already exist.

ii. Methods for creating new forms of collective arbitration

The next issue to consider is how these new forms of collective arbitration might develop. One possibility is that an official body, such as a domestic or international arbitral organization, will decide to amend existing arbitral rules, or create a new set of specialized rules to outline the procedures used in collective proceedings, and will convene a working group to make the necessary recommendations to the institution. That is the approach taken by several arbitral organizations in the United States following the United States Supreme Court's 2003 decision in *Green Tree Financial Corp. v. Bazzle*,[58] which gave national prominence to class arbitration as a dispute resolution device.

The other, perhaps more likely, possibility is that the issue will arise on an *ad hoc* basis as individual cases arise. Indeed, individual courts and arbitral tribunals outside the United States are already being asked to consider the ability of parties to proceed as a collective in arbitration, based on the existence of a valid arbitration agreement and the purported need to bring the claims in a single action.[59] This is analogous to the situation in the United States in the 20 years prior to *Bazzle*.[60]

Those who are asked to consider whether a collective arbitration can proceed in a particular set of circumstances must answer several key questions. The first is whether collective forms of relief are even allowed in the situation at hand. For example, a growing number of corporate entities – in the United States and elsewhere – have attempted to forestall the possibility of being named as a defendant in a group action by inserting a waiver of any collective relief in the arbitration agreement itself. Furthermore, the governing substantive law may prohibit parties from attempting to arbitrate these particular claims. [61]

States are well within their rights to declare certain substantive matters of law non-arbitrable, so the second of these restrictions is unremarkable. On its face, the ability of parties to prohibit certain arbitral procedures also seems straightforward, so long as basic notions of procedural fairness remain in place. However, some forms of collective redress serve both a public and private purpose. In these cases, prohibitions on class or collective arbitration could be viewed as analogous to a party's attempt to circumvent a mandatory provision of substantive law. Indeed, some US courts have struck express waivers of class proceedings as violative of substantive rights.[62] It may be that other countries develop similar policies regarding attempted exclusions of collective relief.

If there is no explicit bar to collective arbitration (or if an explicit bar has been struck as inappropriate), it then becomes necessary to decide whether it is possible for the parties to proceed as a group. It is commonly agreed that arbitral tribunals decide matters of procedure, and judicial opinions in the United States and elsewhere suggest that this approach will be followed in collective arbitrations as well. [63]

Sometimes, the parties can come to an agreement about the collective procedures to be used. In most cases, however, the arbitration agreement will be silent as to the possibility of a collective procedure, and at least one party (typically the defendant) will object, claiming that individual arbitrations are all that should be permitted. In these situations, the question will be whether ordering the parties to proceed collectively is within the scope of the tribunal's discretion and authority. [64]

This paper will now turn to the confluence of policies and principles that affects an arbitral tribunal's willingness to even consider creating a procedure to hear collective claims. These factors will not only affect the shape of the procedure to be used but will likely determine whether the arbitral tribunal decides that it has sufficient discretion to order a collective proceeding.

4. FORCES INFLUENCING THE DEVELOPMENT OF COLLECTIVE ARBITRATION

a. Forces driving the development of class or collective arbitration

Earlier, this paper noted that the international business community is united in its opposition to class proceedings, be they in court or in arbitration. It is somewhat ironic, then, that class arbitration in the United States developed as the direct result of corporate defendants' own efforts.[65] If international commercial actors have been advised to take similar steps to avoid being named as defendants in class or collective proceedings, they should take note that they may actually be contributing to the possible rise of collective arbitration in their home jurisdictions.

Class arbitration in the United States arose after corporate entities who were concerned about being named as defendants in judicial class actions began including arbitration provisions in their contracts so as to force individual claimants to pursue relief in arbitration.[66] As anticipated, the arbitration agreements were upheld pursuant to the strong pro-arbitration policy reflected in the US Federal Arbitration Act. However, it soon became apparent that individual arbitrations did not give full effect to the overriding policy concerns reflected in many of the substantive laws at issue. In particular, it became clear that holders of small-value claims would be unlikely to proceed individually in arbitration and that to require them to do so would result in a breach of their statutory rights.[67] Though many of these issues arose in the context of consumer arbitration, the need (under US law) to proceed as a class is not limited to that area of law.[68]

The failure to pursue individual claims injures more than individual claimants. Rather than create a broad regulatory scheme, the United States has chosen to give private litigants the right and the power to enforce many public laws. When that mechanism fails to operate as intended, society as a whole suffers. Not only are the costs borne by the wrong parties (i.e., the victims rather than the wrongdoers), but deterrence of risky behaviour drops when defendants realize that they will not be made fully liable for their actions.

Thus, when deciding whether to permit class arbitration, US courts and arbitrators had to weigh the relative merits of a broad policy in favour of arbitration against the policies underlying the individual legal claims at issue. Rather than choose one policy over the other, the initiators of class arbitration chose to fulfil both simultaneously.

Critically, it was apparent in all cases that the parties had clearly agreed to arbitrate their disputes, even if they had not necessarily contemplated the form of the procedure to be used.[69] However, the only way that the parties' agreement to arbitrate could be given effect was to permit the claimants to proceed as a class.

This approach describes the 'principle of effective interpretation', which is often used in arbitrations involving pathological clauses. In these situations, the arbitral tribunal adopts the procedure that is most likely to 'establish an effective machinery for the settlement of disputes covered by the arbitration clause'.[70] To the extent that collective redress constitutes not only 'effective' but necessary machinery to resolve certain disputes, arbitrators would appear to have authority to order such proceedings. [71]

Thus, the development of class arbitration in the US required both a strong bias in favour of arbitration as well as the need to provide collective relief to give full effect to the aims of the substantive law. In the United States, this also involved the absence of regulatory mechanisms that could provide alternative means of addressing the public and private injuries suffered. The following sections will discuss whether and to what extent these policies exist in other jurisdictions.

b. Arbitral policy

The first question to be addressed is whether it is necessary that the jurisdiction in question be as staunchly pro-arbitration as the United States, which has been said to favour arbitration perhaps more than any other nation in the world.[72] Certainly, any hostility to arbitration in general on behalf of the national courts or legislature would be fatal to the development of a novel form of arbitration, but there are varying degrees of commitment to arbitration.

Unfortunately, it is difficult to identify any objective standards for evaluating the extent to which any particular jurisdiction supports arbitration. Some attempt to measure global support for arbitration has been made by reference to the increased number of proceedings heard internationally or to the wide adoption of the Model Arbitration Law (MAL), which is said to have an inherently pro-arbitration bias.[73] Others would point to the inconsistent manner in which the MAL is interpreted and applied in different jurisdictions or to the potentially suspect laws or practices in the many countries that have not adopted the MAL as evidence that anti-arbitration sentiments still remain.

However, it may be that the different interpretations of the MAL and other national legislation do not necessarily reflect varying levels of commitment to arbitration. Instead, these variations may demonstrate the range of ways in which individual countries rationalize their support of arbitration. Thus, for example, it has been said that:

> *"[d]ifferent competing theories have been advanced about the nature and legitimacy of arbitration [...]. These differences of opinion over the theoretical basis for arbitration and the nature and legitimacy of the arbitral process, are important because the way in which [...] arbitration is characterized affects the manner in which the extent and scope of applicable rules in arbitration are determined."* [74]

This suggests that asking whether a jurisdiction is 'committed' to arbitration may not be the right question when considering the possible expansion of collective arbitration. Instead, the focus should be on what theoretical approach is used by the entity (arbitral tribunal, arbitral institution, court or legislature) that is considering the use or development of collective arbitration.

Four different theories have been advanced to describe a nation's rationale for arbitration. The first emphasizes arbitration's contractual nature and gives a great deal of weight to the parties' intentions and expressed wishes regarding procedure. Those who embrace this tradition may find it difficult or impossible to craft a collective procedure absent the explicit consent of all parties.

Interestingly, adherents of the contractual theory of arbitration can be found even in nations like the United States, where arbitration is strongly favoured as a matter of public policy.[75] Indeed, this appears to be the view taken by the majority in the recent decision in *Stolt-Nielsen*.[76]

The strict contractual approach has been criticized both for failing to recognize that national courts need to maintain some control over arbitral proceedings to ensure procedural fairness and for failing to recognize arbitrators' need and ability to exercise discretion in procedural matters.[77] These problems inspired the rise of the jurisdictional theory of arbitration, which emphasizes the power of the state to regulate arbitrations seated within its borders. However, this view of arbitration has proven problematic because it fails to give proper precedence to party autonomy and is now largely discounted. [78]

The third approach to arbitration combines the best elements of the contractual and jurisdictional models, charting a middle course between the two extremes. Known as the hybrid theory, adherents of this view of arbitration recognize the role of party autonomy and consent while simultaneously noting the role of national courts in supporting and controlling the outer bounds of the arbitral procedure.[79]

Though popular with many in the international arbitral community, this approach lacks the simplicity of an all-or-nothing mindset and requires adherents to explain why party autonomy should be respected in one circumstance but not another. Nevertheless, the hybrid theory provides a useful description of the rationale underlying the development of class arbitration in the United States, since this theory permits courts, legislatures, arbitrators and arbitral institutions to adopt a more nuanced view of what constitutes consent in situations where the agreement is silent or ambiguous as to certain proposed arbitral procedures.[80] Interestingly, this theory of arbitration has won adherents outside the United States as well.[81]

The fourth theory of arbitration – termed the autonomous theory – could also be used to rationalize the US approach to class arbitration. This technique:

> *"looks beyond contextualizing arbitration within the existing legal framework and instead, focuses on the need of the transnational business community for a private and flexible means of resolving disputes. Its proponents suggest that it is important to look beyond the structure of the arbitral institution and the emphasis on either the contractual or jurisdictional nature of arbitration and instead focus on its goals, objectives and methodology."* [82]

In some ways, this approach hearkens back to the flexible, business-friendly model that is heralded as marking the golden age of arbitration. Furthermore, the autonomous theory could be said simply to reflect a more detailed description of the principle of effective interpretation. While it is true that a robust reading of the autonomous theory may permit a higher degree of procedural formalism than is commonly associated with proceedings held during arbitration's heyday, it can be said that the complex needs of contemporary commercial interests often require similarly sophisticated dispute resolution devices.[83]

Because the autonomous theory looks beyond traditional arbitral structures and strict contractual or jurisdictional interpretations of arbitration, it seems well suited to the development of collective arbitration outside the United States. This conclusion is further supported by the theory's emphasis on flexibility and the need to focus on arbitration's goals and objectives. Thus, those who adhere to this theory of arbitration would likely be amenable to the development of collective arbitration, if other circumstances were right.

No single theory has won universal acclaim, and no known research has identified which states have adopted one theory of arbitration over another.[84] Furthermore, the domestic US response to class arbitrations suggests that there will be different individuals who prefer different approaches even within one national system.[85]

Thus, the possible expansion and development of any form of collective arbitration will likely result in lively debate, both within and between jurisdictions. Those persons who adhere to one of the first two theories of arbitration will be unlikely to embrace the development of collective arbitration, while those who support one of the latter two theories may be more likely to do so. However, the adoption of collective arbitration in any particular situation needs more than just an openness to new arbitral procedures, as discussed in the next section.

c. Policies regarding collective relief

i. Constituent elements

Previously, this paper suggested that the development of class arbitration in the United States relied heavily on the need to give full effect to the aims of the substantive law, typically in the absence of any regulatory mechanisms that could fulfil the same duties. This suggests that new forms of collective arbitration will likely only arise in states or situations where there is not an adequate remedy for the individual and group injuries outside of collective arbitration.

Traditionally, those states with strong regulatory regimes have opposed representative or group relief in court, claiming, among other things, that US class actions and similar procedures are an abuse of individual rights. Partially this is a jurisprudential concern, in that these states have a different view of the content of various rights, and partially this is a pragmatic concern, in that these states have addressed the societal ills through regulatory mechanisms. In other words, there is no need for mass judicial relief in these highly regulated societies.

Thus, the central inquiry should be whether the legal system available to the claimant(s) addresses the injury that is the subject of the purported collective arbitration through one means or another. It may be that states with strong regulatory regimes do not and will not need to develop a form of collective arbitration for domestic disputes, thus answering the pragmatic question.[86] Furthermore, states that fall into this category are most likely to view the concept of individual rights in such a way as to prohibit the use of any collective devices.

However, not every jurisdiction has a suitably comprehensive regulatory scheme. Even those countries with strong traditions of public regulation are supplementing those systems with limited forms of private relief in the judicial context. As these states' legal structures change, so, too, do their philosophical conceptions of individual rights and their ability to address structural issues, such as the res judicata effect of judgments for mass injuries.

Even more importantly, this change in the availability of private redress for group harms demonstrates a recognition on the part of the state that regulation alone does not cure this particular injury. Instead, there is a need – limited, perhaps, but still identifiable – for this type of private cause of action.

These influences are primarily experienced at the domestic level. However, the rising incidence of cross-border injuries suggests the need to develop an internationally acceptable form of collective arbitration, for all the reasons that are traditionally associated with international commercial arbitration. For example, arbitration has the ability to avoid any biases exhibited by national courts, to create a more flexible procedure suitable to parties from different legal cultures and to permit predictable enforcement of arbitral awards. Furthermore, international class arbitrations have already begun to arise.

ii. Practical analyses

In anticipating what might be done in the future, it is useful to see how courts and arbitral tribunals that have contemplated the possibility of collective arbitral relief in the past have proceeded. Notably, many follow a similar pattern of analysis.

First, the court or arbitral panel considers whether the right to collective relief is procedural or substantive. If the right is merely procedural, then the parties may have waived their ability to proceed collectively, either through an express provision in the arbitration agreement or simply by choosing to proceed in arbitration. [87]

Interestingly, those nations that have made the most cautious inroads towards collective relief in state court by only providing for collective redress in specific provisions in specific statutes involving certain substantive areas of law may be most at risk of having those rights construed as substantive rather than procedural, since the injury and the remedy are combined in the same enactment. Nations that take a broader, trans-substantive approach to collective rights might find that the right to proceed as a group is considered 'merely' procedural, since the right is located in a code of civil procedure rather than in the substantive law. However, the United States has overcome that problem by finding that the only way to vindicate certain statutorily protected rights is to permit collective relief.[88] Other states may take a similar view, allowing a purported procedural right to be transformed into a substantive right.

Next, the court or arbitral tribunal needs to consider the different ways in which the goal of the substantive law can be fulfilled. It may be that the procedures relating to collective relief are proscribed (either in the substantive law itself or in the code of civil procedure) by only allowing certain entities to pursue claims on behalf of the group or by only permitting injunctive relief. Such provisions might suggest only a limited need for collective relief. In these cases, it may be that the combination of individual arbitration plus regulatory protections could be sufficient both to compensate victims and to deter future wrongdoing.[89] Alternatively, it may be that the aims of regulatory relief are different from those associated with group relief and that collective redress, even in arbitration, is still necessary.[90]

The best analyses would not only take into account the apparent aims of the substantive law but also any underlying legal realities, including whether holders of small value claims will proceed in arbitration.[91] Although this issue may arise most frequently in consumer arbitration, it can be found in other areas of law as well. In any case, it is important to conduct an independent analysis of these issues in each case. Collective arbitrations can cover a wide range of subject matter areas, and each field of law will likely have its own unique concerns.

Although collective relief in courts need not be coextensive with collective relief in arbitration, the fact that a state has considered it necessary or at least useful to develop even a limited form of collective judicial redress suggests that the regulatory scheme is not enough to protect individuals and society at large. Although this view might increase the likelihood that collective arbitration would develop outside the United States, this expansive principle is offset by the fact that the court or arbitral tribunal should look at the type and scope of relief provided in state courts before deciding the type and scope of relief to be provided in arbitration.

There are two reasons this makes good sense. First, it puts the focus on whether collective arbitration is needed to vindicate the statutory rights of the claimant(s). Development of a new procedural form of relief is not something that should be done by whim. However, under either the hybrid or autonomous theory of arbitration, it is something that may be done as a matter of necessity, in accordance with the principle of effective interpretation and consistent with the larger commercial and legal context.

Second, consideration of the scope and type of relief available in the courts helps ensure that the form of collective arbitration to be developed keeps pace with that state's jurisprudential approach to individual rights and with the overall regulatory regime. Expanding collective relief in arbitration beyond what is necessary and beyond what is permitted in the state courts can lead to difficulties; however, an unduly narrow approach to the development of these types of procedures can allow individual defendants to upset the state's regulatory regime by fleeing to arbitration. That, certainly, was never the intent or purpose of arbitration.[92]

Relying on a strict statutory analysis of needs, goals and available remedies does not elevate judicial forms of relief over arbitral forms, or *vice versa*. Instead, this analytical approach reflects the view that arbitration and litigation are equally competent in vindicating the rights of parties.

It should be noted in passing that the policies regarding collective relief in arbitration do not necessarily mirror the policies regarding what might now be considered more 'traditional' forms of multiparty and multicontract arbitration (i.e., those typically involving three to five parties). For example, Julian Lew has suggested that multiparty arbitration should proceed when to do so would encourage procedural economy, avoid inconsistent awards, increase fairness by facilitating fact-finding and presentation of legal and factual arguments, address any confidentiality concerns and uphold the equal ability to choose arbitrators.[93]

Although these policies would support the use of collective arbitration, these issues were not considered as central to the question of whether to develop class arbitration in the United States. In particular, collective arbitration does not rely on the need to create an efficient mechanism to resolve the parties' dispute, at least not in the way the term is commonly understood.[94] Thus, it is suggested, these rationales need not be central to the development of other forms of collective arbitration. Instead, the question should be whether the relief sought in this particular arbitration can only be realistically provided through collective action.

5. CONCLUSION

The rise of class arbitration in the United States has been highly controversial, both inside and outside the United States, and many people do not want to see this particular procedural device expand to other countries. However, it is impossible to put the genie back into the bottle once it has escaped, and the better course of action may be to adapt the device to better suit parties and societies outside the United States.

Although this paper takes no view on whether collective arbitration is necessary or merited in any particular circumstance or jurisdiction, it does take the view that the development of one or more forms of collective arbitration outside the United States is likely, given recent interest in new forms of collective relief, both judicial and arbitral, in a variety of states, including those that have traditionally shunned such mechanisms. Therefore, the discussion in this paper has focused on what those alternative procedures might look like and what forces might drive a particular jurisdiction to adopt such measures.

One topic that has not been discussed is whether class or collective proceedings in arbitration are preferable to similar proceedings in court. Some commentators have suggested that 'opposing parties [...] may not necessarily be at odds concerning the desirability of resolving a class action in arbitration rather than litigation',[95] and certainly there are many issues to consider, since each procedure has its advantages and disadvantages. For example, arbitration may not require the same kind of heightened pleading that could lead to successful motions to dismiss in court, but proceeding in arbitration may allow for more limited discovery. Similarly, the unavailability of appellate review in arbitration may be problematic, but concerns about errors in liability or damages determinations may be offset by the absence of juries in the trial phase. Certain commercial realities may be such that no local court will have jurisdiction over all injured parties, meaning that a cross-border group arbitration is the only mechanism for effectively dealing with the claims. However, opponents to class and collective arbitration can identify an equally long list of reasons why such procedures are logistically, economically or jurisprudentially problematic[96]. Therefore, that debate is best left until another day.

The limited nature of this paper has required a focus on generalities rather than specifics. However, the discussion is useful to the extent that it helps shape the debate about whether and to what extent collective arbitration is necessary in any particular circumstance. It also demonstrates that the tools for creating such a device – i.e., an expansive theory of arbitration and a legal structure that contemplates the possibility of some form of collective relief in state courts – already exist in many jurisdictions. Whether this is good or bad is somewhat in the eye of the beholder. However, regardless of one's views on the propriety of class or collective arbitration, it is certain that the coming years will bring some very interesting developments.

END NOTES

* Ph.D. (law), University of Cambridge; D.Phil., University of Oxford; J.D., Duke University; M.P.W., University of Southern California; B.A., University of California, Davis. The author, who is admitted to practice as an attorney in New York and Illinois and as a solicitor in England and Wales, is Associate Professor of Law at the University of Missouri and Senior Fellow at the Center for the Study of Dispute Resolution.

1   'The President and Fellows of Harvard College Against JSC Surgutneftegaz', *PLI/Litigation* 770 (2008) p. 127.

2   This paper will not outline those procedures, though further reading is available. See, e.g., Gary W. Jackson, 'Prosecuting Class Actions in Arbitration', *Annotated 2006 Association of Trial Lawyers of America* CLE 1 (2005) p. 829. It is also possible that procedures will change in the wake of recent U.S. Supreme Court decisions, including *Stolt-Nielsen*. See *Stolt-Nielsen S.A. v. AnimalFeeds Int'l Corp.*, 130 S.Ct. 1758 (2010); see also *In re American Express Merchants' Litigation* 554 F.3d 300 (2d Cir. 2009), *vacated and remanded sub nom. American Express Co. v. Italian Colors Restaurant*, 78 U.S.L.W. 3642 (2010).

3   *Stolt-Nielsen S.A. v. AnimalFeeds Int'l Corp.*, 130 S.Ct. 1758 (2010). Although *Stolt*-Nielsen purports to limit the availability of class arbitration in cases where the arbitration agreement is silent as to group treatment, closer reading of the decision demonstrates the narrowness of the opinion and the likelihood of further litigation on a variety of outstanding issues. See S.I. Strong, Guest Post, 'Stolt-Nielsen Opens More Doors Than It Closes', available at: <http://www.karlbayer.com/blog/?p=8880>.

4   These include: (1) class arbitrations that include at least one defendant from a country other than the seat of the arbitration; (2) class arbitrations that involve defendants that may be based in the arbitral forum but that also hold significant foreign assets, which may be relied upon at the enforcement stage; and (3) class arbitrations that include claimants from outside the arbitral seat.

5   See, e.g., *Sheibani v. United States*, 1 Iran-US Claims Tribunal Reporter 946, para 2 (2003); Howard Holtzmann and Edda Kristjánsdóttir (eds.), *International Mass Claims Processes: Legal and Practical Perspectives* (2007); Scott Armstrong Spence, 'Organizing an Arbitration Involving an International Organization and Multiple Private Parties: The Example of the Bank for International Settlements Arbitration', *Journal of International Arbitration 21* (2004) p. 316.

6   *Beccara v. Argentine Republic*, ICSID case No. ARB/07/5, *Investment Treaty News*, 27 April 2007; Mariel Dimsey, *The Resolution of International Investment Disputes: Challenges and Solutions* (2008) pp. 203-218 (describing a second possible group investment arbitration); Veijo Heiskanen, 'Arbitrating Mass Investor Claims: Lessons of International Claims Commissions', *Multiple Party Actions in International Arbitration* (2009) p. 298; Andrew E. Kramer, 'A Victory for Holders of Yukos', *New York Times*, 1 December 2009; Sofia Lind, 'Shearman and Cleary Gear Up for Mammoth Yukos Arbitration', Legal Week, 4 April 2008; Elizabeth Whitsett, 'The Merits of Former Yukos Shareholders' Expropriation Claim Will be Heard', *Investment Treaty News*, 13 January 2010.

7   See, e.g., Manitoba Law Reform Commission, Report No. 115, Mandatory Arbitration Clauses and *Consumer Class Proceedings* (April 2008) pp. 3-4, 22-23; J. Brian Casey, 'Commentary: class action arbitration should be available', The Lawyers Weekly 25(44), 31 March 2006, p. 9; Ian Meredith and Sean Kelsey, 'Treasury and Budget Minister of Luxembourg

Calls for Arbitration of Madoff Claims', available at: <http://www.globalfinancialmarketwatch.com/2009/06/articles/treasury-and-budget-minister-of-luxembourg-calls-for-arbitration-of-madoff-claims/> (4 June 2009); *infra* notes 38-39 and accompanying text.

8   See, e.g., *The Annals of the American Academy of Political and Social Science*: The Globalization of Class Actions 622 (March 2009) pp. 7, 25 (hereinafter, 'The Annals'); Jonathan Hill, *Cross-Border Consumer Contracts* (2008) pp. 6-8; Richard A. Nagareda, 'Aggregate Litigation Across the Atlantic and the Future of American Exceptionalism', Vanderbilt Law Review 62 (2009) pp. 20-28.

9   Nagareda, *supra* note 8, at pp. 32-41.

10   Dana H. Freyer and Gregory A. Litt, 'Desirability of International Class Arbitration', *Contemporary Issues in International Commercial Arbitration and Mediation: The Fordham Papers 2* (2008) p. 171; see also Brief of American Arbitration Association as Amicus Curiae in Support of Neither Party, Stolt-Nielsen S.A. v. *AnimalFeeds Int'l Corp.*, 130 S.Ct. 1758 (2010) (No. 08-1198), at pp. 22-24 (hereinafter, 'AAA Brief'); Christopher R. Drahozal, 'Arbitration Costs and Forum Accessibility: Empirical Evidence', *University of Michigan Journal of Law Reform 41 (2008)* pp. 837-839.

11   The majority opinion authored by Justice Alito leaves several significant gaps that will necessarily lead to litigation (indeed, the Court has already remanded one case to the Second Circuit for proceedings consistent with its decision in Stolt-Nielsen). See *In re American Express Merchants' Litigation* 554 F.3d 300 (2d Cir. 2009), *vacated and remanded sub nom. American Express Co. v. Italian Colors Restaurant*, 78 U.S.L.W. 3642 (2010). For example, although the Court held that '[a]n implicit agreement to authorize class-action arbitration . . . is not a term that the arbitrator may infer solely from the fact of the parties' agreement to arbitrate', the decision also stated that '[w]e have no occasion to decide what contractual basis may support a finding that the parties agreed to authorize class-action arbitration'. *Stolt-Nielsen S.A. v. AnimalFeeds Int'l Corp.*, 130 S.Ct. 1758, 1775 (2010). This issue will surely lead to numerous judicial disputes. Some questions could be resolved through legislative means, but none of the proposed reforms have yet been adopted. See, e.g., Arbitration Fairness Act, H.R. 2010, 111st Cong. (2009) (proposed).

12   See *PLI/Litigation, supra* note 1, at p. 127.

13   See AAA Brief, *supra* note 10, at p. 16-17. Among other things, the practice of permitting intermediate judicial review of certain arbitral rulings styled as 'final partial awards' was criticized by Justice Ginsburg in *Stolt-Nielsen* as being inconsistent with recent Supreme Court precedent. *Stolt-Nielsen S.A. v. AnimalFeeds Int'l Corp.*, 130 S.Ct. 1758, 1779 (2010) (Ginsburg, J, dissenting) (citing *Hall Street Assoc., L.L.C. v. Mattel, Inc.*, 552 U.S. 576, 588 (2008)).

14   Freyer and Litt, *supra* note 10, at p. 175.

15   Elizabeth Chamblee Burch, 'Securities Class Actions as Pragmatic *Ex Post* Regulation', *Georgia Law Review* 43 (2008) p. 85.

16   Deborah R. Hensler, 'The Globalization of Class Actions: An Overview', The Annals, *supra* note 8, at p. 25; see also Freyer and Litt, *supra* note 10, at p. 171.

17   Burch, *supra* note 15, at p. 77. The loss of the ability to bring collective proceedings in both judicial and arbitral contexts would have widespread ramifications, both to individuals (in that access to justice would be limited) and society as a whole (in that states' overall regulatory schemes would be upset). See *Stolt-Nielsen S.A. v. AnimalFeeds Int'l Corp.*, 130 S.Ct. 1758, 1783 (2010) (Ginsburg, J, dissenting).

18 Christopher Hodges, 'What Are People Trying to Do in Resolving Mass Issues, How Is It Going, and Where Are We Headed', The Annals, *supra* note 8, at p. 333.

19 Burch, *supra* note 15, at p. 74.

20 See *infra* notes 28-51 and accompanying text.

21 Hensler, *supra* note 16, at pp. 7-12.

22 This view appears to be adopted by the majority in *Stolt-Nielsen. Stolt-Nielsen S.A. v. AnimalFeeds Int'l Corp.*, 130 S.Ct. 1758, 1775 (2010) (claiming 'class-action arbitration changes the nature of arbitration'); see also Sir Michael J. Mustill and Stewart C. Boyd, *Commercial Arbitration* (1989) p. 283 (noting problems with procedures that are 'fundamentally different' from established notions of arbitration).

23 Katherine Lynch, *The Forces of Economic Globalization: Challenges to the Regime of International Commercial Arbitration* (2003) p. 18.

24 Ibid., at p. 19.

25 Gerold Herrmann, 'Power of Arbitrators to Determine Procedures under the UNCITRAL Model Law', The Annals, *supra* note 8, at pp. 39-40; cf. Dennis R. Nolan, 'Disputatio: "Creeping Legalism" as a Declension Myth', 2010 *Journal of Dispute Resolution* 1; see also Laura J. Cooper, 'The Process of Process: The Historical Development of Procedure in Labor Arbitration', *Arbitration 2005: The Evolving World of Work* (2006) pp. 99-120.

26 See, e.g., Joachim G. Frick, *Arbitration and Complex International Contracts* (2001) pp. 3-8; Bernard Hanotiau, *Complex Arbitrations: Multiparty, Multicontract, Multi-issue and Class Actions* (2005) p. 101.

27 Lynch, *supra* note 23, at p. 302.

28 More limited forms of representative relief have long been available in other jurisdictions. Hensler, *supra* note 16, at p. 13.

29 See The Annals, *supra* note 8; see also Global Class Actions Exchange, available at: <http://www.law.stanford.edu/library/globalclassaction/index.html>.

30 Hodges, *supra* note 18, at p. 331.

31 S.I. Strong, 'Enforcing Class Arbitration in the International Sphere: Due Process and Public Policy Concerns', *University of Pennsylvania Journal of International Law* 30 (2008) pp. 24-25.

32 Hodges, *supra* note 18, at p. 338.

33 Hensler, *supra* note 16, at p. 13.

34 Hodges, *supra* note 18, at pp. 339-340; see also S.I. Strong, 'The Sounds of Silence: Are US Arbitrators Creating Internationally Enforceable Awards When Ordering Class Arbitration in Cases of Contractual Silence or Ambiguity?', *Michigan Journal of International Law* 30 (2009) 1031.

35 See Carole J. Buckner, 'Toward a Pure Arbitral Paradigm of Classwide Arbitration: Arbitral Power and Federal Preemption', *Denver University Law Review 82* (2004) pp. 320-323; AAA Brief, supra note 10, at p. 10.

36 Compare Federal Rule of Civil Procedure 23 with: American Arbitration Association, Supplementary Rules for Class Arbitrations, available at: <http://www.adr.org/sp.asp?id=21936>; Judicial Arbitration and Mediation Services, JAMS Class Action Procedures, available at: <http://www.jamsadr.com/rules/class_action.asp>; and

National Arbitration Forum, Class Arbitration Procedures, available at: <http://www.adrforum.com/users/naf/resources/Arbitration%20Class%20Procedures%202007.pdf>; see also Meredith W. Nissen, 'Class Action Arbitrations: AAA vs. JAMS: Different Approaches to a New Concept', *Dispute Resolution Magazine* 11 (2005) p. 19.

37 AAA Policy on Class Arbitrations, available at: <http://www.adr.org/Classarbitrationpolicy>.

38 *Valencia (Colombia) v. Bancolombia (Colombia)* (24 April 2003) – Arbitral Tribunal of the Bogotá Chamber of Commerce, digest by Eduardo Zuleta for Institute of Transnational Arbitration (ITA), available at: <http://www.kluwerarbitration.com>.

39 McCarthy Tétrault, *Defending Class Actions in Canada* (2007) pp. 107-113; Geneviève Saumier, 'Consumer Arbitration in the Evolving Canadian Landscape', 113 Penn St. L. Rev. 1203, 1204-22 (2009); Strong, *supra* note 34, at pp. 1032-1034.

40 See, e.g., Unfair Commercial Practices Directive 2005/28/EC, OJ 2005 L 149/22; Cross Border Injunctions Directive 98/27/EC, OJ 1998 L 16/51; see also White Paper: Damages actions for breach of the EC antitrust rules, COM (2008) 165 (2 April 2008); Green Paper: Consumer Collective Redress, COM (2008) 794 (27 November 2008); Hill, *supra* note 8, at p. 166; Laurel J. Harbour and Marc E. Shelley, 'The Emerging European Class Action: Expanding Multi-Party Litigation to a Shrinking World', ABA Annual Meeting: The Emerging European Class Action, 3-6 August 2006.

41 Hensler, *supra* note 16, at p. 15.

42 Ibid., at p. 14.

43 Gary Born, *International Commercial Arbitration* (2009) p. 2482.

44 Hensler, *supra* note 16, at pp. 10, 13, 16-17.

45 For further reading on issues in consolidation, see Hanotiau, supra note 26, at pp. 49-196.

46 Barry R. Ostrager et al., 'Andersen v. Andersen: The Claimants' Perspective', *American Review of International Arbitration* 10 (1999) p. 443 (describing ICC arbitration with over 140 parties).

47 See, e.g., Holtzmann and Kristjánsdóttir, *supra* note 5.

48 Ianika Tzankova and Daan Lunsingh Scheurleer, 'The Netherlands', The Annals, *supra* note 8, at pp. 153-155; see also Hodges, *supra* note 18, at p. 342.

49 Burch, *supra* note 15, at pp. 114-120.

50 See, e.g., Article 12 of the Rules of the Mediation Institute of the Stockholm Chamber of Commerce, adopted on 1 April 1999.

51 See Christopher Newmark and Richard Hill, 'Can a Mediated Settlement Become an Enforceable Arbitration Award?' *Arbitration International* 16(2000) pp. 81-87.

52 Hans Smit, 'Class Actions and Their Waiver in Arbitration', *American Review of International Arbitration* 15 (2004) p. 211.

53 W. Mark C. Weidemaier, 'Arbitration and the Individuation Critique', *Arizona Law Review* 49 (2007) pp. 95-98.

54 Pierre Mayer, 'Comparative Analysis of Power of Arbitrators to Determine Procedures in Civil and Common Law Systems', in Albert Jan van de Berg (ed.), Planning Efficient Arbitration Proceedings: The Law Applicable in International Arbitration, VII ICCA Congress Series No. 7 (1996) p. 26.

55 See Strong, *supra* note 31 (discussing the issue in the context of international enforcement).

56 See Jasminka Kaljdzic et al., 'Canada', The Annals, supra note 8, at pp. 41-52; Vince Morabito, 'Australia', The Annals, supra note 8, at pp. 320-327; Nicholas M. Pace, 'Group and Aggregate Litigation in the United States', The Annals, *supra* note 8, at pp. 32-40; Strong, *supra* note 31, at pp. 24-25.

57 See Dietmar Baetge, 'Germany', The Annals, *supra* note 8, at pp. 126-128, 131; Nagareda, *supra* note 8, at pp. 33-41.

58 539 US 444 (2003) (plurality opinion).

59 See *supra* notes 38-39 and accompanying text.

60 AAA Brief, supra note 10, at p. 10.

61 For example, several national courts have decided that pre-dispute arbitration clauses in consumer cases violate the European Union's Unfair Terms in Consumer Contracts Directive. Hill, *supra* note 8, at p. 215. Similarly, the relevant arbitral rules may preclude some forms of collective arbitration. Spence, supra note 5, at p. 316.

62 Ramona L. Lampley, 'Is Arbitration Under Attack? Exploring the Recent Judicial Skepticism of the Class Arbitration Waiver and Innovative Solutions to the Unsettled Legal Landscape', *Cornell Journal of Law & Public Policy* 18 (2009) pp. 492-500.

63 *Green Tree Fin. Corp. v. Bazzle,* 539 US 444 (2003) (plurality opinion); *supra* notes 38-39. But see *Stolt-Nielsen S.A. v. AnimalFeeds Int'l Corp.*, 130 S.Ct. 1758, 1772 (2010) (casting doubt on the effect of the plurality decision in Bazzle but declining to address the issue).

64 The concept of contractual 'silence' and what would be necessary to support a finding that class arbitration was proper was discussed but not decided in *Stolt-Nielsen. Stolt-Nielsen S.A. v. AnimalFeeds Int'l Corp.*, 130 S.Ct. 1758, 1776 n.10 (2010). The author has previously identified a method of interpreting arbitration agreements that are silent as to the possibility of class treatment so as to decide whether group treatment is permissible. Strong, *supra* note 34. The interpretive approach described therein relies on principles and practices commonly used in international arbitration and would, it is suggested, be suitable for use in collective arbitrations seated outside the United States.

65 Lampley, *supra* note 62, at pp. 510-518.

66 See, e.g., Jean R. Sternlight and Elizabeth J. Jensen, 'Using Arbitration to Eliminate Consumer Class Actions: Efficient Business Practice or Unconscionable Abuse?', *Law and Contemporary Problems* 67 (2004) p. 75, n.1.

67 Justice Ginsburg takes the view that any new restrictions or rules laid down by the majority decision in *Stolt-Nielsen* – rules which are, at this point, extremely unclear – do not in any event apply to 'contracts of adhesion presented on a take-it-or-leave-it basis', as would be the case with many consumer contracts. *Stolt-Nielsen S.A. v. AnimalFeeds Int'l Corp.*, 130 S.Ct. 1758, 1783 (2010) (Ginsburg, J, dissenting).

68 The American Arbitration Association (AAA) has administered 283 class proceedings since 2003. Of these, 37% involved consumer actions, 37% involved employment actions, 7% involved franchising, 7% involved healthcare, 3% involved financial services and 11% involved other business-to-business concerns. AAA Brief, *supra* note 10, at pp. 22-24.

69 The majority in Stolt-Nielsen has framed the pertinent question not as what procedure is to be adopted by the arbitral tribunal but 'with whom' the parties agreed to arbitrate. *Stolt-Nielsen S.A. v. AnimalFeeds Int'l Corp.*, 130 S.Ct. 1758, 1774 (2010).

70 Emmanuel Gaillard and John Savage (eds.), *Fouchard, Gaillard, Goldman on International Commercial Arbitration* (1999) para. 478.

71 Hanotiau, supra note 26, at pp. 5-6 (arguing against the 'restrictive' reading of arbitration agreements).

72 Bernard Hanotiau, 'Groups of Companies in International Arbitration', *Pervasive Problems in International Arbitration* (2006) p. 287.

73 UNCITRAL Model Law on International Commercial Arbitration, United Nations Commission on International Trade Law, 18th Sess., Annex 1, U.N. Doc. A/40/17 (21 June 1985), revised by: Revised Articles of the UNCITRAL Model Law on International Commercial Arbitration, UNCITRAL, 39th Sess., Annex, U.N. Doc. A/61/17 (7 July 2006); Born, *supra* note 43, at pp. 68-71.

74 Lynch, *supra* note 23, at p. 65.

75 See Green Tree Fin. Corp. v. Bazzle, 539 US 444, 458-459 (2003) (Rehnquist, J., dissenting); *Yuen v. Superior Court*, 18 Cal. Rptr. 3d 127, 132 (Cal. Ct. App. 2004) (Mosk, J., concurring).

76 *Stolt-Nielsen S.A. v. AnimalFeeds Int'l Corp.*, 130 S.Ct. 1758, 1773-74 (2010) (noting arbitrators' and courts' duty 'to give effect to the intent of the parties').

77 Lynch, *supra* note 23, at p. 68; see also Hanotiau, *supra* note 26, at pp. 5-6.

78 Lynch, *supra* note 23, at p. 70.

79 Ibid., at p. 71.

80 See, e.g., *Green Tree Fin. Corp. v. Bazzle*, 539 US 444, 452-53 (2003); *Mitsubishi Motors Corp. v. Soler Chrysler-Plymouth*, Inc., 473 US 614, 626-37 (1985).

81 See, e.g., ibid.; see also Gaillard and Savage, *supra* note 70, at para. 480; Hanotiau, *supra* note 26, at pp. 5-6.

82 Lynch, *supra* note 23, at p. 72.

83 Ibid., at pp. 20-21, 72-73; see also *Herrmann, supra* note 25, at pp. 39-40.

84 Lynch, *supra* note 23, at p. 74.

85 Compare *Green Tree Fin. Corp. v. Bazzle* 539 US 444, 450-451 (2003) (Breyer, J.,) with ibid. at 458-459 (Rehnquist, J., dissenting).

86 Freyer and Litt, *supra* note 10, at p. 176; Hodges, *supra* note 18, at p. 373.

87 Justice Ginsburg sees this result as highly problematic if it also robs claimants of the ability to proceed collectively in court. *Stolt-Nielsen S.A. v. AnimalFeeds Int'l Corp.*, 130 S.Ct. 1758, 1783 (2010) (Ginsburg, J, dissenting) (questioning whether the 'class-action prospect' can or should 'vanish' as the result of an arbitration agreement).

88 Lampley, *supra* note 62, at pp. 499-502.

89 Burch, *supra* note 15, at pp. 88-114.

90 Ibid., at pp. 97-105.

91 Lampley, *supra* note 62; Sternlight and Jensen, *supra* note 66, at p. 86.

92 Lampley, *supra* note 62, at p. 494.

93 Julian D.M. Lew et al., *Comparative International Commercial Arbitration* (2003) para. 16-92.

94 Strong, *supra* note 34, at pp. 1045-1055.

95 Freyer and Litt, *supra* note 10, at p. 175; Strong, *supra* note 34, at pp. 1052-1053.

96 See *supra* notes 14-27 and accompanying text.

CHAPTER 11

CLASS ACTION IN ARBITRATION AND ENFORCEMENT ISSUES: AN ARBITRATOR'S POINT OF VIEW

Gerald Aksen[*]

I am usually asked to contribute to volumes like this one because of my expertise as an arbitrator. This expertise is based on my decades of handling arbitral proceedings. That is surely not the case here. I suspect that I have been asked to contribute because the only decision in the sole class action arbitration in which I have been involved – the Stolt-Nielsen case – is being argued right now before the US Supreme Court.

The whole topic of class action arbitration is so new that I can pose many questions about it without giving many, if any, definitive answers. This is not a problem, because you cannot start getting the answers until you first ask the questions. And I am an expert in asking questions.

1. IS THERE SUCH A THING AS INTERNATIONAL CLASS ARBITRATION?

The answer to this question is both 'yes' and 'not yet'.

'Yes' – at least in terms of the American Arbitration Association (AAA). It has devised the Supplementary Rules for Class Arbitrations, which have been used in 283 cases (121 of which are active). The AAA Rules are drafted so as to be applicable to international as well as domestic arbitration. The parties in the *Stolt-Nielsen* case agreed to use these rules for the purpose of dealing procedurally with the class action issues. Of course, most of the AAA cases have been domestic, and the fact that the *Stolt-Nielsen* case involves maritime contracts may be a reason why it is now before the Supreme Court.

'Not yet' – because national courts are the ultimate enforcers of arbitral awards. One could say that there cannot be such a thing as 'international class arbitration' until the judiciaries of several major commercial centres enforce awards in such arbitrations. As no such award has yet come up for enforcement, we simply do not know.

2. WHAT DOES IT LOOK LIKE?

The class action as developed in the US court system allows certain named parties to bring claims on behalf of third parties similarly situated. Even in the United States, class action arbitration is so recent that the first institutional rules dealing with such proceedings – the AAA Supplementary Rules for Class Arbitrations – were not drafted until 2003. This was just after the US Supreme Court issued its first class action arbitration decision in *Green Tree Fin. Corp. v. Bazzle*. [1]

These AAA Rules provide for three sequential determinations:

- The first – 'class construction' – establishes whether the arbitration agreement (or agreements) permit class action arbitration.
- If this is the case, the second – 'class certification' – determines whether the arbitration meets the requirements for a class action to proceed.
- If the first two criteria are met, then a decision ensues on the merits.

The *Stolt-Nielsen* case has only reached the first stage. What the Supreme Court is about to consider is whether the arbitration agreements permit class action arbitration.

If international class arbitration is to become a reality, then the second stage set forth in the AAA Rules – that is, whether the particular case meets the requirements for a class action – becomes the most important. The AAA Rules adapt the requirements set forth in the US Federal Rules of Civil Procedure for judicial class actions. Among these rules, there are five important criteria:

(i) *Numerosity:*
Is the class so numerous that the joinder of separate arbitrations on behalf of all members is impracticable?

(ii) *Commonality:*
Are there questions of fact or law common to the class?

(iii) *Typicality:*
Are the defence claims of the representative parties typical of those of the class?

(iv) *Adequacy of representation:*
Will the representative parties and class counsel fairly and adequately protect the interest of the class?

(v) *Similarity:*
Has each class member signed an agreement with an arbitration clause substantially similar to that signed by the other class members?

The AAA Rules recognize that, even if an arbitration clause can be construed to encompass a class action, not all cases are appropriate for resolution as a class action.

3. IS IT VERY DIFFERENT FROM OTHER MULTI-PARTY ARBITRATIONS?

Multi-party arbitrations are no longer unusual. I have been involved in insurance arbitrations with many parties. However, they most often involved a single insured and many insurers where the issues of coverage and amounts owed arose from the same event. Also, all the parties usually had one single arbitration clause with the same terms and applicable law. Examples include the Bermuda Form and ARIAS Rules.

Construction cases, too, often have many parties. They can include owners, architects, engineers and prime contractors, as well as their many subcontractors. In addition, they can often involve different contracts with differing arbitration rules. Nonetheless, some courts have granted consolidation and have ordered such cases to arbitration. When that happens, the arbitral tribunal has to sort out the various procedural problems. A good example of this is the *Boston Tower* case, which involves 26 different parties (albeit that the case was brought pursuant to an insurance policy).

Class arbitration differs even more from ordinary arbitration. It can comprise many different parties, with each member having different arbitral clauses, different rules, different applicable laws and different hearing locales.

The primary difference between multi-party arbitration and class arbitration is that in class arbitration it is important to be (i) especially vigilant about the need to protect the interests of absent members of the class and (ii) especially conscientious about due process and public interest concerns.

4. HOW ARE THE ARBITRATORS SELECTED?

Fairness issues may be raised by allowing the representative parties to select arbitrators without the participation or consent of absent class members. The designation of an impartial appointing authority to select the tribunal may serve to obviate such issues.

5. HOW DO YOU MANAGE MANY DIFFERENT LAW FIRMS?

Again, fairness issues may arise. Usually, in US judicial class actions, one or two law firms are chosen by the court as lead class counsel, and class members are permitted to retain counsel. Both the Federal Rules of Civil Procedure and the AAA Rules require the court or tribunal to make a determination to ensure that lead counsel fairly and adequately represents the interests of the class as a whole.

6. HOW MUCH IS WITHIN THE ARBITRATOR'S CONTROL?

I can personally attest to the fact that this is a matter in flux! One of the questions before the Supreme Court in the Stolt-Nielsen case is whether arbitrators can authorize class arbitration where the arbitration agreement is silent on the subject.

7. WHAT IS THE ROLE OF THE COURTS IN CLASS ARBITRATIONS?

In *Green Tree Fin. Corp. v. Bazzle*,[2] the Supreme Court held – albeit in a plurality opinion – that when parties agree to arbitrate, the question as to whether the agreement permits class arbitration is generally one of contract interpretation, and one to be determined by the arbitrators. The extent of that arbitral authority is one of the issues now before the Supreme Court in *Stolt-Nielsen*.

8. IS AN AWARD DECIDING ON THE CONSTRUCTION OF AN ARBITRATION CLAUSE IN FAVOUR OF CLASS ARBITRATION FINAL?

In *Stolt-Nielsen SA v. Animalfeeds Int'l Corp.*,[3] the arbitrators interpreted a contract clause that allowed for arbitration 'in the City of New York or in the City of London' in order to permit class arbitration. The District Court, in a case of first impression, set aside the arbitral award for manifest disregard of the law. The Appeals Court reinstated the award.[4]

Certiorari has been granted in the *Stolt-Nielsen* case by the US Supreme Court, and the case is scheduled to be argued very soon. We may then get answers to some of the problems faced by arbitrators.

9. WHAT WILL THE SUPREME COURT DECIDE?

As I said at the beginning, I have no answers but many questions. Here are some of them:

(i) Does the Federal Arbitration Act permit arbitrators to conduct class arbitration, where the arbitral clause is 'silent' regarding class arbitration?

(ii) Is class arbitration – where clauses are silent on the issue – consistent with the Federal Arbitration Act?

(iii) Did the arbitrators exceed their powers under the Federal Arbitration Act, 9 U.S.C. 10(a)(4), when they applied ordinary principles of contract interpretation to hold that a broad arbitration clause of '[a]ny dispute' arising from the contract permits class-wide arbitration?

(iv) Is a petition to vacate an arbitral tribunal's interim decision, based upon class construction, ripe for judicial review where the tribunal has not yet made a decision on classification to certify a class ruled on the merits of the claim?

(v) Is a standard maritime broad-form arbitration clause ever subject to class arbitration?

(vi) Can an award involving foreign commerce be set aside for manifest disregard of law by US courts?

(vii) Is judicial review of arbitral awards limited exclusively to the grounds listed in the Federal Arbitration Act?

(viii) Is a broad-form arbitration clause really silent?

(ix) Does the pro-arbitration policy in US courts apply to class arbitration?

(x) Who decides the default rule when the arbitral clause is silent – the courts or arbitrators?

(xi) Is the availability of class action procedures in arbitration an issue for arbitrators to decide?

There are lots of questions that need addressing. Perhaps the Supreme Court will provide us with some answers!

Endnote: "On April 27, 2010, the U.S. Supreme Court in Stolt-Nielsen S. A. v. Animalfeeds Int'l Corp. No. 08-1198 held that arbitrators could not impose class arbitration on parties whose arbitration clauses are silent on that issue."

END NOTES

* Arbitrator and mediator.
1 539 U.S. 444 203 (2003).
2 Ibid.
3 435 F.Supp. 2d 382 (S.D.N.Y., 2006).
4 548 F.3d 85 (2d Cir., 2008).

CHAPTER 12

THE EFFECT OF AWARDS RENDERED IN MULTIPARTY/MULTICONTRACT SITUATIONS

Pierre Mayer*

1. INTRODUCTION

Complex arbitrations involving multiple parties and/or multiple contracts raise various difficulties as previously illustrated in the other contributions to this dossier. Where the arbitrator fails to anticipate such difficulties, or believes that they can be overcome, these difficulties can reappear at the later stage of enforcement of the award.

An arbitral award rendered against multiple parties, or based on a series of contracts, will have little effect if the judge views the award as having violated the laws ensuring its validity and enforceability. At the start of such complex arbitrations, therefore, a claimant can make one of two strategic choices: splitting the dispute into several procedures or bringing all parties and/or contracts into one single procedure. Before making this choice, the claimant must ask itself the following question: in the case of splitting, and assuming the award is rendered in its favour, will it be able to rely on the award, rendered in the two-party and single contract arbitral proceeding in another proceeding (whether judicial or arbitral) involving another party or another contract?

In order to fully address the claimant's options in such multiparty and multi-contract situations, I will cover the two scenarios in the following two sections.

2. BRINGING ALL PARTIES AND/OR CONTRACTS INTO A SINGLE PROCEDURE

An award rendered against (or in favour of) two or more respondents, or on the basis of two or more contracts, risks being refused enforcement on the same grounds as those that were, or should have been, in the mind of the claimant at the time it initiated the proceedings. One need only refer back to the provisions of Article V of the New York Convention on the Recognition and Enforcement of Foreign Arbitral Awards (the 'New York Convention') to understand the challenges an award of this kind faces.

It will first be recalled that recognition and enforcement of the award may be refused if, according to Article V.1.c,

> *"the award deals with a difference not contemplated by or not falling within the terms of the submission to arbitration [...]."*

Under this article, a court can deny enforcement on the basis that one of the parties to the proceedings was not a party to the arbitration clause or because one of the contracts in dispute did not have an arbitration clause or had an arbitration clause that was incompatible with the one upon which jurisdiction was established.

Article V.1.d of the New York Convention mentions another obstacle:

> *"The composition of the arbitral authority or the arbitral procedure was not in accordance with the agreement of the parties [...]."*

This situation can arise when there is consolidation – *stricto sensu* – of two arbitral tribunals into one, based on the fact that the two arbitrations are closely related but against the will of one of the parties.

Another defence to enforcement is lack of due process under Article V.1.b of the New York Convention. According to this provision, an award may be refused enforcement if:

> *"the party against whom the award is invoked was not given proper notice of the appointment of the arbitrator or of the arbitration proceedings or was otherwise unable to present his case."*

This can occur, for instance, when one of the parties is forced to join proceedings already underway.

In an international context, the existence of those potential obstacles to the enforcement of an award raises specific issues in one of the following situations (which can also be combined):

(a) Two co-respondents, both subject to an unfavourable award, reside in different countries.

(b) The award was rendered in one country and enforcement is sought in another.

a. First situation: two co-respondents, both subject to an unfavourable award, reside in different countries

Under this hypothetical set of facts, an order to pay was made against the two co-respondents jointly and severally, or *in solidum*. Alternatively, the main respondent was ordered to pay a certain amount to the claimant and the other respondent was ordered to indemnify the main respondent. A serious problem will arise if the award is recognized in one country and refused enforcement in the other.

In the case of jointly and severally liable respondents, the claimant will seek enforcement for the full amount of the award against the party that resides in the country where enforcement is possible, and that party will not be able to recover the other respondent's share in the debt. Similarly, in the other case, the respondent that will have complied with the award made against it will not be able to obtain indemnification from the other respondent.

There is no doubt that these outcomes are fundamentally unfair. The question remains, therefore, whether there is a remedy to avoid these kinds of situations.

Before the Milan Court of Appeal, a jointly and severally liable respondent pleaded that it could never request its co-respondent, residing in Malaysia, to contribute to its part of the debt.[1] On this basis, it tried to resist enforcement of the award. The Court of Appeal, by a judgment rendered on 5 November 2003, rejected this defence, which it rightly found to be incompatible with the very notion of joint and several liability.

b. Second situation: the award is rendered in one country and enforcement is sought in another

Most arbitral tribunals will not take the risk of seeing the award annulled by the courts at the place of arbitration. They will only find that they have jurisdiction and are duly constituted, with regard to multiple parties or multiple contracts, after having verified that the award will not run any serious risk of being set aside. Notwithstanding Article 35 of the ICC Rules, pursuant to which: 'the Arbitral Tribunal [...] shall make every effort to make sure that the Award is enforceable at law', they will, however, rarely verify at the outset whether the award is enforceable in one or several of the countries in which enforcement can be envisaged. As a consequence, even if the risk that the award will be set aside by the courts of the place of arbitration appears minimal or non-existent, this does not guarantee that the award will be found enforceable in a foreign country.

This is the issue that the claimant might face once it has obtained a favourable award. Supposing, for instance, that the arbitral tribunal assumed jurisdiction over a party that had not signed the arbitration clause and that this appears to be in conformity with what the local courts would accept, it remains to be seen whether the court requested to enforce the award will have the same understanding of the issue regarding the extension of the arbitration clause to non-signatories.

The ICC case of *Dallah Estate v. the Ministry of Religious Affairs, Government of Pakistan* is an illustrative example. [2]

In this case, a contract was concluded between a Saudi company, Dallah Estate, and a Pakistani trust called Awami Hajj Trust, whereby Dallah agreed to build accommodations suitable for pilgrims travelling from Pakistan to Mecca. The negotiations had been led, on the side of Pakistan, by the government, which ultimately decided to promulgate an ordinance providing for the establishment of the trust, that would act as a vehicle to undertake the project. A few months after the execution of the contract, the Ministry of Religious Affairs, by a letter on its headed paper, put an end to the contract, alleging that Dallah had breached certain fundamental obligations. Dallah started an ICC arbitration in Paris against the government of Pakistan. The arbitral tribunal was presided over by Lord Mustill.

The Government rejected any suggestion that it was a party to the contract or that it had consented to the arbitration agreement, and denied the arbitral tribunal's jurisdiction on those bases. The tribunal decided that the question whether the government of Pakistan was a party was to be determined 'by reference to those transnational general principles and usages which reflect the fundamental requirements of justice in international trade and the concept of good faith in business'. [3]

More concretely, the tribunal observed that the arbitration agreement extended 'to parties that did not actually sign the contract but were directly involved in the negotiation and performance of such contract [...]'.

This last formula is a quotation from French case law as it was formulated at the time.

The arbitral tribunal concluded that Dallah had demonstrated that the government of Pakistan had been, and considered itself to be, a party to the contract with Dallah. On the merits, the tribunal found that the government owed Dallah GBP 20 million in damages.

The government did not seek annulment of the award in France. The claimant, on its part, made an *ex parte* application to the Commercial Court for leave to enforce the award as a judgment of the High Court of England.[4] An order giving Dallah such leave was issued, which led in turn to an application by the government to set aside the order on the grounds that the arbitration agreement on which the award was based was not valid within the meaning of Section 103(2)(b) of the English Arbitration Act, which reflects Article V.1.a of the New York Convention. [5]

Article V.1.a provides, in so far as is material to this decision, as follows:

> *"Recognition and enforcement of the award may be refused, at the request of the party against whom it is invoked, only if that party furnishes to the competent authority where the recognition and enforcement is sought, proof that:*
>
> *[...] the agreement referred to in article II [...] is not valid under the law to which the parties have subjected it or, failing any indication thereon, under the law of the country where the award was made."*

Since the parties had not agreed on the law by which the arbitration agreement should be governed, the High Court and, on appeal, the Court of Appeal, found it was subject to French law, as the law of the country where the award was made.[6] One could therefore hope that a convergence might be reached between the position that a French court would adopt, if seized of a request to set aside the award, and the position of the English court. If only English law was applied, for example, the court would have most certainly refused enforcement, since English judges will rarely extend an arbitration clause to a party that is not a signatory to the contract. What remained to be seen, however, is how the English courts would apply the principles of French law.

What the High Court and the Court of Appeal each understood in the application of French law is that: [7]

> *"[...] in order to determine whether an arbitration clause upon which the jurisdiction of an arbitral tribunal is founded extends to a person who is neither a named party nor a signatory to the underlying agreement containing that clause, it is necessary to find out whether all the parties to the arbitration proceedings, including that person, had the common intention (whether expressed or implied) to be bound by said agreement and, as a result, by the arbitration clause [...].*
>
> *To this effect, the courts will consider the involvement and behaviour of all the parties during the negotiation, performance and, if applicable, termination of the underlying agreement."*

The High Court therefore established that it would seek to ascertain the subjective intention of each of the parties through their objective conduct.[8] In doing so, it found that it was not the subjective intention of all the parties that the government of Pakistan should be bound by the agreement or the arbitration clause: [9]

> *"In fact, I am clear that the opposite was the case from the beginning to end. That is why the GoP distanced itself from the contractual arrangements in the Agreement and that is why it sought to argue from the time of the Termination Letter that the Agreement was void and illegal."*

Similarly, the Court of Appeal found that this subjective intention – or implicit intention – was lacking.

According to Lord Justice Moore-Bick, who wrote the lead opinion, there was no doubt that prior to the establishment of the trust, the government of Pakistan was the only party with which Dallah could negotiate. There was, however, a fundamental change in that position when the government established the trust and, most importantly, when the final contract was signed only between Dallah and the trust. Lord Justice Moore-Bick therefore posited, in the most commonsensical fashion, that '[i]f it had been [the parties'] common intention, the Government would surely have been named as a party to the Agreement, or would at least have added its signature in a way that reflected that fact'.[10] As to the termination letter sent to Dallah on the Ministry of Religious Affairs' letterhead, the Court of Appeal found it ambiguous as it was sent by the Minister of Religious Affairs, who is evidently a member of the government but was also the chairman of the board of directors of the trust (although at that point it had already been dissolved).[11] As a consequence, the English courts refused to grant the claimant leave to enforce the award.

While the English judges' conclusions were reasoned and sophisticated, they failed to fully capture some essential points of French law. According to the French *Cour de cassation*, following the most recent version of the rule:[12]

> *"The effect of an international arbitration clause extends directly to parties involved in the performance of the contract and in the ensuing disputes."*

This criteria is in essence objective. If it had been applied to the *Dallah* case, it would have inevitably led a French judge to confirm the arbitral tribunal's jurisdiction over the government of Pakistan.

I do not conclude therefrom that Dallah should not have sought its remedy against the government of Pakistan. Given the circumstances, it did not have much choice, since the trust (the only signatory to the contract) no longer existed by the time Dallah launched the ICC arbitration proceedings. If, however, the claimant had had the option to pursue two respondents, it would have had to consider the *dépeçage* option.

3. SPLITTING THE DISPUTE INTO SEVERAL PROCEDURES

The key question here is whether, if it has opted to split its claims, the claimant will be allowed to rely on the contents of an award obtained in its favour in a subsequent proceeding introduced on the basis of another contract or against another respondent?

The answer to this question will depend on whether the parties are different or the same.

a. Two or more contracts involving the same parties

At this point, it is necessary to make a further distinction.

1. The fate of contract No. 2 depends on the validity or interpretation of contract No. 1, which is the subject of the earlier proceedings.

The outcome of this situation is relatively straightforward. Since the validity or interpretation of contract No. 1 will necessarily have been decided in the dispositive part of the first award, the solution will be binding on the subsequent arbitrator or judge seized with matters concerning contract No. 2.

2. Contracts Nos. 1 and 2 concern the same issues of fact or law, but they are subject to separate proceedings (before two arbitral tribunals or before one tribunal and one court).

The question that arises here is whether the way the issue is resolved in the award concerning contract No. 1 is binding on the tribunal (or court) dealing with contract No. 2.

While each country has its own interpretation of the *res judicata* effects of an earlier and final adjudication by a court, international arbitration would greatly benefit from a system of universal rules of application for arbitral awards.

In this regard, the Recommendations of the International Law Association (ILA) adopted in 2006 on res judicata constitute appropriate guidelines:

> "4. An arbitral award has conclusive and preclusive effect in the further arbitral proceedings as to:
>
> 4.1 determinations and relief contained in its dispositive part as well as in all reasoning necessary thereto;
>
> 4.2 issues of fact or law which have actually been arbitrated and determined by it, provided any such determination was essential or fundamental to the dispositive part of the arbitral tribunal."

The latter part of Article 4.2, which makes the *res judicata* effect of the first tribunal's findings conditional, is justified in that it is preferable not to impose on the second arbitral tribunal the first tribunal's findings on a given issue if such issue was only superficially discussed between the parties in the earlier proceedings, because they had found it to be of minor importance in the context of those proceedings.

b. Different parties

An award cannot be used against third parties, nor can third parties assert the award in their favour. This position is confirmed in Article 3.4 of the ILA's 2006 Recommendations on *res judicata*:

> "3. An arbitral award has conclusive and preclusive effects in further arbitral proceedings if: [...]
>
> 3.4 it has been rendered between the same parties."

Even if the matters at issue are the same – for example if all contracts are identical in content or were negotiated in the same factual context – each arbitral tribunal will in principle issue its own independent decision.

For example, in *Sun Life Assurance Company of Canada*[13], a case that was on appeal with the English Court of Appeal, the *res judicata* issue in dispute concerned two claimants (Lincoln and Cigna), which had been involved in separate proceedings against Sun Life in relation to reinsurance policies entered into with Sun Life. In its arbitration, Lincoln believed it was entitled to avoid the application of its reinsurance on grounds of misrepresentation and non-disclosure as decided by the *Cigna tribunal*. The *Lincoln tribunal*, however, disagreed. It made it clear that an earlier arbitral award would not bind a party to the award in any later proceedings against a third party. Hence, it would generally be free to contradict the findings of the award.

However, the impossibility of invoking the findings of an arbitral award against a third party must be nuanced in the following three ways.

First, an award may be relied upon by another arbitral tribunal as a source of inspiration. In ICC case No. 7061, the arbitrator, while confirming that the arbitral tribunal was not bound by the earlier award, stated that the prior award contained:[14]

> "[...] *a helpful analysis of the common factual background to this dispute. Accordingly, we have borne its findings and conclusions in mind, whilst taking care to reach our own conclusions on the materials submitted by these parties in these proceedings.*"

Second, *res judicata* must not be confused with *opposabilité* (to use a French legal term which has no equivalent in the English language).

The binding effect of an award only exists between the parties – *l'autorité de chose jugée est relative* – whether it relates to findings of law or fact. That being said, what has been decided, that is the decision itself, establishes a legal situation constituting an objective reality that, although it does not directly affect the legal situation of third parties, cannot simply be ignored by the latter.

The *Sun Life* decision of the English Court of Appeal contrasted the *res judicata* issue, which it resolved in the way described above, with a hypothetical situation that would be one of opposabilité in the French terminology, and for which the award could be regarded 'as a relevant fact for the purposes of the second dispute': [15]

> "*For example, if a certain amount of damages had been award by the arbitral tribunal, the party seeking to claim damages from a third party could assert that the amount that he had to pay as damages in the earlier dispute was the amount of damages that he suffered, for which the third party was therefore liable.*"

There may be a third nuance to be made. It would distinguish between the situation in which a finding of law or fact in the earlier award is used *against* a third party and the situation in which it is the third party that *relies* on the prior award against the original party for the purposes of its own case.

In the former case, there would be violation of due process if the third party was denied the right to submit its own arguments and/or evidence.

In the latter case, the original party, against which a finding of law or fact is invoked, had every opportunity to present its case before the earlier tribunal. It can be argued that there is no reason, in that situation, why the third party could not borrow from the prior award to make its case before the tribunal. If anything, it reduces the possibility for contradiction between awards deriving from the same factual context. This is the majority view among the courts in the United States.

END NOTES

[* ...] Professor and Partner, Dechert LLP, France; Council Member, ICC Institute of World Business Law.

1   Polcon Italiana srl (Italy) v. P.T. Perkebunan Nusantara III Persero (Indonesia), Corte di Appello [Court of Appeal], Milan, 5 November 2003, Rivista dell'Arbitrato 2 (2005) pp. 295-298, with note by Atteritano pp. 298-310.

2   Dallah Estate and Tourism Holding Company v. The Ministry of Religious Affairs, Government of Pakistan, in the Supreme Court of Judicature Court of Appeal (Civil Division) on appeal from the High Court of Justice Queen's Bench Division (Commercial Court), [2009] EWCA Civ. 755 (20 July 2009) (hereinafter, 'Dallah, Court of Appeal, [2009] EWCA Civ. 755').

3   Dallah Real Estate & Tourism Holding Company v. Ministry of Religious Affairs, Government of Pakistan, [2008] EWHC 1901 (Comm), [2008] App.L.R. 08/01 (1 August 2008), at para. 49 (hereinafter, 'Dallah, High Court, [2008] EWHC 1901 (Comm)').

4   Ibid., at para. 54.

5   The High Court as well as the Court of Appeal rendered their decisions in application of the New York Convention as embodied in the English Arbitration Act of 1996.

6   Dallah, High Court, [2008] EWHC 1901 (Comm), at para. 3.

7   Ibid., at para. 85 (referencing the Joint Memorandum submitted by the parties to the High Court encapsulating the principles of French law which the parties agreed were applicable to the case). See also Dallah, Court of Appeal, [2009] EWCA Civ. 755, at para. 26.

8   Dallah, High Court, [2008] EWHC 1901 (Comm), at para. 87. See also Dallah, Court of Appeal, [2009] EWCA Civ. 755, at para. 27.

9   Dallah, High Court, [2008] EWHC 1901 (Comm), at para. 129.

10 Dallah, Court of Appeal, [2009] EWCA Civ. 755, at para. 32.

11 Ibid., at para. 34.

12 Cour de cassation, Chambre Civile 1, N° 04-20842, 27 March 2007: 'Mais attendu que l'effet de la clause d'arbitrage international s'étend aux parties directement impliquées dans l'exécution des contrats et les litiges qui peuvent en résulter.'

13 Sun Life Assurance Company of Canada (Canada), American Phoenix Life and Reassurance Company (U.S.A.), Phoenix Home Life Mutual Insurance (U.S.A.) v. Lincoln Life Insurance Company, Judgment by the Supreme Court of Judicature Court of Appeal (Civil Division) on appeal from the High Court of Justice Queen's Bench Division (Commercial Court), [2004] EWCA Civ. 1660 (hereinafter, 'Sun Life, [2004] EWCA Civ. 1660'). See also B. Hanotiau, Complex Arbitrations (2006) para. 546.

14 Award of 28 November 1997 in ICC case No. 7061 (unpublished), cited in Hanotiau, supra n. 13, at para. 551.

15 Sun Life, [2004] EWCA Civ. 1660.

CONCLUDING REMARKS

BY ERIC A. SCHWARTZ *

Multiparty arbitration is a well-trodden topic that, over the course of the last several decades, has been the subject of multiple international conferences, abundant doctrinal writings and the scrutiny of arbitral institutions, courts and users. It is a subject that has long commanded the attention of the ICC, in particular. In 1991, the Institute of International Business Law and Practice published a collection of papers from its 1989 conference in Stockholm, under the title *Multi-Party Arbitration: Dossiers of the Institute of International Business Law and Practice*.[1] This publication was followed in 1994 by the Final Report on *Multi-Party Arbitrations* of the Working Party established by the ICC Commission on Arbitration under the chairmanship of Jean-Louis Delvolvé.[2] This report was the culmination of more than 15 years of study by the ICC Commission. In 2003, the ICC revisited the topic once more in a publication entitled *Complex Arbitrations: Perspectives on their Procedural Implications*.[3]

So why another ICC conference on this subject? Is it the case, as Stephen Bond has quipped, that this is a subject about which everything has already been said, but simply not yet by everyone? The large number of attendees (more than 150), the presentations of the speakers and the discussions that followed demonstrated that, irrespective of the attention that the topic of multiparty arbitration has already received, it continues to fascinate and to challenge practitioners, courts and arbitral institutions.

Part of the reason, of course, is that multiparty arbitration is not a single subject but a multiplicity of different and continually evolving topics. The conference programme was a testament to this. Some of the topics traversed familiar territory (e.g. groups of contracts, groups of companies, the separation and consolidation of disputes and the extension of arbitration agreements to non-signatories), but others covered relatively new ground, such as the development of 'class action' arbitration in the United States and the possible reform of the ICC Rules to cater expressly for some of the issues raised by multiparty arbitration.

During the 20 years since the Institute last explored the different facets of multiparty arbitration, there have been important shifts in both the legal landscape and attitudes towards multiparty arbitration.

Perhaps the most important shift has been the emergence, in the wake of the well-known decision of the French Court of Cassation in the *Dutco* case in 1992,[4] of a widely-accepted solution to the potential problems posed by the constitution of the arbitral tribunal in a multiparty context. Twenty years ago, the difficulties associated with the constitution of the arbitral tribunal in such cases were a source of considerable concern. The subsequent widespread amendment of international arbitral rules (including those of the ICC) to deal with this particular issue appears to have given multiparty arbitration a new lease on life, opening up avenues that previously remained largely unexplored in the predominantly bipolar world of international arbitration. It is notable how the mood appears to have swung, emboldening the ICC, as part of its current review of the ICC Rules of Arbitration (described by Simon Greenberg at the conference and in this publication), to consider incorporating into its Rules new provisions intended to regulate issues arising in a multi-polar arbitration context, such as the joinder of parties and cross-claims.

When the ICC last amended its arbitration rules in 1998, these changes were widely resisted. At that time, multiparty arbitration was generally viewed as a matter that was best left to the parties themselves and one that should not be the subject of regulation. Moreover, the international arbitration community was generally wedded to the view, consistent with the then architecture of nearly all arbitration rules, that arbitration was and should be a bipolar process, with a claimant (or claimant group) on one side and a respondent (or respondent group) on the other. Departing from this model was widely perceived to be fraught with difficulties and risks, beginning with the constitution of the arbitral tribunal, and likely to lead to inefficiency and delay. At the time of the 1989 Stockholm conference, one prominent practitioner noted: 'There is some law [...] and [...] there is some practice. In my view, however, both deter the sensible use of multi-party arbitration. The Holy Grail remains as elusive as ever.'[5]

Twenty years have passed, and while this view still has its adherents – multiparty arbitration (of the multi-polar variety, at least) was described as a 'snake pit' by one of the speakers at this year's conference – the practical issues and potential difficulties arising from the organization and conduct of multiparty cases have generated far less comment and fewer expressions of concern than was the case in Stockholm in 1989. Whether or not, and if so to what extent, the ICC is close to finding the Holy Grail, given its resolve to deal with some of the related issues in its next set of arbitration rules, remains to be seen.

While there appears to be a new openness towards the possible accommodation of multiparty procedures in the ICC Rules of Arbitration, one aspect of the multiparty arbitration discussion that has not changed over the years is the central place occupied by the issue of the parties' consent. Speaker after speaker posited that the consent of the parties is fundamental. However, it was also repeatedly acknowledged that, notwithstanding decades of consideration of multiparty arbitration issues, parties often still do not cater for multiparty (or multicontract) arbitration in their arbitration agreements. This has inevitably led to tension between the recognized need for consent and the widespread desire for arbitration to be able to accommodate multiparty disputes in the interests of efficiency and the good administration of justice. This, in turn, has led to a debate about how faithful courts and arbitrators have actually been to the requirement of consent when finding or imputing consent that has not been explicitly expressed. Although there no longer appears to be much support, as was once the case, for mandating the consolidation of arbitrations by legislative action, the contributions to the conference and this publication demonstrate the continuing vitality of this debate and the differing ways in which consent may or may not be established by courts and arbitrators.

Professor Karim Youssef, the author of a new book on arbitral consent in a multiparty and multi-contract context,[6] set the stage for the discussion by raising the provocative question, based on his review of arbitral case law, of whether consent as a jurisdictional criterion has declined in importance. Do arbitrators and commentators merely pay lip service to consent as a 'fundamental pillar' of international arbitration, while, in reality, stretching the concept in order to do justice in specific cases? Youssef argues that the case law with respect to consent is in a state of flux, claiming that an analysis of the case law reveals the existence of not one, but a multitude of approaches to jurisdiction in multiparty and multicontract cases. Among the doctrines that he considers is the so-called 'group of companies' doctrine, as formulated in the *Dow Chemical* case nearly three decades ago, with its controversial reference to the group as 'a single economic reality'.[7]

The group of companies theory, often perceived as an anomalous French doctrine, is in turn the subject of the contribution of Yves Derains, who, intent on emphasizing the importance of consent in French jurisprudence, stresses that the existence of a 'single economic reality' in the *Dow* case was merely an indication of (and an ambivalent one at that) rather than a substitute for consent. The group of companies theory, he says, has today outlived its usefulness ('a fait son temps').

Whether or not that is the case, there is nevertheless ample room for discussion on who is best suited, and in what circumstances, to seek to divine the parties' intent when it has not been made explicit: the arbitrators, the courts or the arbitral institution? What presumptions, if any, should inform the decision-makers' attempt to determine the parties' intent? Do different or special considerations come into play when one (or more) of the parties is a state or state entity? What laws or rules of law are to be applied in making the related decision?

These difficulties are illustrated by two recent and very different cases, on different continents, that were the subject of considerable discussion during the conference.

One was the decision of the English Court of Appeal in the case of *Dallah Estate and Tourism Holding Company v. The Ministry of Religious Affairs, Government of Pakistan*.[8] In this case, as discussed in greater detail by Georgios Petrochilos, the English Court of Appeal affirmed the decision of a lower court refusing to enforce an ICC arbitration award made in Paris against the government of Pakistan. The lower court's refusal to enforce the award was founded on its determination that the arbitral tribunal had not properly applied principles of French law in deciding that the government of Pakistan was a party to the arbitration agreement. Given that the arbitral tribunal was chaired by an eminent English jurist, Lord Mustill, the decision of the lower English court, as affirmed by the Court of Appeal (but now on appeal to the Supreme Court), demonstrates in a particularly spectacular fashion how a general appreciation of the importance of establishing the common intent of the parties in determining jurisdiction in multiparty cases is nevertheless susceptible to widely different possible applications in specific cases.

Similarly, in a different context, the United States Supreme Court determined, in a much anticipated decision issued on 27 April 2010 in the case of *Stolt-Nielsen S.A. et al. v. AnimalFeeds International Corp.*,[9] that an arbitral tribunal sitting in New York (and chaired by Gerald Aksen) had wrongly found that an arbitration clause that was silent on the subject permitted a class action arbitration.[10] The issue before the US Supreme Court was whether the arbitration tribunal had properly found, in accordance with the Class Rules developed by the American Arbitration Association, that the arbitration clause in question permitted AnimalFeeds to bring a 'class action' arbitration in a case where the parties had stipulated that their arbitration clause was silent on that issue. While the Supreme Court has now found, by a majority decision, that the arbitral tribunal erred in the circumstances of that case, its decision does not exclude the possibility of class action arbitration. More litigation aimed at determining the consent of parties to such an extreme form of multiparty arbitration is thus likely to arise in the United States.

Twenty years after the Institute's last conference on the subject of multiparty arbitration, the community of international arbitration practitioners appears to have grown more comfortable with the concept. Nevertheless, it appears that determining whether all the parties in a specific case have consented to multiparty arbitration will continue to present challenges that are likely to divide practitioners, courts and arbitrators for years to come.

END NOTES

* Partner in the Paris office of King & Spalding International LLP; Council Member, ICC Institute of World Business Law; Member (United States), ICC International Court of Arbitration; former Secretary General (1992-1996), ICC International Court of Arbitration.

1   ICC Pub. No. 480/1.

2   *ICC International Court of Arbitration Bulletin* 6(1) (May 1995).

3   *ICC International Court of Arbitration Bulletin,* Special Supplement (2003).

4   Cour de Cassation, *Sociétés BKMI et Siemens c/ société Dutco*, 7 January 1992, Rev. arb. (1992) p. 470.

5   H. Lloyd, 'A National Experience', in *Multi-party Arbitration: Dossiers of the Institute of International Business Law and Practice*, ICC Pub. No. 480/1, p. 62.

6   *Consent in Context: Fulfilling the Promise of International Arbitration* (West, 2009).

7   Cour d'appel de Paris, *Société Isover-Saint Gobain c/ société Dow Chemical France et autre*, 22 October 1983, *Rev. arb.* (1984) p. 98.

8   20 July 2009, EWCA Civ. 755.

9   559 U.S. ___, 2010 WL 1655826, at *4 (2010).

10 By coincidence, the oral argument in the *Stolt-Nielsen* case was to be conducted the day after the conference, on 9 December 2009.

KEY-WORDS INDEX

A

AAA Policy on Class Arbitrations .... 210 n. 37

AAA Supplementary Rules for Class Arbitrations .... 209 n. 36, 215, 216-217, 218

abuse of rights
    see fraud and abuse of rights

aggregate relief
    consent 192-193
    group litigation order procedure (UK) 192
    multi-district litigation procedure (US) 192
    use of existing arbitration procedures 192-193

alter ego doctrine .... 87, 90, 106 n. 47, 108 n. 77, 128, 149-150

American Arbitration Association (AAA) .... 17, 211 n. 66

amicus curiae 121

arbitral awards
    effects 230-232
    enforcement issues 224-229

arbitral policy
    autonomous theory of arbitration 200
    contractual theory of arbitration 199
    hybrid theory of arbitration 200
    jurisdictional theory of arbitration 199
    US approach 197-198

arbitral tribunals
- *amiable compositeurs* 97
- appointment in multiparty settings 27, 141, 142, 177-178, 179
- complexity of tasks 96-97
- duties 73, 97-98

arbitration
- *see also multicontract arbitration*
- *see also multiparty arbitration*
- 'Americanization' of..188
- by default...83
- increasing complexity of...161-162, 188-189
- level of commitment to 198
- transition from litigation to 112

arbitration agreements
- as ordinary contracts..73
- autonomy of..85
- consolidation of
- see consolidation
- disregarding..54-56
- extension to non-signatories
- see extension of the arbitration agreement
- global/model/umbrella 26-27
- imperfect 26
- (in)compatibility of...166, 168-170, 171
- stand-alone 29

arbitration clauses
- *see arbitration agreements*

ARIAS Rules..217

Australian International Arbitration Act (1974)..........................37-38

B

Belgian case law
  on consolidation/inseparability 54-55, 58

Belgian Code of Civil Procedure .... 54, 55, 57, 58, 60, 68 nn. 40-41

Bermuda Form 217

C

CEPANI Arbitration Rules (2005) .... 46 n. 12

class action (US-style)
  adoption in other countries 189-190
  criticism of 189

class arbitration (US-style)
  see also international class arbitration
  ability to impose 219-220
  alternative forms of
    see collective arbitration
    criteria for 216-217
    gradual expansion of 183-184
    nature of 183
    objections to
      arbitral concerns 188-189
      commercial concerns 186-187
      jurisprudential concern 187

  origins 97-189

collective arbitration
  adoption in other countries 90-191
  alternative forms of
    aggregate relief 192-193
    on ad hoc basis 195
    reliance on judicial procedures 194-195

    representative relief..191-192
    settlement relief..193-194
    via domestic and international arbitral organisations........................195
    forces behind development of
        level of commitment to arbitration..198-199
        policies regarding collective relief..201-205
        theoretical approach...200-201
    limitations on..195-196
    opt in/out..191-193
    relative merits of court proceedings and..205

collective redress
see collective relief

collective relief
see also collective arbitration
    as a procedural or substantive right...202-203
    EU directives on harmonisation of..192
    in specialized arbitral contexts 184
    need for...203-204
    not the same as multiparty/multicontract arbitration...............204-205, 217
    substantive law...203
    versus regulatory mechanisms...201-202, 203-204
    waiver of...195

Concordat intercantonal sur l'arbitrage (CIA) [Switzerland].......................28

consent
    applicable law...98-99
    as basis of jurisdiction...76-77
    as default criterion..103
    centrality of...76
    competing principles..36-37, 71-72, 74-75, 94-95
    consent per se...75, 93, 96
    decline
        background 71-72
        implications 72-73
        rationalisation of 92-95, 100-101
    degrees of..74-75, 87-88
    forçage de consentement 72

    genuineness 98
    implied..51-52
    importance of...23- 44
    in emerging jurisdictions..91-92
indicia
    contractual intent of states 124
    costs 43-44
    economic unity..19-20
    involvement in contract....................................16-18, 77, 82-83
    involvement in performance...........................74, 82-83, 94
    knowledge of the contract/arbitration agreement......16-19, 84-85, 94, 135-
   136
    principe de l'apparence.......................................80-81, 87, 94, 98
    relationship between contracts...41-42
    relationship between parties..43
    role of applicable law...26
    single economic reality.........................14-16, 76, 77, 78, 135, 237
indifferent..75, 87-88
limits on
    context...75-83
    equity..88-90
    national contract law..86-88
    objective assessment of jurisdiction..................................84-86
    types of...100
presumption of..86
substitution of..84-85, 86
unwilling non-signatories...116, 117
willing non-signatories.......................................114-116, 116-117

consolidation
    arguments in favour of...36-37, 50
    based on individual arbitration agreement(s)....................39-43
    based on institutional rules..38-39
    based on national law..36-38
    consequences of non-consolidation
      see tierce opposition
court-ordered
    objections to...51-52
definition 163
difficulties caused by...52-53
distinct from multicontract arbitration............................166, 167
grounds for

    general..163
    similarity of parties...164-165
    strictness of...54-56
ICC Court practice...38, 164-165
international 53
presumption for or against..39-41
procedural alternatives 52
quasi-consolidation..164-165
versus *tierce opposition*..60, 64-65

counterclaims...171, 179

cross-claims..179

D

dépeçage
    see consolidation

droit commun..86, 87, 95

E

Egyptian case law
    on limits of consent 91-92

enforcement of arbitral awards.....................................62-63, 124-126, 224-229
    see also *New York Convention*
    impossibility of simultaneous enforcement
    see *tierce opposition*

equitable estoppel..112, 116

equity 89-90

Euro Disney arbitration clause 27

European Convention on Human Rights
Article 6(1) ....104 n. 13

European Union
Cross-Border Injunctions Directive ....210 n. 40
European Commission 54
Unfair Commercial Practices Directive ....210 n. 40
Unfair Terms in Consumer Contracts Directive ....211 n. 61

extension of the arbitration agreement
as transition from litigation to arbitration 112
based on consent
see consent
based on other grounds 36-37, 71-72, 74-75, 94-95, 148-149
based on substantive law obligations 121-122
inaccuracy of concept ....95, 157 n. 5
to individuals ....182 n. 15
to non-signatories
see non-signatories
to states/state entities
see states and state-entities

F

fraud and abuse of rights ....87, 108 n. 75, 128, 136, 149, 151, 152-154

French case law
on consolidation/inseparability 38-39, 56
on contract law 87
on equity 90
on extension 124
on the group of companies doctrine 15-19, 23-25, 82, 134-136, 138-141
on the group of contracts doctrine 20-21, 23-25
on jurisdiction 84-85
on piercing the corporate veil 152-153
on tierce opposition 58-59

French Code of Civil Procedure 57-58, 61, 63, 64, 138

G

group of companies doctrine
  see also extension
  ambiguous indicator of intent 140
  as exception to requirement of multicontract arbitration 167-168
  as substantive or procedural rule 137
  constitutive elements 133-134
  criticism of 12
  definition 131-132
  differences with group of contracts doctrine
    consent 13-14
    economic considerations 14-22
    procedural aspects 22-23
  differences with piercing the corporate veil 149-150
  distorting effect on consent 77-79, 82
  dosage of consent 75-76
  economic considerations 14-19
  evolution 82
  French case law 15-19, 23-25, 82, 134-136, 138-141
  global assessment of jurisdiction 81-82
  in arbitration case law 132-141
  jurisdiction 22-23
  lack of autonomous standing 77, 14,
  limited effect of 138
  presumption of consent 83
  principe de l'apparence 80-81, 87, 94, 98
  role in case of consolidation 141-142
  role in case of joinder 141-142
  role in revealing intent 138-141
similarities with group of contracts doctrine
  common solutions 26-29
  consent 25-26
  diminishing relevance of national laws 26
  increasing obsolescence 30
  overlap 23-25
usages of international trade 139, 140

group of contracts doctrine
  see also consolidation
  see also group of companies doctrine
      differences/similarities with

economic considerations 19-22
French case law... 20-21, 23-25
jurisdiction.. 22-23
scenarios 13-14

H

Hong Kong Arbitration Ordinance (1963).................... 45 n. 5, 53, 56, 69 n. 20

I

ICC Commission on Arbitration.. 165, 235

ICC Institute of International Business Law and Practice............................ 235

ICC International Court of Arbitration
practice regarding consolidation... 38, 164-165
practice regarding cross claims... 179
practice regarding joinder.. 173-178
practice regarding multicontract arbitration..................................... 166-172
practice regarding third party intervention.. 178
role of.. 161-162

ICC Rules of Arbitration (1998)
Article 1.. 181 n. 3
Article 4... 38, 163-165, 172
Article 6.. 166-167, 173-174, 182 n. 13
Article 10..................................... 46 n. 17, 141, 165, 177-178, 179
Article 18... 181 n. 7
Article 30.. 179
Article 35.. 226
revision of... 165, 171, 178, 179-180

ICJ Statute
    Article 38..97

ILA Recommendations on *res judicata*...230-231

incompatibility..54-56 168-171, 224, 225

indivisibility of group of contracts..19-21

inseparable disputes..54-65
    see also tierce opposition

intent
    see consent

international class arbitration
    criteria for..216-217
    difference with multiparty arbitration..217-218
    existence of..215-216

intervention
    see third-party intervention

involvement in performance
    as basis for extension of the arbitration agreement......74, 82-83, 84-85, 94

involvement in the contract
    as basis for extension of the arbitration agreement............16-18, 77, 82-83

Irish International Commercial Arbitration Act (1998)..........................46 n. 6

Italian case law
    on enforcement of arbitral awards..225

Italian Code of Civil Procedure..63-64

J

JAMS Class Action Procedures ....209 n. 36

joinder
    and counterclaims 175
    conditions for
        see joinder test
    definition 172
    grounds for 54-56
    ICC Court practice 173-178
    not the same as inclusion of non-signatories 22
    respondents v. claimants 172
    states and state entities 176

joinder test
    before constitution of arbitral tribunal 177-178
    claims against new party 176-177
    signature requirement 173-176

joint and several liability 225

jurisdiction
    based on consent
        see consent
    based on other grounds 74, 78-79, 84-85, 94-95
    consolidation 53
    ex aequo et bono 89-90
    group of companies doctrine 22-23
    group of contracts doctrine 22-23
    impact of overly expansive approach 73
    mutual or common intention 80-81
    post-modernist approach to 90
    tierce opposition 60-62, 63-65

jurisdictional assessment
    global assessment of jurisdiction 81-82, 89
    objective assessment of jurisdiction 84-86
    sophistication of 92-93, 96-97

jurisdictional exposure
    exclusion clauses 101
    express choice of law 101
    risk of entrenching current practice 102

jurisdictional theory of arbitration 199

jurisdictions, emerging 91-92

K

knowledge of the contract/arbitration agreement
        as basis for extension of the arbitration agreement....16-19, 84-85, 94, 135-136

L

lex fori 99
    see also national contract law

lex mercatoria 83, 86, 94, 95

liability
    see piercing for liability

M

multicontract arbitration
    see also consolidation
    see also group of contracts doctrine
arising from counterclaims 171
awards in
    see arbitral awards

conditions for
    see multicontract test

definition..166
distinct from consolidation..166, 167
ICC Court practice...166-172
multicontract test
    compatibility of arbitration clauses................................. 166, 168-170, 171
    contracts signed by all parties..167-168
    group of companies exception...167-168

    same economic transaction...171

multiparty arbitration
    see also extension
    see also group of companies doctrine
awards in
    see arbitral awards
increase in..161-162

N

NAF Class Arbitration Procedures..210 n. 36

national contract law
    application to arbitration agreements...86
    consent..87-88
    continental jurisdictions..87
    general principles of contract law..86-87, 94
    US law...86-87, 115

Netherlands Arbitration Act (1986)..46 n. 5, 53, 55, 56

New York Convention on the Recognition and Enforcement of
    Foreign Arbitral Awards(1958)...73, 74
    Article II...67 n. 16
    Article IV..44
    Article V...45 n. 2, 51-52, 53, 224, 227

New Zealand Arbitration Act (1997)...51, 54

non-signatories
    claimants and defendants..112, 116
    unwilling

    and consent..116, 117
    definition of..112
    motivation to compel participation of................................114
willing
    and consent...114-116, 116-117
    definition of..112
    motivation to participate...113-114

O

opposabilité..232

P

Permanent Court of Arbitration (PCA).......................................192

    piercing the corporate veil.................................87, 90, 94, 98, 99, 127-128
        distinct from alter ego doctrine.....................................149-150
        applicable law..155
        as a basis for extension..148-149
        French case law on...152-153
        Swiss case law on..153, 155
        US case law on..128, 148, 151-152
        definition..147-148
        differences with group of companies doctrine..................149-150, 151
        distinction between jurisdictional issues and liability.........................154
        effects...157
        fraud and abuse of rights.......................................149, 151, 152, 153-154
        in arbitral awards..150-151
        'piercing for liability'...148, 154

principe de l'apparence..80-81, 87, 94, 98

privity...86, 87, 89, 122, 127

R

representative relief
- consent ... 191
- injunctive relief ... 192
- intermediate entities ... 192
- limited v. unlimited ... 191

res judicata ... 192, 202, 230-232

right or obligation to arbitrate ... 86
- diversification of sources ... 94-95
- relationships that give rise to ... 111
- theories of law that give rise to ... 112

rule of reason ... 93

S

settlement relief
- as enforceable arbitral award ... 193-194
- in the Netherlands ... 193

Singapore Arbitration Act ... 46 n. 6

single economic reality ... 14-16, 76, 77, 78, 82, 135, 237

states and state entities
- attribution of conduct to ... 120, 121-123
- contractual intent ... 124
- difference between private law agency and administrative delegation of functions ... 122, 122
- grounds for extension in absence of substantive private law liability ... 126-128
- joinder ... 176
- reasons for special status ... 119-120

Stockholm Chamber of Commerce Arbitration Rules ... 46 n. 12, 210, 48

Swiss case law
    on groups of companies...136-137
    on piercing the corporate veil...153, 155

T

third parties
    see joinder
    see third-party intervention

third-party intervention
    criteria for...54-56
    ICC Court practice 178

tierce opposition
    absolute effect..59-60
    against arbitral awards
        before arbitral tribunals..61
        before courts...61-62
        enforcement of awards..62-63
        jurisdiction..63-65
        parties' expectations...63
        unity of the legal order..62
    definition and scope...57-58
    drawbacks..60
    French case law on..58-59
    jurisdiction...60-62, 63-65
    versus consolidation...60, 65-65

U

UK Arbitration Act (1996) 36-37, 53, 227

UK case law
    on applicable law...99
    on attribution of intent to states..122, 126-127
    on consolidation 41
    on effects of arbitral awards 231-232

on enforcement of arbitral awards/consent...............124-126, 226-229, 240
on groups of companies 137

UNCITRAL Model Law..73, 91, 198-199

US case law
    on class arbitration...183, 184, 199,
                                                                                                215-220, 238-2391
    on consolidation 40
    on equity...89-90
    on extension..112-116
    on groups of companies..137-138
    on piercing the corporate veil 128, 148, 151-
                                                                                                                       152

US Federal Arbitration Act 187, 217-218

US Federal Rules of Civil Procedure ....66 n. 4, 190,
                                                                                                              209 n. 36, 216, 218

US Uniform Arbitration Act 51, 54

W

waiver of collective relief 196

TABLE OF CASES

Abu Dhabi Gas Liquefaction Co. v. Eastern Bechtel Corp. [UK]......41, 45 n. 1
Adams v. Cape Industries plc. [UK]..104 n. 14
Alexander v. Gardner-Denver Co. [US]...45 n. 2
American Centennial Insurance Co. v. National Casualty Co. [US] 40
Arthur Andersen Business Unit (AABU) Member Firms v. Andersen
Consulting Business Unit (ACBU) Member Firms (Andersen case)..................
   [Switzerland] 28-29
Arthur Andersen v. Carlisle [US]...115-116
Azhar Ali Khan v. Parsons Global Services [US] 112

Birmingham Associates v. Abbott Labs. [US]...112
Bridas SAPIC v. Government of Turkmenistan (Bridas I) [US] 127
Bridas SAPIC v. Government of Turkmenistan (Bridas II) [US]..106 n. 49, 108
   n. 77, 1279
Burlington Insurance Co. v, Trygg-Hansa Insurance Co. [US]............108 n. 76

Carte Blanche Pte v. Diners Club International Inc., et al. [US] 148
Coastal States Trading, Inc. v. Zenith Navigation SA [US]............................151
Compagnie les Assurances générales de France-Vie (AGF) v. Mme Rignon-
   Bret e.a. [France]..68 n. 44
Compania Española de Petreolos, S.A. v. Nereus Shipping, S.A. [US]..46 n. 17
Connecticut General Life Insurance Co. v. Sun Life Assurance Co. of Canada
   [US]..40

Dallah Estate and Tourism Holding Co. v. Ministry of Religious Affairs,
   Pakistan [UK]...124-126, 137, 226-229, 238
Dell Computer Corp. v. Union des consommateurs [Canada]...............45 n. 2

EARL Les Domaines de la Mette v. M. Gilles Sautarel [France].............68 n. 45
Eurosteel Ltd. v. Stinnes AG [UK] 99

Farkar Co. v. RA Hanson Disc. Ltd. [US]...158 n. 19
Federated Title Insurers, Inc. v. Ward [US]..............................158 nn. 19&21
Fisser v. International Bank [US]..151
Fletamentos Maritimos SA v. Effjohn International BV [UK].................47 n. 29
Freeman v. Complex Computing Company, Inc. [US]...............158nn. 19&21

General Electric Co. v. Deutz AG [US] 114
Glenn v. Wagner [US] .... 158 n. 21
Green Tree Financial Corp. v. Bazzle [US] 195
.... 211 n. 63, 214 nn. 75&80&85, 216, 218
Hamburg Chamber of Commerce, Friendly Arbitration Award of 27 May 2002 [Germany] 43

ICC case No. 1434 .... 76, 132
ICC case No. 2375 132
ICC case No. 3493 124
ICC case No. 3879, Westland Helicopters Ltd. v. Arab Organization for Industrialization (AOI) .... 85, 90, 129 n. 2

ICC case No. 4131, Isover-Saint-Gobain v. Dow Chemical Company 13-
.... 14, 75-76, 80-81, 133-134, 157 n. 16
ICC case No. 4367 41
ICC case No. 5721 .... 144 n. 4, 153-154, 157 n. 13
ICC case No. 6000 .... 47 n. 25, 85, 157 n. 16
ICC case No. 6519 .... 105 n. 28, 108 n. 48
ICC case No. 7061 231-232
ICC case No. 7245 95
ICC case No. 7453 99
ICC cases Nos. 7604 and 7610 .... 76, 106 n. 45
ICC case No. 8385 .... 149, 167 n. 15
ICC case No. 8420 .... 41-42, 46 n. 18
ICC case No. 8910 .... 144 n. 2
ICC case No. 9058, Bridas SAPIC and others v. Turkmenistan and others .. 127
ICC case No. 9151, Joint Venture Yashlar and Bridas SAPIC v. Turkmenistan 127
ICC case No. 9517 79
ICC case No. 9762 122-123
ICC case No. 9873 .... 157 n. 13, 158 n. 31
ICC case No. 11209 .... 158 n. 32
ICC case No. 11405 136
ICSID case No. ARB/07/5, Beccara v. Argentine Republic .... 184, 207 n. 6
InterGen NV v. Grina [US] .... 118 n. 5

J.J. Ryan & Sons v. Rhone Poulenc Textile, S.A. (Ryan case) [US] 113, 137-139

Khatib Petroleum Services International Co. v. Care Construction Co. and Care Services co. [Egypt] 93-94
Kis France v. Société Générale [France] 23-25, 140-141

Laborers' Local Union 472 & 172 v. Interstate Curb and Sidewalk [US] .....158 ....n. 19

Merrill Lynch Investment Managers v. Optibase, Ltd. [US] 116
Milan Chamber of National and International Arbitration, Award of 2
    February 1996 43
Mitsubishi Motors Corp. v. Soler Chrysler-Plymouth [US] ....212 n. 80
Municipalité de Khoms El Mergeb v. Société Dalico (Dalico case)
    [France]... 135-136

Nisshin Shipping Co. Ltd. v. Cleaves & Company Ltd. [UK] ....104 n. 12

Orri v. Société des Lubrifiants Elf Acquitaine
    [France] ....107,nn. 53&67, 135, 141-142, 154-155, 158 n. 17

PCA Case No. AA 227, Yukos Universal Limited v. The Russian Federation.....184
Peavey and Company v. Organisme Général des Fourrages e.a. [France]..68 n. 38
Polcon Italia srl v. P.T. Perkebunan Nusantara III Persero [Italy] 225
Pritzker v. Merrill Lynch, Pierce, Fenner & Smith [US] ....108 n. 73, 113

Quarto Children's Books v. Editions de Seuil and Editions Phidal [France].....56

République Arabe d'Egypte v. Southern Pacific Properties [France]...........124

Sam Reisfeld & Son Import Co. v. S.A. Eteco [US]..............................108 n. 76
Sarhank Group v. Oracle Corp. [US]...108 n. 97
Sheibani v. United States [Iran-US Claims Tribunal].............................207 n. 5
Shui On Construction Co. Ltd. v. Moon Yik Co. Ltd. et al. [Hong Kong] .66 n.
    ....8, 67 n. 19
Siemens AG and BKMI Industrieanlagen GmbH v. Dutco Construction Co.
    (Dutco case) [France]..38-39, 141, 177, 236
SNCFT v. Société Voith [France] 98
Société Alcatel Business Sytems (ABS) et al. v. Société Amkor Technology
    e.a. (Alcatel case) [France] 17-18
Société des Grands Travaux de Marseille v. République Populaire du
    Bangladesh et Bangladesh Industrial Development Corporation
    [Switzerland]..129 n. 8
Société Glencore Grain Rotterdam BV v. Société Afric (Glencore case)
    [France] 20

Société Isover-Saint-Gobain v. Société Dow Chemical France (Dow Chemical case) [France]..........15-16, 98, 134, 135, 141, 237-238
Société Korsnas Marma v. Société Durand-Auzias [France]..........85
Société Ofer Brothers v. The Tokyo Marine and Fire Insurance Co. Ltd. et autres [France]..........86
Société Uni-Kod v. Société Ouralkali (Uni-Kod case) [France]..........21
Société V 2000 v. Société Project XJ 220 ITD et autre (Jaguar case) [France]..........16-17, 90, 107 nn. 53&56
Sociétés Suba France et Suba & Unico v. Société Pujol (Pujol case) [France]..........18-19
Sponsor A.B. v. F.L. Lestrade, J.-L.P. Lestrade and M.H. Lestrade [France]..........106 n. 47, 134-135, 139
Stolt-Nielsen S.A. v. AnimalFeeds International Corp. [US]..........83, 184, 199, ...208 nn. 13&17, 209 n. 22, 213 nn. 63&64&67, 212 nn. 69&76&87, 217-..........220, 238-239
Sun Life Insurance Company of Canada, American Phoenix Life and Reassurance Company, Phoenix Home Life Mutual Insurance v. Lincoln Life Insurance Company [UK]..........231-232
Sunkist Soft Drinks, Inc. v. Sunkist Growers, Inc. [US]..........113
Svenska Petroleum Exploration AB v. Lithuania [UK]..........122, 126-127

Thomson-CSF, S.A. v. American Arbitration Association [US]..........107 n. 62

UNCITRAL case UNC 39/DK, Zeevi Holdings v. Bulgaria and the Privatization Agency of Bulgaria..........121-122
United Kingdom v. Boeing [US]..........46 n. 17, 53

Valencia v. Bancolombia [Colombia]..........190

Western Oil Sands v. Allianz Insurance Co. of Canada [Canada]..........66 n. 5
Wm Passalacqua Builder, Inc. v. Resnick Developers South, Inc. [US].....157 n. 3

Yuen v. Superior Court [US]..........195, 214 n. 75

Zurich Chamber of Commerce, case No. 273/95 [Switzerland]..........42

About the authors

Gerald Aksen
Independent Arbitrator, New York City, United States;
Council Member, ICC Institute of World Business Law

Gerald Aksen has been a full time independent arbitrator since 2003. He was previously the partner in charge of international arbitration at the firm of Thelen Reid & Priest (now dissolved) in New York. He is a former Vice Chairman of the ICC International Court of Arbitration and General Counsel of the American Arbitration Association. He is a co-founder and former president of the College of Commercial Arbitrators (USA). He holds a JD degree from New York University School of Law where he taught the course on international arbitration as an adjunct professor of law for thirty years. His wide background in the arbitral field includes four different perspectives, having served as an academic (NYU), administrator (AAA), attorney and arbitrator in numerous international arbitrations. He is a member of the New York Bar and was Chairman of the Section of International Law of the American Bar Association. He is the 2005 recipient of the ABA Dispute Resolution Section's D'Alemberte/Raven Award and is consistently ranked as one of New York's notable international arbitrators, up to an including in Chambers Global Arbitration Review 2009.

Christian Albanesi
Deputy Counsel, ICC International Court of Arbitration, Paris

Christian Albanesi is Deputy Counsel in the Ibero-American team of the Secretariat of the ICC International Court of Arbitration. He was previously an associate at Marval, O'Farrell & Marial in Buenos Aires, Argentina. He was admitted to the Buenos Aires Bar in 2002. He is a former scholar of the Ministry of Education of the Russian Federation. He holds a degree in Law from the University of Buenos Aires, where he also taught law, and a LLM in French and European Law from the University Paris I Panthéon-Sorbonne.

Sébastien Besson
Partner, Python & Peter, Switzerland

Sébastien Besson is a partner at Python & Peter, Geneva. He represents companies before arbitral tribunals and state courts in commercial disputes, and serves as arbitrator.
He has acted as chairman, party-appointed arbitrator, sole arbitrator, counsel or legal expert in numerous international arbitrations under a variety of arbitration rules, and in different jurisdictions. Mr Besson has published extensively on arbitration. Notably he has co-authored with Professor Jean-François Poudret the well-known treatise Comparative Law of International Arbitration (Sweet & Maxwell, London, 2007). He also teaches several courses on arbitration and settlement of commercial disputes at the University of Geneva and as part of the Geneva Master in International Dispute Settlement Program. He was educated at Lausanne University, where he received his Doctorate in Law, and at Columbia University (New York), from which he holds an LL.M.

Stephen R. Bond
Senior of Counsel, Covington & Burling LLP, United Kingdom; Former Secretary General, ICC International Court of Arbitration, Paris; Associate Member, ICC Institute of World Business Law

Stephen R. Bond is Senior of Counsel in the law firm Covington & Burling LLP in London. He was the US Member of the ICC International Court of Arbitration for the period 1994-1999 and Vice Chairman of the ICC Working Group that produced the 1998 ICC Rules. Prior to joining Covington & Burling, he was co-head of the White & Case LLP International Arbitration Practice Group and a resident partner in the Paris office of White & Case from 1991 to 2008. He was Secretary General of the ICC International Court of Arbitration from 1985-1991. He has served as counsel or arbitrator in numerous international arbitrations under the arbitration rules of the ICC and various other arbitration institutions and ad hoc rules. These arbitrations relate principally to disputes in the natural resources, construction, defense and international joint venture, sales and distribution fields and involve the application of various civil and common law legal systems and international public law. He is on the panel of arbitrators of numerous arbitral institutions and is a frequent writer and speaker on arbitration issues.

Kristof Cox

Senior Legal Consultant, Deloitte; Affiliated Senior Researcher, KULeuven Faculty of Law, Institute for International Trade Law, Belgium

Kristof Cox is a Senior Legal Consultant at Deloitte Belgium since November 2009. His practice focuses on commercial law in general and international contracts of sale in particular. He is an affiliated senior researcher at the Institute for International Trade Law of the Katholieke Universiteit Leuven, Belgium. Before joining Deloitte, he was the assistant of Professor Hans Van Houtte at this Institute. He has written a doctoral dissertation on the effects of an arbitration award vis-à-vis third parties, which he will defend on 21 December 2009. Mr Cox is a member of the Steering Committee of CEPANI-40 and has appeared as arbitrator. He is the founder of the Leuven Pre-Moot for the Willem C Vis Arbitration Moot and was head of organization of the first four editions.

Yves Derains

Founding Partner, Derains Gharavi, France; Former Secretary General, ICC International Court of Arbitration; Vice-Chairman, ICC Institute of World Business Law, Chairman, French Committee of Arbitration

Yves Derains, former Secretary General of the ICC International Court of Arbitration and Director of the Legal Department of the ICC, is member of the Paris Bar and a founding partner of the law firm Derains Gharavi. He is specialized in international arbitration and is acting both as arbitrator and counsel of parties in arbitration proceedings.

Mr Derains is the Chairman of the Comité Français de l'Arbitrage and Vice Chairman of the ICC Institute of World Business Law. He has been the Chairman of the Working Party on the Revision of the ICC Rules of Arbitration in 1998 and Co-Chairman of the ICC Task Force on the Reduction of Costs and Time in international arbitration. He is a member of the French Committee on Private International Law since 1978. He is member of the French Section of the International Council for Commercial Arbitration (ICCA) and member of various other organizations specialized in international arbitration and in international business law. Mr Derains is also author of many publications on International Commercial Arbitration and on International Business Law, in particular: "Evaluation of damages in international arbitration", ICC Institute of World Business Law, 2006 – "A Guide to the ICC Rules of Arbitration" (Second edition, with E. Schwartz), Kluwer Law International, 2005.

José Ricardo Feris
Counsel, ICC International Court of Arbitration, Paris

José Ricardo Feris is Counsel of the ICC International Court of Arbitration in Paris, France. He also acts as Secretary of the ICC Latin American Arbitration Group. He received his law degree "magna cum laude" from the Pontificia Universidad Católica Madre y Maestra in the Dominican Republic and his LL.M. in International Legal Studies from New York University. He is admitted to practice in the Dominican Republic. His experience in international dispute resolution includes being a law clerk at the International Court of Justice in The Hague and representing the Dominican Republic before the Free Trade Agreement of the Americas' negotiation rounds.

Simon Greenberg
Deputy Secretary General, ICC International Court of Arbitration, Paris

Simon Greenberg is Deputy Secretary General of the ICC International Court of Arbitration where he manages teams administering more that 1,300 international arbitrations taking place across the globe. He was formerly a Senior Associate with the international arbitration department of Dechert LLP, Paris, and has previously practised with other firms in Paris and Australia. He has published various articles on international arbitration, lectures international commercial contracts at the Institute of Political Science of Paris (Sciences Po) and lectures international arbitration at the University of Aix-Marseille and Erasmus University of Rotterdam.

Bernard Hanotiau
Professor; Partner, Hanotiau & Van den Berg, Belgium; Council Member, ICC Institute of World Business Law; Council Member, ICCA

Bernard Hanotiau is a member of the Brussels and Paris bars. In 2001, he established in Brussels a boutique law firm concentrating on international arbitration and litigation. He is also a professor at the Law School of Louvain University where he teaches international arbitration. Mr Hanotiau has a PhD from Louvain University and an LLM from Columbia University (1973).Since 1978, Bernard Hanotiau has been actively involved in international commercial arbitration as party-appointed arbitrator, chairman, sole arbitrator, counsel and expert in various parts of the world. He is a member of ICCA, the ICC International Arbitration Commission and a Council Member of the ICC Institute. He is also Vice-President of CEPANI and of the Institute of Transnational Arbitration (Dallas). He has written a major treatise on complex arbitrations (Complex Arbitrations: Multiparty, Multicontract, Multi-issues and Class Actions, Kluwer, 2006).

Serge Lazareff
Founding Partner, Lazareff Le Bars, France; Chairman, ICC Institute of World Business Law

Serge Lazareff is a founding partner of Lazareff Le Bars. He is Doctor of Law of the University of Paris and holds an LL.M. from Harvard. He is Chairman of the ICC Institute of World Business Law and Chairman of the French Arbitration Commission of ICC France. He was formerly General Counsel for International Operations and Vice-President Asia-Pacific of Pechiney, then the leading French industrial groups.

Fernando Mantilla Serrano
Partner, Shearman & Sterling, France; Member, ICC International Court of Arbitration

Fernando Mantilla Serrano is a partner at Shearman & Sterling LLP in Paris, where he practises in transnational litigation and international arbitration, mainly focused on Spain and Latin America. A graduate from the Pontificia Universidad Javeriana in Bogota where he received his Law degree (JD) and Economics degree (MSc), Mr Mantilla-Serrano has also received a MCJ (LLM) from New York University (Fulbright Scholar), a DEA in International Private Law and International Trade and a DSU in EU Law from the Université de Paris II. He conducts arbitrations and appears as Counsel before arbitral tribunals in numerous venues, mainly in Europe, the United States and Latin America. Mr Mantilla-Serrano is the Colombian member of the ICC International Court of Arbitration and Fellow of the Chartered Institute of Arbitrators. His articles on arbitration have been published in Arbitration International, the French Revue de l'Arbitrage, the Journal of International Arbitration and the Spanish Revista de la Corte Española de Arbitraje. He was one of a four-member commission created by the Spanish Minister of Justice to draft Spain's new arbitration act (Law 60 of December 23, 2003). He is admitted to the bars of Colombia, New York (USA), Paris (France) and Madrid (Spain).

Pierre Mayer
Professor and Partner, Dechert LLP, France; Council Member, ICC Institute of World Business Law

Pierre Mayer is a partner at the Paris office of Dechert LLP and a professor at the University of Paris-I Panthéon-Sorbonne, where he teaches private international law, arbitration law and the law of contracts since 1984. He practises arbitration, both as counsel and arbitrator, mainly in the fields of international trade, joint ventures and industrial cooperation, oil and gas, technology transfer and distribution, under the rules of ICSID, ICC and UNCITRAL. President of the French Committee on International Private Law, he is also associate member of the Institut de droit international, a Council member of the ICC Institute of World Business Law and member of the Comité Français de l'Arbitrage. He is a former President of the Committee on International Commercial Arbitration of the International Law Association and former President of the Committee on Private International Law of the International Law of the International Union of Lawyers (UIA). Mr Mayer is the author of numerous articles and several books, including a treatise on Private International Law, "Droit international privé", Montchrestien (first edition 1977, in its ninth edition in collaboration with Professor Vincent Heuzé), and the 2003 General course at the Hague Academy of International Law.

Georgios Petrochilos
Partner, Freshfields Bruckhaus Deringer LLP, France; Avocat à la Cour and Advocate of the Greek Supreme Court

Georgios Petrochilos is a partner in the international arbitration and public international law groups of Freshfields Bruckhaus Deringer LLP and is based in the Paris office. He specializes in public international law and international arbitration, with a particular emphasis on energy-related matters. His extensive arbitration experience includes acting as counsel or advisor for numerous clients, under the arbitration rules of the main arbitral institutions. He has represented governments, international organizations, and private parties on a broad range of cases involving long-term energy contracts, investment protection, boundary disputes, entitlement to natural resources, and immunities from jurisdiction. Mr Petrochilos is a member of the International Arbitration Committee of the International Law Association and a Member of the Chartered Institute of Arbitrators. Together with Jan Paulsson, he has served as advisor to the UNCITRAL Secretariat. He now represents Greece as a delegate to UNCITRAL. He is also a rapporteur for the Institute for Transnational Arbitration.He has published extensively on subjects related to international law and international arbitration. Notably, he is the author of Procedural Law in International Arbitration and co-author of the forthcoming edition of International Chamber of Commerce Arbitration (both at Oxford University Press). He holds degrees from the Universities of Athens, Strasbourg, and Oxford, including a doctorate in international arbitration law. He is fluent in English, French and Greek, and also speaks Dutch and German.

Eric A. Schwartz
Partner, King & Spalding, France; Former Secretary General, ICC International Court of Arbitration; Council Member, ICC Institute of World Business Law

Eric Schwartz is a partner in King & Spalding's Paris office and a member of the International Arbitration Practice Group. He is a former Secretary General of the ICC International Court of Arbitration. Over the last 30 years, he has acted on behalf of some of the world's largest companies, public authorities and sovereign states in international arbitration proceedings in all of the principal European arbitration venues, as well as in Asia and the U.S. He is the co-author (with Yves Derains) of A Guide to the ICC Rules of Arbitration and is presently a member of the ICC Court as well as being a Council Member of the ICC Institute of World Business Law.

S.I. Strong
Associate Professor of Law, University of Missouri School of Law, Columbia, Missouri, United States; Senior Fellow, Center for the Study of Dispute Resolution

S.I. Strong is currently Associate Professor of Law at the University of Missouri and Senior Fellow at the award-winning Center for the Study of Dispute Resolution, having previously taught law at the University of Cambridge and the University of Oxford in the United Kingdom. Prior to joining the faculty at Missouri, Dr Strong was Counsel specializing in international dispute resolution at Baker & McKenzie LLP and a dual-qualified practitioner (U.S.-England) in the New York and London offices of Weil, Gotshal & Manges LLP. Dr Strong has acted in arbitral proceedings under a wide range of institutional rules and is listed as a neutral on various national and international rosters. Dr Strong is the author of numerous works on international arbitration, including the award-winning article, The Sounds of Silence: Are U.S. Arbitrators Creating Internationally Enforceable Awards When Ordering Class Arbitration in Cases of Contractual Silence or Ambiguity? 30 Michigan Journal of International Law 1017 (2009), as well as the books Research and Practice in International Commercial Arbitration: Sources and Strategies (2009) and Class Arbitration and Collective Arbitration: Mass Claims in the National and International Sphere (forthcoming), both from Oxford University Press. Dr Strong, who is qualified as a lawyer at the New York and Illinois bars and as a solicitor of the Supreme Court of England and Wales, holds a Ph.D. in law from the University of Cambridge, a D.Phil. from the University of Oxford, a J.D. from Duke University, an M.P.W. from the University of Southern California and a B.A. from the University of California.

John M. Townsend
Partner, Hughes Hubbard & Reed LLP, Washington DC, United States

John M. Townsend is a partner in the Washington office of Hughes Hubbard & Reed LLP and is chair of that firm's Arbitration and ADR Group. He specializes in international disputes, including complex litigation and arbitration. In February 2008, President Bush appointed Mr Townsend as one of the four American arbitrators on the Panel of Arbitrators of the International Centre for the Settlement of Investment Disputes. He is Chairman of the Board of Directors of the American Arbitration Association. He is a Trustee and a member of the Arbitration and Competition Law Committees of the United States Council for International Business, and chairs the USCIB's Task Force on European Privilege Issues. He is a member of the CPR Panel of Distinguished Neutrals and of CPR's Challenge Review Board. Mr Townsend served as the first chair of the Mediation Committee of the International Bar Association (2005-2006). He is a member of the American Law Institute and of the College of Commercial Arbitrators. He obtained both his B.A. (1968) and his J.D. (1971) from Yale University. He has been with Hughes Hubbard & Reed, in New York, Paris, and Washington, since 1971. He speaks fluent French.

Karim Youssef

Associate Professor of Law, Cairo University, Egypt; Associate, Cleary Gottlieb Steen & Hamilton LLP, France

Karim Youssef is an associate at the international arbitration group of the law firm of Cleary Gottlieb Steen & Hamilton LLP. He also lectures private and international law at Cairo University, School of Law, and is non-resident Counsel at the Cairo Regional Centre for International Commercial Arbitration. He is also member of the National Law Commission of Egypt (NLC), and the Commission Working Group on the Reform of the Egyptian Arbitration Law. Dr Youssef holds degrees from Yale Law School, Paris

University (Sorbonne) and Cairo University School of Law. His previous positions include acting as Counsel for the Ministry of Justice of Egypt, the Egyptian Capital Market Authority, and the International Human Rights Law Institute of Depaul University in Chicago. He is a member of the ICC Commission on International Arbitration and the Commission Working Group on the Reform of the 1998 ICC Rules. He has served as arbitrator in a number of domestic and international proceedings, ad hoc (UNCITRAL) and institutional. Among his recent publications: "Consent in Context or Fulfilling the Promise of International Arbitration, Multiparty, Multi-contract and Non-contract Arbitration", West, 2009 (Preface by Jan Paulsson); The Death of Inarbitrability, in Loukas Mistelis and Stavros Brekoulakis (eds), Arbitrability: International and Comparative Perspectives, Kluwer Law International 2009; and The Independence of International Arbitrators: An Arbitrators Perspective, ICC Intl. Court of Arb. Bull., 2007 Special Supplement, 2008 (with Professor Ahmed S. El-Kosheri, Former Vice-President of the ICC International Court of Arbitration).

ICC at a glance

ICC is the world business organization, a representative body that speaks with authority on behalf of enterprises from all sectors in every part of the world.

The fundamental mission of ICC is to promote trade and investment across frontiers and help business corporations meet the challenges and opportunities of globalization. Its conviction that trade is a powerful force for peace and prosperity dates from the organization's origins early in the last century. The small group of far-sighted business leaders who founded ICC called themselves "the merchants of peace".

Because its member companies and associations are themselves engaged in international business, ICC has unrivalled authority in making rules that govern the conduct of business across borders. Although these rules are voluntary, they are observed in countless thousands of transactions every day and have become part of the fabric of international trade.

ICC also provides essential services, foremost among them the ICC International Court of Arbitration, the world's leading arbitral institution. Another service is the World Chambers Federation, ICC's worldwide network of chambers of commerce, fostering interaction and exchange of chamber best practice.

Business leaders and experts drawn from the ICC membership establish the business stance on broad issues of trade and investment policy as well as on vital technical and sectoral subjects. These include financial services, information technologies, telecommunications, marketing ethics, the environment, transportation, competition law and intellectual property.

ICC enjoys a close working relationship with the United Nations and other intergovernmental organizations, including the World Trade Organization, the G20 and the G8.

ICC was founded in 1919. Today it groups thousands of member companies and associations from over 120 countries. National committees work with their members to address the concerns of business in their countries and convey to their governments the business views formulated by ICC.

For more information, please visit **www.iccwbo.org**

Some ICC Specialized Divisions

- ICC International Court of Arbitration (Paris)
- ICC International Centre for Expertise (Paris)
- ICC World Chambers Federation (Paris)
- ICC Institute of World Business Law (Paris)
- ICC Centre for Maritime Co-operation (London)
- ICC Commercial Crime Services (London)
- ICC Services (Paris):
    - **Publications**

ICC Publications Department is committed to offering the best resources on business and trade for the international community.

The content of ICC publications is derived from the work of ICC commissions, institutions and individual international experts. The specialized list covers a range of topics including international banking, international trade reference and terms (Incoterms), law and arbitration, counterfeiting and fraud, model commercial contracts and environmental issues.

Publications are available in both traditional paper and electronic formats from the ICC Business Bookstore.

- **Events**

Through conferences and trainings, ICC Events promotes and brings ICC's expertise to a wider audience - helping to make the international business and legal community aware of ICC's main policy issues and tools.

Always highly topical, these events cover a vast array of some of the most pressing matters for global business from international commercial arbitration and dispute resolution to banking techniques and practices. ICC courses on international arbitration and negotiating international contracts for business-people, corporate counsel, lawyers and legal practitioners involved in international trade are considered to be the best continuing education in these fields.

ICC Events offers courses in all corners of the globe, in collaboration with ICC national committees.

Source Products for Global Business

ICC's specialized list of publications covers a range of topics including international banking, international trade reference and terms (Incoterms), law and arbitration, counterfeiting and fraud, model commercial contracts and environmental issues.

ICC products are available from ICC national committees which exist in over 80 countries around the world. Contact details for a national committee in your country are available at **www.iccwbo.org**

You may also order ICC products online from the ICC Business Bookstore at **www.iccbooks.com**

Publications Department
38 Cours Albert 1er
75008 Paris
France
Tel.   +33 1 49 53 29 23
Fax   +33 1 49 53 29 02
e-mail   pub@iccwbo.org

The world business organization